THE RIGHT TO BE

For our children: Iris, Ilse, Amylin and Justin and all their peers.
Beyond every border I let my heart's desire resound that they,
and all succeeding generations, may come to know their uniqueness.
That they will live, dance, and celebrate their right to be in freedom,
surrounded and permeated by the Great Spirit who breathes love into all life.

MOTHER EARTH BY ILSE OVERSIER

The Right to Be
Publisher: London Books

First printing: September 2021 (Dutch edition)
Second printing: October 2021 (Dutch edition)
Third printing: November 2021(Dutch edition)
Fourth printing: March 2022 (Dutch edition)
Fifth printing: July 2022 (Dutch edition)
First printing: November 2022 (English edition)

Lay-out cover and inside of book: Ellen Langendam – artwisedesign.nl
Photo author: Laurens Morel
Editing Dutch edition: Tanya van der Spek/Evelien Dommerholt
Editing English edition: Jill van der Aa-Shand
Illustrations: Irina Filcer – irinafilcer.com
Printer: Drukwerkconsultancy – Jeroen Boereboom
ISBN: 97 894 93280 15 1
NUR: 320
BISAC code: OCC022000 BODY, MIND & SPIRIT / Afterlife and Reincarnation
OCC011000 BODY, MIND & SPIRIT / Healing / General

www.maartenoversier.com

THE RIGHT TO BE

EXPOSING THE SUPPRESSED HISTORY WE STILL CARRY WITHIN US

Maarten A. Oversier

Translated from the Dutch by Scott Rollins

LondonBooks

ENDORSEMENTS

"The shit from your past is the fertilizer for your future" is the encouraging text clients read before entering Maarten Oversier's practice. A powerful expression of the connection that Maarten and I have as a professional and as a person. Maarten understands the past, I am concerned with understanding the future.

Let me introduce myself. My first study was psychology which, like my past, was something I was interested in but that did not really fascinate me. From a very young age, I had the feeling that a drunken stork had accidentally dropped into the wrong nest. After quickly leaving that nest, a search for my future began. It turned out to be the future itself.

I developed a sense for recognizing signals, sometimes faint, that would determine the future. Increasingly I saw that our present and what comes out of it are not so unique at all. Similar patterns repeat themselves again and again as laws of nature that do not care about man. I was driven to delve more into the 'shit from the past', which radically changed my view of the future, and of people. While studying psychology, I learned about the importance of the subconscious, but that did not really resonate with me. Nor had I gotten much wiser from what I had picked up from other areas of interest such as parapsychology, the Egyptian pyramids, and similar fields. In short, the accepted descriptions of our history did not resonate with my observations and intuition. As I explored history more deeply to truly understand the future, I was struck by the cruelty of man. I was overcome by the pain of victims of human trafficking and came to realize that it is not only passed on for many generations but also settles 'somewhere'. My own past, which goes back several generations, also began to fascinate me more in this context. It turned out that I had not been dropped in the wrong nest, but rather in a different time. I recognized traits that had played hide and seek for at least a generation. Just like with Maarten, the Sherlock Holmes awoke in me.

Since the day we met, my intuition told me that we had known each other for some time. Probably from a past life. My first associations called to mind the adventures I had read in my youth to make boredom bearable, written by the internationally acclaimed 19th century German author Karl May, noted for his adventure novels set in the American Old West, and best known for the characters Winnetou and Old Shatterhand. As a young man, I found the combination of Winnetou's wisdom, with the knowledge of Old Shatterhand particularly fascinating. And how together they managed to defeat evil in the Wild West. Two opposites forming an unbeatable team. The yin and yang of virtue. When I started to come up with Karl May-like stories myself, I ended up being able to empathize best with the more down-to-earth Old Shatterhand. In his role, I experienced the exciting adventures I had missed in my youth. Many invented crooks have ended up behind virtual bars. Was it a coincidence that Karl May had died on my birthday, March 30th?

No mention was made about whether Chief Winnetou could cook, but certainly about his bringing wisdom from previous generations. Maarten Oversier can do both; he was Chief Chef and is now Chief Reason to Be. His book has given me new perspectives on life that I had actually been looking for in psychology. It brought new insights into the importance of rituals and the reliving of painful events. His visions are mind-expanding in the literal sense and are supported by the documentation of his many sessions with clients. Their testimonies illustrate how much Maarten had helped them in the processes of healing and gaining new insights. I now also realize that our similarities may be greater than the differences. In any case, we share the present, our future past in the present Wild West. Have we met again to catch the present-day bad guys in the Wild West together? And are the two of us also 'the hands and feet of The Creator?'

I have concluded after many years of voracious curiosity that, 'The more I know, the more I realize I don't know'. Countless times I expanded my boundaries to acquire new knowledge and each time this gave me unprecedented opportunities to understand life more deeply. 'The Right to Be' has expanded my boundaries again and 'reminded' me that I know nothing. I can therefore wholeheartedly recommend the book to anyone who wants to learn to look beyond borders.

– Prof. dr. Bob de Wit
Professor of Strategic Leadership at Nyenrode Business University in the Netherlands

Maybe he was born in the wrong country. Or at the wrong time. The fact is that this man in the present can see behind the curtains and mists of time and cultures of the past. With compassion he makes them very much alive and relevant to the patterns in your life. Like a Saint Germain in a cowboy hat, he wanders with the greatest of ease through the folds of time of individual and collective history. The fact that he makes a delicious bouilla-baisse can also be savored in his tasty and perfectly seasoned texts.
– ***Geert Kimpen****, author of The Kabbalist, among others.*

This is the cookbook of the recipes of your lifetime. It all has to do with preparation. On the fire for a long time, gently sim-mered, slightly browned, seared, mari-nated, spicy, sour, bitter and mild flavors. That's life. Everything can be traced back to the kitchen, the end result. The perfect harmony, the most beautiful creation in every season. The seasons of life in which Maarten switched around the ingredients for people. If you couldn't keep down those Brussel sprouts, then they were either forced to taste palatable or never eaten again. That is of course a shame, because you have to find out where it once went wrong.
– ***Herman den Blijker****, head chef*

We still carry inside us every experience that is not recognized and processed. However, the trauma is pushed aside and buried, sometimes so deep that we seem to have forgotten it, but it's not gone. It has been stored in the subconscious and from there directs us in the form of restrictive convictions and patterns, which are knotted together.
In his work as a reincarnation therapist and with this magnificent book Maarten Oversier helps us to untangle those knots. With wisdom and patience, he uncoils the rope right back to the very beginning where the issue originated. Our soul wants nothing more than to bring unresolved past from all incarnations to the surface so that it can be seen and healed, both at an individual and collective level.
*– **Susan Smit**, author*

Yvette Kulkens Photography

As a patented seeker of truth, it is it has been clear to me for a long time that there is a nefarious clique of particularly cunning people who are trying to keep and hold us down in all manner of ways. In this era of the great existential emancipation there is a need for brave visionary forerunners and scouts, who show us the way out of this slave plantation. My good buddy Big Chief Oversier is such a prominent figure. For years he has been telling us: know thyself and your ancestors. We are brought to tears at the realization how, without exception, each of us is unimaginably hurt, often by traumas from past lives, of not only ourselves, but now also of unknown relatives who came before us. Tears flow when you understand that you can detect these injuries. Through this, you acquire the liberating opportunity to heal and restore yourself in the unio mystica with everything that is.

*- **Peter Vereecke**, Former Belgian politician, ex-mayor of Evergem, researcher, and author*

TABLE OF CONTENTS

LETTER FROM A NATIVE AMERICAN FAITHKEEPER

My name is Ken Maracle, Hao Hyo, faithkeeper of the Lower Cayuga Longhouse. I am a member of the Cayuga Nation, Iroquois Confederacy, Deer Clan.

I have had the privilege of receiving instruction from our traditional chiefs and wisdom keepers such as Chief Jake Ezra Thomas, Cayuga chief (1922-1998) and others who have remained true to the original values and knowledge of our peoples, the Haudenosaunee. In addition to my responsibility as a faithkeeper, guardian of traditional values and stories from my culture, I am an artist – I fabricate authentic cultural objects with their spiritual messages and symbolism, keeping alive and propagating the wisdom and customs of our people.

For forty years I have been teaching people about our culture and traditions. The so-called Wampum Belts are an indispensable guideline for this. These symbol-rich necklaces, made of white and purple shell beads, have been a fundamental part of our culture for centuries. They represent the most important events in our history, which are captured in the simple symbolism used. In this way, our history will never be forgotten, and the significance of these events will be passed on to the current generations. I see a huge overlap with the work of my dear friend Maarten Oversier. An official historical treaty (1613) between our peoples, the Iroquois and the Dutch, our white brothers, is also recorded in a Wampum Belt. The so-called TwoRow-treaty, guided by The Friendship Belt. The belts were made

TWOROW WAMPUMBELT & FRIENDSHIP WAMPUMBELT

to protect future generations. The message that speaks from this is an international agreement that we must respect the life path of all peoples in the world. We have all come here with an appointment from our 'Creator', to take on some responsibility in our lives.

In the course of your life, you will discover which special talent wishes to speak through you. A "gift" that tells you to have faith in the universe, as a personal gift that the Creator has given you to carry out into the world. The spiritual names we receive from our parents, sometimes grandparents, refer to those talents, so that they are empowered.

Since my meeting with Maarten at the powwow of the Six Nations of the Grand River reservation in 2005, we have become very good friends. We met almost every year after that, both in Canada and in the Netherlands, and there was an intensive exchange of ideas, dreams and plans for the future.

In the fall of 2006, I was with a Mohawk brother, William Woodworth, La-weno-gwas, (He Dips the Words), Bear Clan of the Mohawk Nation, in the Netherlands teaching people about our traditions. For this occasion, we organized a 'Bringing back to life of old connections' meeting in Drenthe. I had noticed how green the Netherlands was and that blackberries were growing everywhere.

I remember a dream. Maarten and I came walking towards each other from two different directions. I had a large bowl of strawberries in my hands and he a bowl of blackberries. Strawberries have a very special spiritual symbolism for our people, about the sweetness of life. In the dream Maarten and I mixed our fruits in an even larger bowl. We also invited people to taste the combination. The dream told us that it is important to connect and taste the authentic values and fruits of everyone's habitat, without affecting its authentic form and taste.

Seeing is believing and so I witnessed various sessions that Maarten did based on his working method. We were invited by a man and a woman to attend their sessions. I was so touched and honored when I saw what was happening and realized that thankfully these ancient ways of healing had not been forgotten. They all serve the same purpose our fundamental values and traditions stand for: to keep intact, and where necessary heal, what lies behind us but must never be forgotten.

Our many Wampum Belts, each with its own story and meaning, passed through the hands of many people who 'knew'. These people lived and died, but their essences are kept alive in these beaded necklaces by the spirits of our ancestors. The Wampum Belts contain so much power and inspiration, which will never expire. In this way we maintain the well-being of our peoples, by relating our history to the present. After all, what we decide now has an effect for the next seven generations – and our distant ancestors also realized this.

My partner, Mellinda, and I feel a close kinship with each other and with Maarten, as if we know each other as old friends from previous lives. A friendship that has been revived, teaching us that we have to embrace the past and also that we have to forgive and accept the dark sides of that past so that we can move on.
I send a blessing to *The Right to Be* from overseas. May it touch many in forgotten memories.

"Onah Gonolonkwa" ("Embrace and look after each other", in Cayuga)
Ken Maracle

KEN MARACLE, CAYUGA FAITHKEEPER AND MELLINDA TRUDEAU, OJIBWE SEER.

FOREWORD BY MARCEL MESSING

Maarten Oversier has several published articles to his name, but this is his first book and hopefully not his last. It appears from this work that the many people who came and continue to come to him to be healed of old wounds, find him to be a sincere healer. A reincarnation therapist who understands the art of making the pain, trauma and sadness visible that takes place in the human soul. In his own life's flow, the author has gradually mastered the art of starting a process of self-healing from insight into life and knowledge of the human soul and spirit. It is no coincidence that the original meaning of the Dutch word *arts* (meaning doctor) is related to the Latin word 'ars', which means art. The art of healing what is broken. The author taps into the history of the ancestors in the shafts of the unconscious. He does this by listening carefully and recognizing how things fit together. The reader meets with man's life stories in *The Right to Be* and can taste from a richly filled jar of wisdom. In a moving way the author also talks about his own path, for example about how he experienced the death of his father as a child, which led to a decisive change in his life.

Fate brought us together during a theme day on 'The Transhuman Man' in Zeyen on March 28, 2015. During the interval there was instant recognition. From soul brother to soul brother. Ancient roots that connected us. Maarten Oversier. A freethinker in the truest sense of the word. An authentic person. Many people are born as originals but die as copies. But certainly not Maarten! A deep unconditional friendship flared between us from beyond the borders of birth and death, followed by many encounters and exchanges.

Anyone who might doubt the existence of reincarnation or believe that this is not possible or allowed based on ecclesiastical dogmatics, and who has come up with all kinds of clever ideas to dispute this, is apparently not aware that most people on earth have adopted this 'theory' for centuries. There are numerous scientific publications that demonstrate reincarnation. Abundant examples of reincarnation include those found in Hinduism, Buddhism, the Gospels and Christian gnosis, among others. In my own life I had already become familiar with the reality of reincarnation early on, which increasingly I began to see as a kind of life's flow. At a later age it became clear to me that the wheel of birth and death keeps turning, as long as the fire of desire burns in us, which always leads to grief, sorrow, and suffering. It also became clear to me that ignorance, the "mother of all diseases" (the Buddha), keeps the flame of desire burning. Contact with wise people and teachers, reading Buddhist texts and staying in a Buddhist monastery in India all contributed to this insight.

In his own life Maarten Oversier has been able to thoroughly examine the essential laws of life. Having grown through many experiences and encounters, life itself led him to the profession of reincarnation therapist. Healing through insight, showing how things in life keep on turning and how a person can free himself from heavy burdens. He is acutely aware of the many roles that a person can assume in successive incarnations. He is thoroughly acquainted with this role play and knows that consciousness sustains everything.

Maarten's book regularly demonstrates the close relationship between victim and perpetrator. But that requires insight into how our lives are determined by thoughts, words, actions, emotions, trauma, and memories. This immediately brings us to the unique area that Maarten has managed to uncover so successfully and beneficially: ancestral culture.

"Countless experiences lie dormant in our consciousness, yes, in our DNA, that are passed on, inherited in life's flow. They become active again, right down to cellular memory," he says. We now know that DNA is indeed connected to cosmic energy and even emits light. Epigenetics tells us that our thoughts and emotions influence DNA. Therefore, the feelings, impulses, emotions of our parents and ancestors continue to impact us. Could we then understand the "fall" of man to be on a different and deeper level? A fall that has led to a brokenness in our consciousness and our bodies.

For some clients, Maarten is a traveling companion who journeys with them beyond the border of death, to unlock insights into the extent to which influences and manipulations from previous incarnations can carry on working in a new birth. Insight liberates, redeems. Socrates went to work like an "obstetrician". He brought people to liberating insights. No doubt Socrates was influenced by his mother, who was a midwife.

Using countless examples from his practice, Maarten demonstrates the flow and influence of past lives and especially how the influence of our ancestors, upbringing, religion, ideas, and dogmas can often still have a devastating impact on our lives.

The Right to Be provides many examples of this – moving, shocking, tender, painful. The past is tapping on the window of the soul of countless people. Emotional memories of a war, the Holocaust, a concentration camp, sexual abuse, religious oppression and exploitation, persecution 'in the name of God'. These are not projections or fantasies of clients, but true events, which can be relived and liberated and so bring people back to their right to be, their ground of existence. In short, great therapeutic treasures can be found in the catacombs of the family chronicles, the author writes. It is there, where all "the old traumas" are tucked away and continue to affect subsequent generations.

Maarten Oversier does not interpret, does not insinuate, does not judge. Above all, he listens to his clients in order to ask an essential question at the right time. The body speaks its own language. It acts as a sounding board of inner feelings, moods, the language of the soul. That materialistic science completely ignores the existence of the soul, is deeply tragic. Awareness of the soul's existence and being able to listen attentively are the basis of any real therapy and healing.

Maarten never claims to be the agent of healing, but the person himself. By listening, paying attention, and speaking at the right time, the heart and head cooperate, together making one sound. Maarten's spiritual ingredients consist of mature insights, experiences, and encounters. Especially the encounters with Native North Americans, with whom he has regular contact. Exchanging and sharing wisdom with them has made him a practicing anthropologist. His medicine wheel is made up of spokes from various cultures, which meet in the hub of consciousness. It is not for nothing that many Native North Americans, especially the 'guardians of the traditional stories', feel a great respect and love for their 'white brother'. This mutual warm friendship flows through their hearts like a clear mountain stream. But before this water can be discharged into the ocean of Consciousness, a person must overcome many obstacles and barriers. Such as a few floating tree trunks or accumulations of stones in the river, or too dense undergrowth or hostile animals in the water or on the banks.

The author also exposes the major conflicts in today's traumatized world. As a sincere researcher, in accordance with previous crises that traumatized people, he also discovered a worldwide network of manipulations behind the corona crisis that he interprets within the context of his field of work. He is well-informed and aware of the sinister workings of power elites, of existing satanic bloodlines, secret societies, and the planned arrival of the so-called 'new world order'. Partly because of this knowledge, he can help people further along their life path – people who sometimes have a hard time of it psychologically in today's world. Helping people can only be accomplished from the inner light.

He also points out the dangers of modern technology (smartphone, internet, artificial intelligence, the cloud, 5G), control techniques that try to keep us captive in a closed, slavish system. As a kind of pseudo-religion, this technology works into our souls and threatens to alienate us, from what I would call our divine essence.

The end of the book includes some heartbreaking stories and reports from several clients. *The Right to Be* is a very well written, fascinating work full of surprises and original approaches, in which wisdom and humor alternate. It is always focused on learning to recognize and confirm one's own right to be from within. May this book touch the hearts of many.

Marcel Messing
Anthropologist, philosopher, author

FOREWORD BY DOUTZEN KROES

Maarten Oversier's book *The Right to Be* was a gift for me. For years I felt I had been carrying around certain unresolved traumas from my childhood that I could not get to. Two years earlier I had embarked on a huge quest. Familiar to many as: who am I, where do I come from and why am I here?

I started living more consciously, dived into all kinds of spiritual books, got to know special people, used plant medicines, meditated, and learned a great deal. What I learned most of all is that I wanted to 'unlearn' a lot and look at life in a new way. With an open mind and with my ego in a new place. It was no longer about 'getting even or being right' but about understanding things differently, as much as possible, and contributing to a new energy balance that benefits the community to which we are all connected.

Mirrors are not always fun, but they have taught me so much and that is still an ongoing process. When I am triggered by something or someone, I try not to take it personally. On the contrary, I ask myself: why is this happening? What is there, still to be seen inside of me? Maarten explains quite lucidly how you can recognize unprocessed trauma. Also, how they are allowed to come out through emotions and physical blockages that present themselves and which can then be investigated as to their genesis. I wish we could learn this from an early age. That we start looking for answers in ourselves and not always outside ourselves. I am very grateful to Maarten that he and many others are helping to pave the way for us. Today he is one of the guides who can teach us how to do it ourselves.

Imagine what it would be like if we all dared to look at our traumas and burdens, to learn to process them. I'm not saying it's always fun. It was sometimes quite heavy, and I don't want to lay claim to instantly 'being there'. It is a natural process in which I always encounter something in myself. But then I think: isn't that also the reason we are here on earth? To learn, to heal? I'm not sure and I know that I can still learn a lot, but one thing I do know for sure: I have become much better for myself and therefore also for others. The physical complaints that I carried with me for such a long time have also disappeared. I believe that my reality is a projection of what is going on inside me. So, everything is a mirror. As within, so without.

Doutzen Kroes
One of the world's most famous supermodels, actress, mother, and wife with a conscious view of the world.

©Paul Bellaart

PREFACE

Unexpected circumstances in life can sometimes put you on a certain path. A path whose destination, you only realize much later, was much further than you initially suspected.

It was March 1994 when a woman from The Hague asked me if I might be able to help her. She was desperate. Her child had died from cot death five months earlier and since then she wasn't really living anymore. I went to her and did something that turned things around for both of us.

Although I didn't charge fees at the time, it became my first officially paid session. Unofficially, in addition to my regular job as a chef in one of Rotterdam's most beautiful hotels, I often assisted in this field, but at the time it was nothing to write home about. I am still doing sessions today, more than twenty-five years later. In the meantime, I have trained, been truly tried and tested, and working with just as much fun and drive as when it all started. It's special how you can be gripped by an irrepressible fascination life throws your way. Curious and determined, I entered a world that, though obscure to the eye, is very much alive to the mind; a world that inspires fear and is framed by taboos. In principle I wanted to investigate this for myself, but the reincarnation therapy that resulted from it also made it visible to others.

My insights and methods formed like the moist clay in the hands of a novice potter. A mass of saturated rough earth that willingly sought to be given form by inexperienced fingers. Sometimes much too wet, so it could not be molded at all, then too dry, causing it to crumble and crack. Fortunately, my courage never failed me. Was something driving me on?

Everything gradually started to amount to something the more practical experience I gained, together with all the fruitful refinements. I became proficient. I frequently visited the regions on either side of the beaten track. First and foremost, I was challenged by earthly life with its human inhabitants to understand it in a different way than I had learned from home and school. I received encouragement just at the right time from various mentors who crossed my path. Because teachers do not always immediately show themselves as such, I sometimes experienced them as a thorn in my side, and only understood the usefulness of their interference afterwards. What kept me on track most of all, were the remarkable results of the sessions. They fueled my drive and increased my confidence. Because of that, the many tricky learning moments have never discouraged me.

HUMOR

The field of work of reincarnation therapy is basically aimed at reliving traumatic events from the past, to be able to break free from them. These events can be experienced in just as many ways as people are diverse. It requires a flexible, curious, and patient attitude from the therapist. As a result, I regularly adjusted my point of view. Just when I thought I had something I could hold on to, I had to let it go. Ultimately, clients themselves tell us how the logic behind their problems is constructed. And even in what context. I discovered that when I learned to ask more focused questions. Based on my work agenda notebooks, I count more than 14,000 sessions over the years up to the end of 2020. That makes me feel blessed.

An official nameplate on the door of my workspace states that I am a reincarnation therapist affiliated with a professional association. In addition, just before they cross the threshold, clients are offered a laconic consideration on a sign nailed next to that door: 'Beer is cheaper than therapy'. Once they have taken the plunge, they encounter yet another encouraging sign that says: 'The shit from your past is the fertilizer for your future'. A truism. Humor is a powerful and indispensable teacher, that I gratefully embrace.

Every stream I have navigated for the past twenty-years cost sweat and tears. It even allowed me to feed four children and make quite a decent living. At the same time, I am sure that the strong winds that frequently billowed the sails of my therapist ship were partly blown my way by dedicated and helpful forces from an unseen world. From the visible world it was my then dear partner Arjanne who was always a stable, supporting factor at the base of our large family, so that my capricious, ground-breaking, and at times restless nature did not capsize the ship. My gratitude cannot be expressed in words.

ARTICLES AND LECTURES

I have written various articles about my practical experience for various magazines over the years. I have given quite a few lectures and readings throughout the country, and for many years I have provided intensive training programs for therapists, coaches, trainers and care providers in the Netherlands, Spain, Germany, and Canada. I did the same on Iroquois Indian reservations. Many people asked me when a book would be coming out. I always cleverly managed to dodge answering with an array of evasive replies. Lack of time usually did the trick best. A busy practice, a large family on a farm in the Dutch province of Drenthe, surrounded by a very large garden, guitars everywhere, and a piano, chickens, a dog, two cats, fish, a refrigerator with tasty things, great friends, and lots of travel, do not leave much room to write a book. And it also happens to be a bit true.

Meanwhile, my laptop was overflowing with reams of text. Reports of sessions, worked out lectures, published and unpublished articles. Encouraged no end by some good friends, I finally buckled down and got to work.

If you're reading this, it has succeeded. It is my ultimate wish to share my practical experience on behalf of thousands of clients, who exposed their souls in all their vulnerability revealing a wealth of essential information in the process. I'm filled to the brim with them: thousands of stories. Stories that in their own right are worth a book, film, or stage performance, but in most cases will never be known by the general public. Stories that are the real cornerstones of our society; that provide understandable explanations and clear answers to the most basic life questions we ask ourselves. Stories that taught me about what really goes on inside people and what lies at the root of the many riddles in the world that we create together. There is also something strange about that world. I gradually discovered that it is being cunningly manipulated by powers with very dubious objectives. Consciously. At first, I shrugged off these discoveries and then began to protest. I'd rather stick to my therapeutic trade than broaden my horizons to some grim field of dark influences. However, the better I began to recognize the signals, the more I could not escape them. It became increasingly clear, and it explained a lot. There are powers, manifesting themselves in an elitist club that place themselves above humankind, that are quite consciously seeking control over people and the world. Their influence is of a much greater magnitude than I could ever have realized. They travel through time, always presenting themselves in a new camouflage suit, but with agendas and working methods that have not changed.

This book would be incomplete, and not do justice to so much anger, surprise, and bewilderment at the true genesis of the traumas we were caught up in over the course of many lifetimes, if I failed to address this matter. At the same time, reincarnation therapy also reveals that we may have contributed to these distorted power relations in previous lives. The so-called 'perpetrator lives'. It is better to expose this in individual therapeutic trajectories to really break free of something, than to keep blaming. And the former is already a tough enough job as it is, especially since most people opt for the latter.

CASE HISTORIES

In addition to a great deal of my own research and detective work, the basis of this book is formed by the stories that surfaced from thousands of clients, over a twenty-year span, during approximately 14,000 sessions of intensive therapeutic processing. This gave clients new insights; sometimes subtle, but usually quite clear. This was often accompanied by significant release of emotional and physical energy, followed by remarkable, and usually lasting, change. The client's mindset was also often naturally adjusted to more original, less fraught visions. There was a structural change to the self-image and the image of loved ones and circumstances. People often experienced that every person who was or is important in their life, holds up a mirror to them and vice versa. Their mindset was also often adjusted when for example, it came to God, government interests, one's world view or issues of assigning meaning and spiritual views. They are the volumes of a history that tell a very different story than we are usually taught in school.

What I discovered above all was that there are four sources that more than anything else influence the state of mind and well-being of the current population – past lives, ancestors, war, and the church. That is this book's significant conclusion. Depending on which continent you grew up, religions, all histories of war and oppression and the extent to which one's family was involved, are the factors that determine the well-being of present-day generations. Traumas from the current life, as well as past lives, are all related to this.

Many personal experiences that were discovered in the subconscious and given a voice were relived, and that re-experience was often accompanied by a simultaneous undertone of indignation. In fact, these sensations of indignation are an important part of the therapeutic process. They separate the wheat from the chaff. Through processing, clients gain in-depth insights. Many people discover, when it comes to a certain role in a past life, that under all kinds of circumstances he or she has relinquished his or her autonomy and in essence has not remained true to themselves.

In war situations, for example, it concerns the wrath at the authorities who gave orders to take part in some war or battle under all sorts of pretexts that, in retrospect, are judged to be extremely irresponsible. The feeling of being cannon fodder. The same goes for lives under strict ecclesiastical influence. When it came to the church, what makes people the most indignant is having been lied to about the fallacy of heaven and hell. It often involves the dismaying realization of having fallen prey to a theater of deception. In general terms, this has been the final verdict reached by countless sessions, after having lived through church-related roles. The joint conclusion of clients, independently of one other, seems to point to an institution of power that apparently needs to exert conscious control and even enslave the population. To that end it sucks people into a field of false truth. The story of Jesus seems to have been manipulated and interpreted in such a way that it would have a profound effect on the sentiments of the populace on many levels - making it easily manipulated.

This is a conclusion with far-reaching implications. A conclusion based on inferences drawn by clients. I don't want to present them as established fact, but I do want to present them emphatically for consideration. My aim is not to demonstrate that this conclusion is correct in any way. As a therapist I am only interested in the result of a treatment trajectory. In the end I am only reporting on my extensive practical experience. If clear improvements repeatedly arise from these kinds of conclusions, I think that should be taken very seriously. I hope to give these insights gained through blood, sweat, and tears a wider reach. After all, broadening our horizons is an ongoing process.

TRANSFORMATION

The present day is dominated by major transformations on earth. There is a real awareness of this at various levels of the soul. Because of this, many have seized the opportunity to break free from the effects of old, painful events with their restrictive themes and beliefs. To put it disrespectfully: to come and clean up a lot of old clutter. It explains why so many people are incarnated now. As a therapist, it takes courage and perhaps some aptitude to venture into these initially gloomy areas. But it can clarify the perception of yourself, the environment, and the world around you. And certainly, if more recognition is gained with (one of) your own ancestors. They might just feel heard and pleasantly touched, if only because you have traveled with them for a little while in a world in which they themselves had been lost.

Hand in hand with all my practical experience, I was nurtured by the intensely deep wisdom and knowledge I received from several teachers from indigenous peoples.

All these ingredients from a quarter of a century of intensive therapy, have resulted in a concoction of my own. Under the name of *The Right to Be*, I am very happy to be able to communicate what I have experienced.

GRATEFUL

First, I am extremely grateful for all the stories of my clients, especially those whose personal stories I have been allowed to use. I would also like to thank Archie Fire Lame Deer, Lakota Medicine Man, Dancing Thunder-Ralph Oquendo, Ken Maracle, Deer clan and faithkeeper of the Iroquois Cayuga Indians, Ojibwe Seer Mellinda Trudeau, Oneida Clanmother Beatrice Nicholas, Charlene Deleary, Chandra Maracle and Rick Hill, Mohawk-Tuscarora, William Woodworth, Bear clan of the Iroquois Mohawk Indians. My dearly beloved grandmother SARA Smith, of the Iroquois Mohawk Turtle clan, who officially adopted me as her grandson in 2009, Tom Porter, Bear clan Mohawk. And Toltec - Grandfather of the Grandfathers - Tlakaelel, a highly respected Sundance chief and spiritual teacher, with whom I had the opportunity of sharing many wonderful moments in life, ranging from boogie-woogie behind the piano to pouring water and singing during sweat lodge ceremonies, always together with bearer of the Sacred Pipe and dear friend, Bert Gunn.

Tanya van der Spek, Nienke Lantman, Nicolyn Dijstra and Evelien Dommerholt for their fantastic editing work, involvement, and expert substantive reflections. Marcel (and Marijke) Messing, for his/their warm (soul) friendship. Marcel is a primal mentor and wonderful human being whom I admire immensely for his pioneering work, wisdom, and publications and who is always an enormously inspiring, steady, and loyal driving force behind my own quest. Good friend Ewald Stöteler for his valuable contribution to this book, for his openness, incredible knowledge, and the many insanely inspiring exchanges in which two disciplines embraced each other. Prof. Bob 'Old Shatterhand' de Wit and the beautiful, on the outside and inside, Doutzen Kroes, graced the English and German translation and fourth and fifth Dutch editions of the book with lovely forewords. How grateful can you be as an author? Dr. Hans Moolenburgh, Peter Vereecke, Irina Filcer, Geert 'bouillabaisse' Kimpen, Michelle Shanti, Herman den Blijker, Guido

Jonkers. Extra big thanks to Coen Vermeeren, who was an important stimulus to the writing of *The Right to Be*, Eelco de Boer, Peter Toonen, Robert Bridgeman, Trudy van Batenburg, Robert Rolloos, Laura Menger, Dirk Post, Rob Bontenbal, Tineke Noordegraaf, Daisy Schilder and others whose names are not mentioned, but that doesn't make me feel any less their contributions, support and loving, sometimes much-needed moral and emotional support that kept me going when needed.

Maarten A. Oversier
Roden, 2022

ONEIDA CLANMOTHER BEATRICE NICHOLAS, KEN MARACLE, MELLINDA TRUDEAU 'AT GRANDMA'S', ONEIDA RESERVAAT, LONDON ONTARIO, CANADA.

PART I

INTRODUCTION TO REINCARNATION THERAPY

CASE HISTORY OF CLIENT LISANNE SPAANDER

Summer turns to autumn and autumn to winter. The seasons flow into one another, as do my feelings. From anger and pain, to rest and peace and vice versa. Today I am allowed to see and intensely feel my emotions. That's why I'm sitting opposite Maarten in a big comfortable chair. He looks at me, and I feel he sees me so I can surrender to this moment. I am 16 years old, and I have a tumor in my pelvis that is 12 by 12 centimeters. I want to do something about this myself; also, spiritually, and mentally.

Maarten and I dive into my life story together. I look at my mother sitting next to me and realize it's about our life story. My mother's mother, my grandmother, died of non-Hodgkin's lymphoma when I was seven. Out of loyalty I still carry her within me. Maarten speaks to her through me, and I feel my mouth start to move. A torrent of words gushes out and it becomes clear that she does not realize that she has died. She is partly the cause of my being sick, by her presence in my system, so in my body too. Grandma now addresses my mother, via my voice, and together they have a conversation. When she was young grandma had very nasty sexual experiences in World War II. She always kept that to herself for fear of a lack of understanding and condemnation from her family. As a result, the bond with her future daughter, my mother, became seriously cool and aloof. But because of this exchange the congealed energy dissolves and starts flowing again from my grandmother to my mother and then back to me. After all that time the natural flow of life comes back on track. Through three generations.

Together we tell grandma that we really see and understand her now and that we respect her place in the family. We also let her experience her passing so that she can continue on and can let me go. Suddenly she is standing in front of me instead of inside me and I see in my mind's eye that she is smiling at me.

"THE UNEXPRESSED FEELING WAS STUCK IN ME"

After contacting my grandmother on my mother's side, I also have an exchange with my paternal grandmother. She was orphaned in the Second World War and because she missed a mother's love, she clings to my father so hard that I can hardly reach him. I am learning to see that the cause of events lies with how people are raised and with what they have experienced under the influence of ancestors and their often drastic and suppressed history. Everyone ultimately acts out of loyalty to one other. I suddenly feel my lips curling into a smile. As if I can understand everyone now. The profound incomprehension, the unexpressed feelings of both my grandmothers was stuck inside me. Together with Maarten I talk about it and feel it intensely. In the car on the way home I look at my mother. "Wow, I feel lighter, I let it all go."

In my world it is taboo to talk about deceased relatives who can make you sick because you carry them inside you. I pushed aside my feelings because of that and labeled it "crazy". Through Maarten I realize that what you feel is right. He saw the same things I did. That gave me confidence to keep working on family ties and on myself. After the session I had surgery to remove my tumor, but the doctors said they could hardly see any tumor anymore. And now, at twenty-two, I can say that I am completely healthy.

Lisanne 'Lies' Spaander

Three weeks after the consultation, this message came from Lisanne's mother, Ilona:

Dear Maarten,
Just an update on Lisanne. A miracle has happened. Lisanne was in the OR on Tuesday, and they first opened her up to see whether the tumor was clear of her sphincter so they could proceed with surgery. We received notification that it is incredible – there was no more tumor to be seen and felt. The bone also looked good. They cut her open even further and moved the artery to one side to remove bone. They found a small ball of living tumor tissue in a small blood vessel on the vein. It's probably left over from the big tumor that receded. This spot was outside the area of operation and after consultation they decided to close her up and stop operating. They have seen and felt that the bone looks good and strong.

Sincerely,
Ilona Woestenburg
Lisanne

Lisanne Spaander was told at the age of 16 that she had a malignant tumor. Music was her outlet. She released an album also including her own song *Vechtersbaas* (Warrior Woman). It was seen on the Dutch national commercial television program RTL Late Night, at the opening of the Princess Máxima Center for Pediatric Oncology and at the *Symphonica in Rosso* concert with popular Dutch singer Marco Borsato, with whom she remained friends. In 2020 her book was published, Vechtersbaas: *Childhood cancer; grown up overnight.*

INTRODUCTION

From bone collector to reincarnation therapist

"Children look magically at the world they live in. There is no room for this in the logic and reason that many grownups cultivate to the extreme. They are no longer able to understand a child."

Rodenrijs, around 1970. Once plied by black tarred barges supplying the famous fruit and vegetable market and the Hordijk box factory with timber, across the Rodenrijs canal, is the spacious polder landscape that stretches into the distance. Dark green meadows, as far as you could see. Frisian cows gobbled tussocks of tender grass with their powerful tongues, before settling in to graze quietly at a rhythmic pace. Long rows of crooked pollard willows marked the ditches full of sticklebacks, salamanders, and frogs. The fences next to the windmills, intended to regulate the water level, were always sagging. A timeless view under the typical Dutch gray-blue skies with clouds constantly scudding by.

The canal was a stone's throw from our flat-roofed house, at the end of Schadeestraat, in the Penninghlaan. I grew up there, seven months after having been born in Rotterdam, in the Cornelis Heinricksestraat, under the smoke of the Feyenoord football stadium. The endless canal was the red thread through our village, the longest one in the Netherlands, at thirteen kilometers, if I remember correctly. Quite a few prominent people had houses that overlook it, such as writer Annie M.G. Schmidt, the bicycle dealer Thomassen, mayor Reekers and taxi company owner van Leeuwen. But the polder region had to be prepared for new residential areas.

The elongated village of *Berkel en Rodenrijs* with its rows of houses stretching along a single road, expanded. Van Winden's farm in the countryside was on its last legs. It was demolished to make way for new building projects. Most places had already collapsed by themselves. Transience had struck with a vengeance. Had everybody gone way from here, I naively wondered.

The rubble and the countless scattered pieces of debris gave my creative mind ample opportunity to put the farm back together in my imagination. Everywhere I looked I saw roof tiles, fencing and pieces of discarded furniture. Earthenware, dented enamel pans, white clay tobacco pipes with decorative sections and an assortment of broken glass preserving jars with a sour-smelling gunk. But the pears that flew in all directions after I had thrown the only intact preserving jar against a stone, still smelled fine. Chunks of wall with several layers of floral-patterned wallpaper still sticking to them, stuck straight up from the wet grassland. A sorry sight of a dilapidated place that for generations had been bustling with activity. A place where hundreds of Christmas trees once stood, babies had been born, people had died, chickens and pigs had been slaughtered, where thousands of liters of soup and mountains of potatoes had been boiled and the toilet flushed thousands of times, and where fruit trees gratefully bore fruit year after year. This was a great place for an eight-year-old kid to play. Nobody else felt attracted to this playground, which you could reach only after having braved a large swathe of muddy field.

JAW OF A MAMMAL

Suddenly, I stumbled upon an object. It made my heart pound faster, even before I knew what it was. It was quite different from anything I had already put on the pile of stuff I wanted to save and take home. Turned brown from the infused clay, and with all its molars still present, pulled out the jaw of a large mammal. An unreal but at the same time innocent encounter with death, orchestrated by a play of factors that were way over my head. Had I found a germ of something I had once lost here? I breathed heavily and felt like a prospector finding his first nugget. In a split second I made an important decision: I will become a bone collector. I wanted more of this, a lot more.

A welcome shiver ran through my inner world. The sudden loss of my father some five years earlier, and all the veils of mystery that shrouded it, had made me feel quite desperate. Amid the countless questions thrusting themselves upon me, one thing became increasingly clear: he wasn't coming home anymore. How acceptable was that? Not at all. No matter that I wanted to understand the story behind those veils.

And now death had become tangible again, because of the bone. It wasn't just the ghost of the cow who had once chewed her grass, but my father who also came back to life for me. I knew all about cows from the meadow behind our house. They briefly merged with the memory of my father in a hopeful moment full of new perspectives. The deeper connections which I, of course, only unconsciously made myself, – it was unlikely they would be understood at home. And that worked fine in 1970. It was going to unfold throughout my life.

As soon as a decision is made, isn't it magical how you immediately feel a new alignment? Now that I had decided to become a bone collector, I suddenly discovered all kinds of things. Thanks to the many trophies I found, wandering through the meadows, over the dike behind our house, between the flowerbeds and the bushes in the park and even in our own backyard, I built up a considerable collection in a short time. The child's respect for nature in a living being radiated from my collection. We often ate chicken at home. I was surprised to recognize the similarities with the skeletons of the many birds I had found.

Whenever we had chicken, we always looked forward to finding the collarbone, the wishbone. It was plucked greedily from the carcass with greasy hands. Anyone at the table, lucky enough to get the top of the wishbone, and longest piece after pulling it apart, could make a wish. I still know how often I wished Daddy was back home, but I slowly came to realize that it did not lie within the power of chicken bones to bestow wishes. Nor could the result of a soccer game be influenced. I noticed that when the Dutch national team lost the World Cup final to West Germany. What remained was the cracking sensation, and who won it.

In my childlike perception of the world, I perceived the wonder of nature that also included transience. A confrontation with that transience, through the death of my father came during a phase in my life where it should have been more about connecting than leaving. Unless... I had to learn early on how to look at life differently. And that, without having the slightest notion that life could be a learning process.

As an international salesman my father was often on the road. My little brother and I were told that he had gone on a trip to a faraway country, and that things were better there, which I childishly interpreted to mean that he had traded us in for something bigger and better. A reckless drunk driver had hit him in the middle of the night, killing him instantly when he was innocently crossing the street; so we were told when we got older. This watered-down version of what really happened had been concocted with the best of intentions in the belief it would be the least harmful to the children. Later I discovered to my mother's and the family's great dismay that the actual truth involved a much more violent version of the accident. Namely, that a serious argument had taken place between two men beforehand. It had to do with business and our father was deliberately run down by a car. So, manslaughter. A fact that was confirmed more than thirty years later by my uncle, who was there that pitch-black night. "When he came back, after having been accosted unawares by two men shortly before, he was staring death in the face", my uncle later admitted about my father. At a single stroke he breached all the built-up secrecy for me that was supposed to keep us from this raw naked truth. "Half an hour later he was dead," he added, confirming a deeply uncomfortable suspicion I had held. After my mother's death in 2000, I read in one of her many notebooks, handwritten in pencil that the official police report of this 'accident' had been immediately destroyed because, "the children should never be burdened with that." It gave me an intensely sad feeling to realize how deeply this truth had to be hidden and how that must have burdened her life and those of everyone else who knew.

All that was left of Papa, were photographs, stories, and personal belongings like his many suits. That was all considerably less exciting than his real body. The way he moved, how he acted. The stubble on his chin and the smell of his skin, his wrist with that gorgeous watch, and the warm voice as he sang and told stories.

Those strong, hairy hands that pulled me onto his lap, with those fingers that moved, played the piano and tickled me. That interplay of his limbs and head, yes especially his head, his most distinctive feature, the way he smoked his pipe, had a drink with mommy, wound up the clock and snapped the chicken's wishbone with me. That was real and that was what had to come back.

The very fact that my father was not there anymore, never came home again, was something I did not want. I wanted to dig down to the bone so that I would never ever have to feel like that again. Every time I discovered something new, death momentarily came alive again. It was on that borderline where there was the greatest chance of obtaining information, from the place my mother had told me, no one had never returned. But how did she know that, I kept asking myself. I wanted to squeeze myself into death to prove otherwise. And by doing so I created unconscious experiences that were actually traumatic, such as surgery on my skull causing me to leave my body. All those unusual phenomena I regularly saw, my ability before falling asleep to consciously leave my body and float around in my surroundings. Why was all that strange to my mother? Why didn't she know or say anything about that? Why was all that fantasy, and certainly not real?

INNER TURMOIL

Leaving the parental home marked the beginning of a long journey that lasted eighteen years before I went from bone collector to reincarnation therapist. I needed the culinary career which culminated in me becoming chef, in a magnificent Rotterdam hotel on the Westersingel, to distract me from my sensitive nature. The renowned Dutch top chef Herman den Blijker, who ran the restaurant *De Engel* on the other side of the street, regularly dropped by to goof around in my kitchen, and vice versa. It had to do with whether we had 'stirred up anything interesting' that day, coupled with enthusiastic tasting sessions where usually no silverware was required. A fantastic time. A world that was full of life, by the way. The bones that passed the review there were either gnawed clean or used to make soups and sauces.

Still, an inner turmoil continued to gnaw at me. I kept wondering how the unseen world was related to the seen. And especially how they influenced each other. That things were like that was beyond dispute to me. I could touch people with my hands without having to lay a finger on them directly and sometimes I saw things that others apparently did not see. A penchant for the occult ensued, for mystical worlds, for spirits and for the logic of the soul born after a body dies.

It wasn't just my co-worker Jos who came to my office for non-business business. The door was then locked, and the blinds shut so that everybody knew the boss was 'in a meeting'. Jos brought about a change. He had been suffering from chronic migraines for years. We noticed that placing my hands on his head significantly reduced his pain. One time while doing this an image suddenly came to me of a man in a dark blue suit, that was in fashion in the 1970s. He was slapping a seven or eight-year-old child hard over the ears with a rolled-up newspaper. When I told Jos about this and elaborated on the details, tears welled up in his eyes. In this scene, he recognized himself as the child with his father. His father who had been dead for many years, turned out to have done this frequently and a moment of reconciliation had never taken place. The emotional process that was triggered in Jos made all sorts of pennies drop. Shortly after that he told me he had an intense dream about his father. He came to say goodbye and apologized. The most amazing upshot was that his migraine never came back after that.

What I learned from all this is that there is an underlying story behind a complaint that manifests itself physically. And that the complaint and story are inextricably linked. And with that a deeply held suspicion was confirmed. If the story itself is not given any attention and only the complaint is treated, not much will change. Or more succinctly, the complaint is a signal of an unprocessed event. That realization played on my mind for a long time before I decided to learn how to work with it effectively.

COT DEATH (SUDDEN INFANT DEATH SYNDROME)

I changed course in 1997 and hung up my chef's jacket. Instead, I began 'cooking up' other things. After a long motorhome trip through Europe with my wife and two children, I did a three-year reincarnation therapy course in Utrecht. I already had a practice, regularly doing sessions with people based on magnetizing and things that came to me clairvoyantly. Something always happened. It reminds me of how Els, a good friend of mine, approached me about a couple living in The Hague who were friends of hers that were having problems.

It was March 1994. Since their three-month-old child had died from cot death, the mother no longer dared leave the house, nor enter the nursery where the death had taken place. "I think you should go there," said Els. And that's what I did, even though I really had no idea what I would find.

Somewhat unsure, I rang the bell. A young woman with a frightened and tense look on her face opened the door. We chatted for a while over a cup of coffee. But she didn't relax. And I didn't really know what to do. "Do you want to see the baby's room?" she asked in a soft voice. I was nervous but agreed. She showed me the way but stayed downstairs. Reluctantly I climbed the steep stairs to the attic. It had been five months since the baby had died and no one had been there since.

A shiver ran through me when I saw the crib with a pink blanket that was still curled up. I even saw a bit of discoloration on the sheet, maybe from some saliva. It was clear by looking at all the things around the abandoned bed, everything was well prepared to provide the necessary care for a new human life. The chest of drawers with Walt Disney figures, and various toys from which I concluded it was a boy. And even a table with some teacups for visitors.

I found it all musty, silent, and lackluster. Indeed, a somewhat gloomy atmosphere, but somehow that didn't bother me. Sitting on a chair, I created a moment of silence, before spontaneously opening the bedroom window wide. I closed my eyes and imagined that the baby's soul was still there. And that I could talk to it. I said something along the lines of it being time to let go. That it served no purpose anymore to stay here and that there might still be new opportunities to start living. I thought I experienced a kind of breeze going through the room. Logical, you would think, because of the open window, but it was something else. It felt noticeably lighter in the room. I took the sheet out of the crib and flapping it back and forth outside the window I saw light clouds of dust being released that glittered because of the dim sunlight that shone on it. It felt liberating and refreshing. As if spring could now come inside. Then I folded it over the edge of the crib.

I think I must have been there for about twenty minutes. Once downstairs I took the shaken mother to the room by the hand. She went without any resistance as if she were sleepwalking. She stopped in the middle of the room and looked aimlessly around. She began softly crying, from the memories that reawakened in her. That touched me deeply and I had an inner image that only now would her uterus be able to finally contract. It didn't take long. I just stood next to her, behind the crib. We chatted for little while afterwards, but not even about anything concrete. After that I went home. I later understood from Els that peace had returned to the house. The trapped energy had been released.

I didn't even know exactly what I had done, but thought it was nice that it had helped her. I now believe that I had managed to contact the baby's soul, which couldn't break free for all sorts of reasons. Apparently, my presence, my intervention, brought a certain vortex that had triggered a process of release. It was my first real session, for which I even received fifty guilders. One of those orange banknotes I found hard to spend afterwards as it represented such a special story. I suspect that this baby's soul has returned through another pregnancy so that it could still become part of a family.

NEW LIFE IN PAST EVENTS

Do the bone collector and the reincarnation therapist have something in common? I think they do. In fact, here too one was born out of the other. Both focused on the original spirit behind what was physically observable. The reason for trying to fathom such things was apparently the death of my father. Would it now be possible to continue to nurture myself with the confidence that this therapeutic path also had fruitful perspectives in a world dominated by rational bodybuilding? Naturally, that wasn't something I dwelled upon all that often. And yet, one of these days I will probably have a good chat about it with my father, over a heavenly cup of tea. Then we will learn to understand things that are far beyond my present earth-oriented comprehension. Every quest has a reason, and this reason was mine.

The bone collector became the fertile ground for the later reincarnation therapist. Breathing new life into past events that were supremely painful, and left unprocessed as a result, appears to have a potent therapeutic effect. Whatever the complaint, I now know that there is always a misunderstood story we carry within. And a need to tell it. And from what I have been told by my clients, it is so inexpressibly valuable, so essential, so stripped of frills and above all so healing that I can't help but bring it all together in this book in a context it absolutely deserves, and to propagate it in this way. I haven't got my father back, but I'm at peace with that now. I am filled with an immense feeling of fulfillment that all those stories via this book, *The Right to Be*, can travel again and so touch and inspire others. Like teamwork. Dear daddy, how I love you.

CHAPTER 1

Reincarnation and Therapy

"We are not human beings on a spiritual journey, we are spiritual beings on a human journey."

Every complaint or condition that you can have as a person has a cause in an unprocessed past. Regardless of whether this complaint is mental, physical, emotional, or spiritual. It usually involves a combination of these.

Human behavior is largely determined by pain that is hidden away, arising from violent events. In our modern world this is hardly acknowledged and certainly not in this context. Crucial situations, which in so-called past lives have not been properly concluded, continue to demand attention. Also painful events from one's present life, as in my case the death of my father. All these connections form the basis of a spiritual law that only becomes comprehensible provided you realize the proper inner process of alignment. The past lives that have not yet been integrated into the current personality still want to be worked out, processed, and completed. That is the reason why we cannot yet let go of some old situations. They cling to us, even as we take on different personalities from life to life. Characters in diverse habitats, that stay connected to old themes and patterns. All things considered; these diverse personalities can never be seen as separate from each other. To me it's simply called reincarnation. Metempsychosis (transmigration of the soul) is also a good term. Through many incarnations and human experiences, by taking on many human forms the soul comes to know its true, divine nature. Bygone eras merge and flow into each other like the seasons. And we humans remain manning them – for example a Corona-dominated society, which includes hidden agendas as well as growth opportunities for the soul. Someday this wave and its aftermath will become a thing of the past. For the soul, however, such an episode is not completed until all the accumulated overtones and restrictive beliefs have been fundamentally discredited. And that doesn't necessarily have to take place in the same life.

There is a strong resemblance between the origin of reincarnation therapy and the method of the shamans or traditional medicine people from various indigenous cultures (including the North American Indians). There it is called 'soul retrieval', in which presumed lost parts of the soul are returned to the current incarnation. Reincarnation therapy is based on two assumptions. Firstly: man is more than just a body containing all kinds of random processes. There is also a soul, or a non-physical human aspect, which throughout all phases of life is more or less conscious and has experiences. The second assumption is that the human soul goes through a cycle of multiple lives or incarnations.

Regression or reincarnation therapy is a form of psychotherapy, the central tenant of which are processes of acceptance and processing and as a result learning to understand subconscious patterns. It's nice that you don't have to believe in reincarnation or study it to achieve favorable results. Regression or reincarnation therapy is based on a simple principle. Processing of pain leftover from the past is still quite possible, while the original event(s), linearly speaking, either comes or come from a bygone time. The time that is behind us, sometimes even very far, can quite emphatically leave its mark on our current life and thereby determine our quality of life. If we divide the past period into segments, in technical terms we refer to them as 're-experience areas'.

Of course there are theories that say that time and space do not actually exist and that all lives exist parallel to each other, but with reincarnation therapy I start from the assumption of chronology and successive lives, because this is how I come across it in my practice. That time and space do not actually exist is particularly noticeable during out-of-body experiences, dreams, or experiences under the influence of hallucinogens. But also, during trance sessions, such as with reincarnation therapy. With our limited comprehension during waking consciousness, it boggles the mind. Although many people can have very deep spiritual experiences in time and space during sessions, they often wonder afterwards whether they haven't confabulated their experiences. As soon as rationality takes over again, horizons immediately narrow.

THE SOUL RESIDES SOMEWHERE

Assuming that we have a soul, it always 'resides' somewhere. Embodied, disembodied or in a body in the making, a fetus. We can have memories of experiences and events from our present life, in a time frame ranging from yesterday to our very first moments of life and early childhood. Influential events during pregnancy, birth or even conception may also be present. The term reincarnation in a therapeutic context indicates that this past is still taken more broadly. Extensive international research and experience in this field have taught us that during sessions, people can also have very lifelike impressions in the perception of their environment that they do not (cannot) recognize from their current life because they have not occurred in this capacity. For example, because they experience themselves as soldiers even though they are born after the war. Or like a medieval figure who died of the plague. Or they experience having died under the exact same circumstances as grandma or grandpa's little sister or brother who died in an accident. In short, these fates are accorded the highest priority and afforded meticulous therapeutic care.

Something that also occurs is that during regression people undergo experiences in which they are disembodied, as in the period between earthly lives, the so-called intermediate existence. From the soul's point of view, an earthly life is regarded as an intermediate existence, but we look at this through our terrestrial glasses.

Experiences from past lives seem to connect seamlessly with all kinds of current themes from the present life, making it more and more difficult to imagine that they are all based on figments of our imagination. And why would we want to do that? Why do we often think it is so difficult to see ourselves in a much more extended picture? Mostly because it is so difficult to comprehend within the frames of thought imposed on us that we can safely go beyond the confines of our conditioned powers of imagination, as well as find much deeper insights there about ourselves and the surroundings in which we live. Ever since childhood most people have consumed information in a very passive way and are discouraged from forming an authentic picture of the world. And that is also how the teacher fared who did this. The natural curiosity inherent in every human is thereby strongly discouraged, leaving countless possibilities that we have at our disposal as human beings to remain untapped – to learn essential things about ourselves and make discoveries about the world. In fact, before you know it, you are a dissenter who does not fit into the system, because all the important insights that manifest themselves as soon as the imposed ideas fade, ultimately refer to our spiritual nature.

EVERYTHING IS CONSTANTLY EXPIERIENCED

In a general sense we remember everything that was impressive, valuable, profound, special, difficult, or emotional. But when experiences are genuinely traumatic, we tend to suppress them into subconscious worlds. All kinds of denial or dissociative mechanisms are then deployed so that we do not have to fully experience the shocking reality and pain. They are strategies that under the circumstances, or shortly thereafter, are effective but eventually take their toll. We continue to adhere to and nurture these mechanisms even though the actual event is over. That leads to survival. That is why we speak of survival strategies.

It is strange for the soul to speak of memories. Everything is constantly experienced, lived, and registered, regardless of the circumstances. Like water is always wet and fire hot, so too the soul constantly experiences its own essence. The soul makes no effort to do that, it is its nature. There is a continuous perception, more or less conscious, depending on the circumstances in which the person it animates finds himself.

An unprocessed past is characterized by the development of patterns of symptoms, arising from event(s) that could not be completed. Sometimes quite clearly traceable and recognizable, sometimes quite dormant, unconscious, kept secret and/or covered up. All the sensations involved and the energetic imbalance arising from a such a burdened past, like fear, obsession, physical injury, trapped tension in the body, or inability to express emotions, subsequently no longer harmonize (completely) in someone's system. The unprocessed past attaches itself and the flow of the vital energy, also called prana or qi, gets blocked in all sorts of ways. This is translated in the form of various symptoms and complaints.

In this context, we do not recognize the cause of the complaints initially, which means that we tend to treat them in their outward form. We combat disturbing thoughts with cognitive behavioral therapies, forced positive thinking, tranquilizers, or meditation. Physical disorders with the well-known symptomatic medical treatments. Emotional blockages with drugs and methods that are supposed to regulate our moods, ranging from influencing hormonal processes to shock therapy. This usually yields little result and when it does, it is usually temporary, and symptoms reappear. Reincarnation therapy searches precisely for the deepest disturbances, the crux of pains, which are the underlying cause of these complaints. In this sense, the only reason for reincarnation therapy to be preoccupied with the past, is precisely to detach people from it so that they can do more and more in the here and now.

UNFINISHED BUSINESS

All experiences, gained over countless lifetimes, remain with us. They form a personal database, a private akasha. Our own library containing the oeuvre of our life experiences. Our unique and self-acquired history. What I personally find most fascinating about regression and reincarnation therapy is that people can remember an untold number of stories. Literally endless. All experiences are remembered in our subconscious. It not so easy to define exactly what consciousness is, but I'll try. Consciousness is a personal, intelligent, limitless, and at the same time structured field of life energy in which information is stored that is decoded by our brain. It is invisible to the naked eye but creates a clearly noticeable effect in our perception and behavior. Phew, now let it go.

It is useful to distinguish between those experiences in life that have been lived through and therefore completed, and those that stagnated due to all kinds of circumstances and so could not 'finish vibrating'. After all, the potential of these events also contains life energy, but now in an area demarcated and sometimes even closed off by the trauma. In other words, vital energy is locked in by an anxiety-induced contraction. Because this trapped energy needs to flow freely again, it attracts those circumstances that once caused it like a magnet. The original embedded experience is brought back, is recalled now in a different time, under different conditions, but with the same ingredients. In fact, in this way consciousness creates a second chance for the individual to 'step in' again, but now with the possibility of release and completion.

We have all lost ourselves at one time or another in intrigue, life and death battles, war, jealousy, extreme loneliness, (religious) frenzy, illnesses and injuries, excesses, alienation, or hubris. From the soul's point of view, these are the unfinished chapters from our life's parade. And those pieces, too, ultimately want to be fully seen and embraced. We are allowed to reconsider matters in those new confrontations with old remnants. In doing so, we are reminded once again of the consequences of our past actions. We may also make different choices than before to experience a different outcome. Until those old split-off remnants are no longer alien to us, and we can integrate them as whole parts of ourselves. These unfinished matters partially define who we are. Our comings and goings are strongly driven by them. In professional parlance we speak of 'the soul's unfinished business'.

SOCCER

Imagine seeing a soccer ball on a field with a goal behind it. You're walking towards it and on the way to the ball you feel a growing desire and need to give it a good swift kick towards the goal. Preferably with an imaginary goalkeeper who you want to show a thing or two with a brilliant shot in the top corner. You start your run up and kick out with one leg until… the ball unexpectedly disappears for some totally unforeseen reason. The feeling that lingers inside you is a good example of an unfinished experience. You still feel the need to give that ball a good wallop, especially your leg, but now there is no ball and no goal (and no goalkeeper) anymore. When you are walking down the street the next day and see an empty can on the sidewalk, that situation can give you the opportunity to complete what wasn't finished the day before. Agitated, you will kick the can away, with or without a feeling of satisfaction, while the countless people passing by did not even notice it was there. They were not thematically connected with it. Although this simple example obviously doesn't do justice to describing a real trauma, the similarity is there. When someone is in a life-threatening situation and cannot escape, the need to free oneself and run away is still present. So, he attracts a similar situation again. When someone had been hopelessly locked up for a long time and eventually died, the need to be liberated from an enclosed space is still there. So, that person attracts a similar situation again. When someone was not allowed to make a sound, under life-threatening circumstances, the need to do so remains. So, he attracts a similar situation again. When someone was not allowed to attract attention, because this once had disastrous consequences, the need to become visible again remains present. An example: when a Jewish boy in 1943 is told emphatically by his parents to hide behind the old stuff in the attic only to be found a night and day later (and taken away), in the next life such a person may become overly attached to old stuff. He is unable to let go of stuff because of old fear. A conviction has been etched from the previous, unprocessed experience: so long as I surround myself with old stuff, I won't be found out (and taken away). When someone died of hunger, that hungry feeling continues to connect him to 'life'. After all, it was the most intense sensation he experienced before he died. In other words: so long as I experience hunger, I'm still alive. And remember that that sensation might also give him the hope to be reunited with a child or loved one. In a new existence he therefore wants to experience that feeling of hunger again, if need be, by not eating. That is happening now in a subconscious area because the old story has receded into his memories. The logic of the soul behind it, however, is that now a different turn can be experienced that unlinks him from the association of hunger with life.

RELIVING, HAVING DIED

The completion of a past human life goes hand in hand with an intense reliving of the death at a previous time. This is an extremely important focus area of reincarnation therapy since many aspects of a past life could not be completed properly. It results in confusion about that dying, as if that was some residue that still adhered to it energetically. Such a past life could not be integrated sufficiently into the total essence of the soul. Reliving it offers the opportunity to clear up much of that confusion and bring it to consciousness. Essentially, a kind of final aftercare for the soul.

In addition to a life that can be classified as one's past life, a reincarnation therapist also pays attention to the lives of one's ancestors or direct relationships – something I certainly do – either to the death of a blood relative, friend, foe, or someone with whom they had close personal ties.

If this dying has not been completed properly, there is now a chance to do so. The soul of a deceased person can still emotionally and physically experience what it is like to die, by utilizing the client's physical capacity. With guidance, it becomes receptive to the unresolved experiences of the deceased. In that sense I make my client a temporary medium, as it were. I only do this when it comes to relationships of close kinship, almost always a blood relative, or a parent or ancestor. By a concentration of attention, reinforced through very specific questions, you can contact another soul other than your own. In a milder form, this is also visible in family constellations. The difference there is that strangers are drafted in, in the name of someone else's ancestor. Fine for those who achieve a good result with that. For me it feels more appropriate to connect the soul of a deceased person's soul to one of his own descendants.

If a person 'does not die well', the cleansing effect that naturally forms the basis of the process of dying is unable to take place properly on every conceivable level. In this way all sorts of ambiguous residue still cling to someone's being in energetic form. One's experience is stagnated and incomplete. Nothing is cleared up. Reliving a death experience, even if it has taken place physically, and within our perception of time, means clarity can still be obtained concerning the circumstances when it occurred. The clarity that this brings about instantly accelerates to the present, and merges with our current understanding.

As dying under therapeutic guidance becomes a more accepted practice, this mortal 'becomes rarefied'. As if the original personality starts to condense. Thereby withdrawing from the personality he himself once was in, in the living environment at the time. Much broader realizations seep naturally inside by themselves, on a wider scale than they had when he was still in his old personality, his old role. Every question I ask during this alignment is usually met with a fluent and 'to the point' answer. The balance of the past life is drawn up, which is always accompanied by a feeling of liberation, of letting go. Let me again emphasize this phenomenon: a person can in fact have been dead for many years, but the soul can still dwell in a kind of timelessness on that front, not realizing what has happened. It is disassociated from itself as it were. Shamans here speak of the fragmentation of soul energy or "soul loss".

FROZEN PARTS

Consciousness not only remembers experiences, but it also directs the second chances. It is intelligent. But consciousness in the waking state is an invisible realm to the naked eye. How can we discover its efficacy? Anyone wanting to prove there is wind can only do so by suspending a petal in it. As it flutters back and forth, one 'sees' the action of the wind. The petal is the symptom, the indicator that someone experiences, driven by an invisible past time that still has an influential impact. The simple past never allows itself to be lost. It wants to be liberated, discharged, and understood, no matter how painful it was. People who go through trauma freeze in time, as it were. The shock still exists in timelessness, connected to the event with the relevant circumstances. While ordinary clock time goes on, this piece remains. This way you can carry frozen parts in yourself as an adult that have not grown and evolved into the present.

In the metaphor of the wind and the petal, consciousness is like the wind. We could simply say that memories that have become distant and which were of therapeutic importance were once too shocking to experience in full. They have shifted to our subconscious, into the simple past tense department. Another striking metaphor for consciousness is that of the iceberg. The part of consciousness that is visible above the surface of the water is the part that is consciously known. It is immediately retrievable and has logic and context for the bearer. The much larger part, the subconscious, lies below the surface. It is no longer easily accessible, but always present, and influences the visible part.

It should of course be noted that memories must have a degree of relevance for the whole, to be actively remembered. It is of lesser importance to consciously recall how many pancakes someone ate thirty years ago on Thursday evening when he came home after playing soccer. Unless he nearly choked on the eighth pancake because someone unexpectedly slapped him on the back. In that case someone will develop a hang-up about eating food (too quickly), about swallowing. Or the person will always be anxious and restless when eating and people walk past him from behind. Anyway, an indicator remains active that refers to the original experience. And that indicator is experienced as annoying, as a complaint or problem, which can cause a person to decide to seek therapy.

Certain techniques reenable one to make contact again with those events that have passed. In a way we zoom in on the petals in therapy, the symptoms of someone's complaint, so that the story comes back into the picture and can be touched. It can now finally be told, experienced, and released where necessary. Closure, completion, and integration are the goal.

Over the years, reincarnation therapy has grown into a very active field in which more and more therapists and clients feel at home. People's progressive nature always brings new developments. Included among the ranks of reincarnation therapy's biggest pioneers are: Morris Netherton, Roger Woolger, Hans ten Dam, Ian Stevenson, Rob Bontenbal, Tineke Noordegraaf (who did groundbreaking work in the field of working with children), Thorwald Dethlefsen, Helen Wambach, Carol Bowman and Michael Newton, just to name a few. The current day reincarnation therapist builds on their legacy and adds another dimension to the whole. And this is how the working methods and insights continue to develop and advance. More and more people are making grateful use of the possibilities it offers and marvel at the results.

TRANCE

Trance, a preliminary stage of hypnosis, is the desired state for a client to reconnect with old experiences in the therapeutic setting. This concentration of attention makes it possible to build a bridge to the original experience. This original experience usually presents itself in parts, sometimes even fragmented, and not directly in a complete context. The trick is to put those fragments back together into a logical whole under therapeutic guidance.

Trance is an ordinary, natural state of being. Somebody engrossed in a good book or enthralled by a movie, for example, is already in a trance. Just minutes before I wrote this in my motor home, I decided to open a carton of organic vermicelli soup. It's boiling on the stove now and its smell reminds me of my grandma who always did that in a green enameled pan (but without the carton). And during this afternoon's walk in the woods, in which I was accompanied by quite a few great tit songbirds, the memory of my grandfather sprang vividly to mind. Great tits were his favorite birds. In my mind's eye I saw him sitting on his huge lawn with pine nuts in his hand, waiting with endless patience for them to eat from his hand. I must have been around seven years old. All quite natural trance moments, and for everyone recognizable as such, that cause spontaneous memories, regressions. Trance in therapy is more concentrated, but certainly does not necessarily have to be hypnotic. If someone asks me about my grandmother's kitchen, with the vermicelli soup as a trigger, all kinds of details seem to come to mind again. Afterwards I may wonder at still being able to recall them, but for consciousness it is natural to save everything and release it if tapped into. It is like a forgotten diary that resurfaces. If something or someone calls on a set of certain specific circumstances, the page in question will open again. Experiences, no matter where they are in the past can be reached and reinvestigated through trance induction.

CASE HISTORY PETER AND TRUUSJE

Peter (1952) suffers from passivity, respiratory blockages, and great fatigue. "In life things are never about me," he says. We go back in time. His mother was first pregnant with a girl. The baby dies during childbirth. Father and grandfather buried the body with no name in a coffin in the cemetery. Mom doesn't want to be there when they do. When she gets pregnant again, Truusje is born. Truusje is big, clumsy, and very strong. Because of a handicap, she is unable to distinguish fiction from reality. She has no control over her body and knows no boundaries. "An enormously brute and unpredictable power", says Peter with corresponding tension rising in his voice. "She once hugged a bunny rabbit so tightly that the poor animal suffocated," he adds with emphasis.

This is followed by a third child, Peter, Truusje's little brother. Truusje develops an obsession for little Peter and seizes every opportunity to grab him, squeeze him and cuddle him (practically) to death. Little Peter develops a mortal fear of his sister. He is constantly on the alert and anticipating her whereabouts, aware of how to manipulate her so she doesn't pounce on him. He develops a survival mechanism in the process. Out of self-preservation he learns above all, not to be in touch with himself but to a much greater extent with his surroundings, where Truusje is constantly present. His parents, now quite desperate and behaving awkwardly due to this unexpected twist in family life, are not always vigilant. Sometimes little Peter is asked to keep an eye on Truusje when they have to run an errand.

"I was so scared stiff then that I couldn't even say to my mother I didn't want her to leave."

At a certain moment mother comes home in the nick of time. Three-year-old Peter is already turning blue in his sister's stranglehold. There is almost no air left in his lungs. Peter has a narrow escape, but somehow unconsciously remains trapped in this oppressive feeling. An energetic frozen state that lodges in his body to this day. He can no longer breathe normally.

During the therapeutic work, when we contact Truusje's soul, (she passed away twelve years earlier), we discover that Truusje is the next incarnation of the baby who died during childbirth. You could say that Truusje carries the death of the previous baby from the same mother in her as a traumatic experience. And on top of that it is also compounded by her disability, due to oxygen deficiency during the (second) delivery, so that there are no normal bounds to her behavior towards another human life. Truusje has a very high level of "I'm not fit to live." She literally grabs at everything and without meaning to, practically hugs everything to death that has any life in it. She wants to devour it, as it were, because she doesn't feel it herself. Her main project becomes her little brother Peter. "He is my existence," she now says during the session.

After Truusje died at the age of 54, much older than initially expected, her soul is still clinging to Peter. Truusje did not consciously experience her physical passing. She is still confused about the fact that she is dead. In this way, pre-existing patterns and manners can continue to persist between two creatures, while one of the two is no longer physically here. Peter's troubled childhood, in turn, made him become accustomed to constantly being vigilant for his sister's presence in his surroundings. Because of this fear, Peter developed a program in his system that ensures that there is always an instinctive threat in the world around him. It causes an energetic magnetic effect to remain active between him and his sister, even though there has been no physical contact for quite some time.

EARTHLY ATTACHMENT

After we let Truusje relive her death experience through Peter, this time quite consciously and step by step, her soul is released from earthly attachment. Their mother's previous stillbirth also receives proper attention. This is a tremendously liberating experience for both Truusje, now as a soul, and Peter. In fact, only now have these two broken free from each other so that Peter no longer instinctively feels there is any threat in his surroundings. He breathes a huge sigh of relief with the necessary emotional release – realizing that the 3-year-old boy inside him has survived and is allowed to come out of his shell. The inner child can now integrate into Peter as an adult.

When we analyze this entanglement between Peter and Truusje from a reincarnation therapeutic background, a deeper dimension unfolds behind the dramatic relationship between them. Peter experiences himself in another, previous life, as a Belgian peasant living under extremely poor conditions somewhere around the turn of the previous century. Hard work, unsanitary conditions and survival characterize day to day reality. He is unable to control the frustration he has that he will not amount to anything as a man and that he lives under these miserable conditions. His son, a teenage soldier during the First World War, has been gone for quite some time. He and his wife have no idea whether he is still alive. The peasant farmer exhibits even more dominating and aggressive behavior towards his wife than before when he caught her showing interest in a wounded soldier. He taunts her constantly and threatens to kill her if she so much as thinks of packing her bags. They are devastated by news of their son being killed in action. His wife, whose only prospect for the future was her son, hangs herself. Shortly after, the Belgian farmer follows her example. He cannot live without her and feels guilty and responsible for her death to his innermost being. He tries to identify himself with her by hanging himself in the same place, "I want to find her in death, I destroyed her life, and I don't deserve to exist anymore." His not being able to breathe while suffocating to death is the connecting factor with his wife. Peter and Truus were each other's partners in this extremely sad, past existence. Not only were they never able to let go of one another, they found each other again in a new incarnation. The detail is incredible. Even the bunny rabbit that was hugged to death refers to their son at the time, who Truusje missed terribly and 'wanted to devour in her despair'.

By letting go of his sister Truus, now, in his current life, the painful karmic background of this story is dispelled. Love and connection can be felt again. Huge emotional release gives an immense sense of liberation. "I can start living again, it's good now", says Peter with relief.

CHAPTER 2

How real are our memories?

"I think in general there is a yawning gap between the facts as they really are and what people imagine them to be."
– George Santayana

Are the memories that come to a client during a session authentic? Or can they also be made up, manufactured? Science draws rather one-sided conclusions in this area. Reincarnation therapy is a profession and it is a holistic approach that is required to understand the phenomenon of 'remembering'.

The controversial 'false memory syndrome', referred to in scientific-psychological literature, says that we can conjure within ourselves pretty much fantasied stories created by external influences. Fabrications are confused with memories, so that memories are no longer reliable. They could sprout from someone's brain without them being based on personally experienced facts. The cause of this phenomenon is sought in influences in the environment. Energetically transmitted impressions, emotions, words, pains, and ideas can blur one's own authentic experiences so that something else can take root. This impact would increase someone's associative capacity in such a way that it is no longer possible to distinguish what belongs to whom. Influential people such as parents, certain family members, bystanders or those present in tense situations (such as an accident or fight), gurus, even movies, books, or TV series, would not only be able to leave an indelible mark on someone, but also be capable of hijacking someone's inner world. The receptive person, who has no conscious control over, or is unaware of this incorporated information, could turn it into a story internally, which he then comes to believe he has experienced himself. Especially when it concerns sexual abuse where this syndrome is often invoked, people could wrongly perceive this experience as having been real. Here the human memory could be "false". Since in my area of expertise it is extremely important to stay alert to those internally transferred impressions that are not your own, it makes sense to subject the syndrome to further research.

TEN DOGMAS

It is relevant to emphasize here that the phenomenon of 'memory', as well as false memory syndrome, according to scientific criteria, takes place solely in the brain. The brain is said to be the physical carrier of memories and information. The material from which these conclusions are drawn is quite meager. It even excludes the existence of a soul, or immeasurable consciousness. While the soul or consciousness could add a much deeper dimension to this concept. The English biologist Rupert Sheldrake conducted extensive scientific research into the phenomenon of telepathy. He made a neat list of the things on which modern science bases all its investigations and conclusions with "the ten dogmas of modern science."

1. **Everything is essentially mechanical.**
2. **All matter is unconscious.**
3. **The total amount of matter and energy is always the same.**
4. **The laws of nature are fixed. They are the same today as they were at the beginning, and they will stay the same forever.**
5. **Nature is purposeless, and evolution has no goal or direction.**
6. **All biological inheritance is material, carried in the genetic material, DNA, and in other material structures.**
7. **Minds are inside heads and are nothing but the activities of brains.**
8. **Memories are stored as material traces in brains and are wiped out at death.**
9. **Unexplained phenomena like telepathy are illusory.**
10. **Mechanistic medicine is the only kind that really works.**

That has rather far-reaching implications regarding our memory and the false memory syndrome. What conclusion remains, if any reference to something spiritual, energetic or to a form of consciousness is excluded, is the following: due to a disturbed correlation between the different brain groups and nerve connections the transfer of information falters for all sorts of physically identifiable, random reasons. If necessary, with an explanation, sought in genetic predisposition. The technical, medical terms used are synaptic disconnections and disrupted impulse transfers. This is how stories can arise out of the blue and their authenticity be inherently questionable.

These are one-sided conclusions. The functioning of spiritual intelligence from fields of consciousness or from soul influences is not included in the study of the phenomenon of 'memory'. According to reincarnation therapy, it is impossible to get a clear picture of what is really going on inside someone if any spiritual component of human nature has not been given a fully-fledged role. A holistic view is by definition crucial, and the exclusion of a soul or spirit is unthinkable, even negligent.

NOT-OWN ENERGY

What is abundantly clear is that outside influences can be enormous, and indeed can take root in someone's perception of the world. We call this Not Own Energy, in short NO. It can thoroughly disturb a person's state of mind and for a long time. People who go through a trauma, freeze as it were. They are therefore unprotected and are all the more open to external influences: emotions, thoughts and sounds from their environment. These can now nestle unfiltered in someone, and indeed are therefore not one's own. In this regard, I can go along with the effect of influences coloring memories of events that give an imaginary turn to what was experienced in fact.

Still, it is precisely about discovering where the original experience and the original thoughts and feelings of a person have remained, among all that information introduced by the outside world. Various therapeutic methods make it possible to have clients distinguish during sessions, between what is their own and not their own, to separate the wheat from the chaff again. The crux of the matter is a consideration of the following: which fundamental disturbance, due to which circumstances and events, and with whom, makes one so susceptible to influences that start to lead of life of their own? There must be a reason when someone invents terrible and perverse dramas that did not (or would not have) happened. Nobody does that for no reason. Curious, I started watching the 2015 film Regression by Alejandro Amenábar with Emma Watson and Ethan Hawke. The end credits betray its intent, packaged in a generalizing conclusion: nowadays people call regression therapy into question because it evokes false memories. Any specification as to who is meant by 'people', is unfortunately omitted. Although the therapist involved does not exactly exhibit much competence, which already puts regression therapy in a dubious light, the bottom line is that the authenticity of information generated in regressions is not only seriously questioned and therefore incapable of being substantiated by facts but can also cause enormous damage to people and their close relations.

BLIND SPOTS

If you assume that stories can be twisted, then the next question is: would the inability of some researchers to look at problems in a larger context also be why the true story of a patient does not enter the picture?

After all, the researcher is programmed to believe that everything takes places in the brain. His own limits deny him access to the deeper reality of his patient. Therefore, he lacks the logic and empathy to be able to look behind the information expressed by his patient. And he is then also unable to adjust it where necessary and make it transparent. The real story does not come to light. The blind spots in his own perception explain away in advance that which does not fit into his own framework of thoughts. The true depth and coherence of a story that emerges are not accessible to the observer. As a result, there is a lack of specific questioning and focus and conclusions are drawn prematurely. A story based on false memories is the most disastrous thing of all. Everything that is dismissed as such disappears into an even deeper, more inaccessible place. These conclusions give a very misleading turn to a treatment. Patients feel even less heard or understood, and they no longer make a constructive contribution to their own therapeutic process. Any motivation that was left to clarify matters, however hesitant and vulnerable, is nipped in the bud. Especially when it comes to memories of past lives.

How can a client who gets very vivid impressions of a terrified and hounded soldier, whom he experiences to be himself, then be taken seriously? Or someone who, as a young girl, remembers being raped by a crazed brutal villain in a bygone era? The therapeutic counselor, imprisoned by his limited comprehension, can only conclude that this is not possible. After all, his client has never experienced a war, according to his biographical details. His experiences must be based on a figment of his imagination. A hallucination, a fantasy that cannot be based on reality. If a diagnosis from this care provider were expected, he could only report that his patient suffers from (forms of) delusions. He might still assume that his patient is disturbed by the invasive stories of a father, brother, grandfather, or grandmother, who did experience the war. But the possibility that these are real experiences from a previous life of this patient himself, is excluded. To use a metaphor: when a therapist only has a hammer as tool at his disposal, he can only work with nails. He can't handle screws; he doesn't even recognize them.

ENDLESS CONSCIOUSNESS

To my knowledge, memories are not physically stored in the brain, but the brain is the great decoding machine of energetically stored data. As Cardiologist Pim van Lommel nicely demonstrates in his book *Eindeloos Bewustzijn* (Endless Consciousness) (2007), in which many people report on their so-called near-death experiences (NDE), that had all kinds of traceable experiences while they were – medically speaking – (brain) dead. Well then, that's clear. We do not depend on our brain to have experiences and perceptions. What we need our brains for is to process events and associated perceptions. And then to be able to analyze and translate them into a context that can be understood. Incidentally, it appears a person on average only uses a very limited part of his brain capacity. The rest is dormant. One can just imagine what we all might remember if the whole mechanism was functioning. But that aside.

You can compare it to a radio. The receiver is then the brain and the received waves are the carriers of the original information. As soon as the translation or decoding has taken place, this information becomes contextually audible and understandable through the amplifier and loudspeaker. Depending on the position of the radio's antenna, someone can tune in to various channels, in the same way you can listen to multiple sources or people at the same time. In a therapeutic practice, that coordination, of course, is focused on the request for help. The enormous diversity of vibrations energetically stored in a person's database, contain the memories yet to be decoded by the brain. All these vibrations are basically within the range of a client. And so, it is not really possible to forget something forever. Forgetting – and so dementia and a disease such as Alzheimer's – is only a temporary affair in which the frequencies of the (repressed) stories can no longer contact that specific region of the brain that ought to translate them. There is a disturbance or damage on a physical level. But that doesn't mean the information isn't there anymore. Hence someone gradually starts to remember everything after his death. And in that capacity the person does not require a brain.

MEMORY LOSS

In a state of shock, one loses contact with the content and the gravity of the event. That reality is too shocking to experience in full. Especially if the head as a home for the brain, has been given a good clout. But memory loss can also come into play using anesthetics, ranging from alcohol, narcotics, chemical medications, and heavier drugs. We call that unconscious, but in fact what we are saying is that consciousness is unable to contact the radio, so we think we didn't receive anything.

During a therapeutic setting, the radio dial is tuned so specifically that it connects to the less easily accessible transmitters, or sometimes even to those that are almost lost – in other words, the memories that were once too painful to receive which are tucked away out of contact. In this way it is perhaps easier to understand that their reception may be a phased process. All elements must eventually be downloaded in conjunction with one another, so that the original image, sound and feeling of the story comes back. The wonderfully beautiful thing and the essence of reincarnation therapy is that this process of retrieving forgotten, and lost stories goes hand in hand with the accompanying emotional and physical sensation.

Memories from subconscious regions therefore do not always directly emerge in a streamlined and complete way and in a logical context. They don't come in successive chapters and paragraphs. They come to the surface as part of a process, often as fragments, which, if misinterpreted or interpreted too quickly, may distort the original version. It takes some patience, insight, and experience to understand the true meaning and purpose of an emerging history. Therapeutic treatment of stories that are not based on truth do not have beneficial results. That is also an easy indicator, as well as the reason why haphazard suggestions or interpretations put forward by the therapist are meaningless. Stories that are not true are particularly verifiable by the absence of emotion – even if they are sometimes simulated to make them appear true. And that is an important discovery. What truth is being camouflaged by the created story? Or put a tad more subtly, what true history unfolds if the content of the created story is readjusted? In summary, what is the root of making up an event? Not being too quick to dismiss the realm of fantasy as irrelevant could provide a surprising twist to a therapeutic process.

CHAPTER 3

Suggestion and placebo

"Facts do not cease to exist because they are ignored."
– Aldous Huxley

It is sometimes argued that the effect of reincarnation therapy is based on suggestion and placebos. An explanation that may be reassuring to some because the content of all those intense stories that 'just happen to arise' does not necessarily have to be true. Or, more simply, it could be that this therapy might work because someone received a great deal of attention, in which a kind of placebo effect takes place. The stories that bubble to the surface would meanwhile have no truth value. It is important to emphasize that a (good) reincarnation therapist does not suggest past lives. It is correct to say that on average a client is given more focused attention than with any other form of therapy.

VIBRATION IN A FROZEN SOLID AREA

Suggestion literally means 'putting an idea into one's mind from the outside' or 'a generated representation of something that does not actually exist.' When a suggestion has a truly remarkable effect of bringing about change and healing, an intervention from outside can provide the impetus to new movement in the original story. As if the ball is thrown back into the field, so that the game that was put on hold can start again. In other words, the right suggestion is a welcome intruder that disrupts the framework of an old, fixed story. A desirable disruption, that is, because stories only get stuck because they were traumatic.

I will try to explain this in more detail. We already knew that the main side effect of trauma and shock causes something to freeze. A restriction of the original, free flow of movement is then the result, like when you pinch off something, hold it back or freeze it. Now, with the right suggestion, such a frozen field of elementary particles becomes stirred up again. As a result, a strong impulse from the outside releases the forgotten story from being blocked. And just to be clear: that story does not change the content, it is only released. The ball is fired into the pinball machine so that everything is reactivated, and the story starts flowing. And so, the released nanoparticles can now rearrange themselves. This then leads to a new structure in the energetic pattern. Essential, liberating sensations and changes can be experienced in this way, just like with the dam made of stones in a river. Moving just a single stone can cause several stones to be washed away in the current and the stagnant water will start flowing again.

A firm, well-aimed suggestion can therefore certainly lead to a change, just like a properly chosen homeopathic remedy. This also brings a vibration into an area that is frozen solid. However, many internalized stories are so painfully frozen that suggestions cause only a temporary change, or often no change at all. He who sincerely hears 'I love you' while hardly able to love himself, is hit by a well-aimed bomb of suggestion that can cause a great deal of turmoil. It often brings a temporary pleasant sensation. However, as soon as one becomes dependent on this external I- love- you- input source, it doesn't have a curative effect. It's all about self-love being restored and permanently activated, independently of others.

THE IDEA MAY BE ENOUGH

Placebos suggest that something can change. It has been widely demonstrated that this can affect one's system of belief or even a transition from sickness to health. A person does not know whether a particular drug administered contains an active substance or not. The idea alone that this might be the case may be enough to bring about a change. Or even better, such as when someone comes to a doctor with a certain pain, and it goes away without any treatment. An energetic exchange is activated between the source of the pain and what the doctor symbolizes for that person. That's called placebo. When someone is administered the same placebo completely unnoticed in the form of a drug, as used among a group of test subjects, i.e., without an active substance, this has no effect. It is therefore not part of the area of suggestion. But to be clear he is then not even a test subject. Provided that power of thought can achieve a great deal, both in yourself and in someone else, there must be a certain conscious connection with the source of a place-bo. When someone has a firm idea about someone else, without making it known in an outward form, that does not mean no exchange takes place between these two persons. Of course, the nocebo effect also exists. Anyone who hears about a very dangerous virus on a large scale and is simultaneously a breeding ground of fear, more easily provides fertile soil for a disease by the intrusive and repeated influx of the threatening suggestion. I remember the telling statement of a well-known Dutch acupuncturist, Yan Schroën. He said the effect of a needle being placed in one's meridian system is mainly determined by the intentions of the person inserting the needle and not by the needle itself. Afterwards, someone shouldn't need repetition of new or similar suggestions or placebos. Otherwise, actual transformation hasn't yet happened. And naturally we also see the other side of suggestions and placebos. If they do not touch upon the original history, then they do not work, or only work temporarily, after which the energetic field will assume its 'familiar' frozen state again. Then it takes heavier guns to move it.

IDENTIFICATION WITH A FAMILIAR IMAGE

When people tend to manufacture fantasy stories, or construct incoherent fairy tales, something more is going on. It is then necessary to find out what motivates that person to make-up a non-existent story. What drives them to do that? And then also with specific themes. Anyone who deeply considers themselves to be worthless or unimportant, can therefore give an extremely confusing account of made-up stories of heroic characters. For adults they may be about tales of fame and success in business or sport. Or they hide their deep insecurity about themselves behind the imposing appearance of someone who has an answer for everything or is a know-it-all. If people already start from the premise of reincarnation, then there can also be some venomous snakes in the grass. Accounts of past lives are then given free rein. After all, there is nothing in them that can be verified. The high priests, generals, leaders, wise seers, shamans, and kings are flying in everyday direction, while the characters who really need attention seem to be lingering in some unreachable place. Some people also identify with evil. I have had dozens of clients in my practice who claimed to have been Adolf Hitler in a past life. Those people mix their own life as a perpetrator, which they vehemently condemn, with the life of Adolf. Since they find themselves to be 'evil to the core', and at the same time try to find some sort of justification for it, they identify with a well-known paragon of evil. You must literally learn to see through that and to distil very precisely that part people were responsible for, in which they did have a share. Stories that are fabricated are recognizable to experienced listeners as having a certain transparency. There is no meat on the bones. And yet in principle they serve an important purpose, as they are the gate to the real story. The real story doesn't always come easily. People are sometimes incredibly sensitive about it. Especially when they are about themes of sexuality that entail shame and guilt. Or extremely twisted power relations. In that case they should be taken extremely seriously by the listener. They are made from desperation and self-defense. After the necessary painstaking breakdown of its elements, one finds the true history of what lies behind these stories, that contains the unvarnished truth that is so painful, shameful, or astonishing that a fantasy is draped around it like some protective cloak. The naked truth ought to be revealed with the greatest candor and care.

From a therapeutic point of view, that really makes sense. Particularly if a client comes to realize that the confabulated story served a kind of survival purpose.

CHAPTER 4

Stringing of lives

"Those who cannot remember the past are condemned to repeat it."
– George Santayana

As a client begins to realize more and more how their current life is intertwined with various past lives, we speak of the stringing of lives. Different beads, representing different past lives, with different colors and shapes, suddenly appear to be part of the same chain. Or, put in another way: the many pixels on a screen that at first seemed to move completely randomly relative to each other, appear to form a coherent picture. For that, you must first assume the right vantage point. Johan Cruijff's "You can only see it when you see through it' totally applies here. During therapeutic sessions, but of course also during such other groundbreaking life experiences, such as taking ayahuasca, one can also arrive in that kind of state. You see yourself, your relationships, and the deeper meaning of certain events in your life in a much larger context. The cohesion in the image arises because the pixels correspond to each other, and that is what is observed. They even work in perfect coordination together, regardless of whether they repel or attract each other. They are interactive with each other in a way that depends on the experiences they shared together.

DROWNED SLAVE

If we learn to look at our symptoms in this way, and especially at their specific details, we see that they are actually valuable clues. These symptoms draw attention to deep, forgotten, or repressed stories. And those stories concern very specific human situations that ultimately enable you to see yourself in a greater whole. What might be confusing to some is that these stories cannot always be placed directly in a recognizable context. Not everyone can immediately accept that these are past life events. That's mainly because we didn't grow up with this wisdom. In fact, the information with which we have grown up has in fact greatly distracted us from this knowledge.

Suppose someone has suffered for many years from a painful eczema-like skin condition around his wrists. Ointments don't help. How can the consciousness of this person integrate such an event from the past when this experience appears to come from a slave that was handcuffed by his wrists in a sinking galley ship? In fear of his life and in total panic in his final moments, before ultimately drowning, he tried with all his might to wrench his wrists free from his chains until they bled. Even though he had in fact died, his wrists were still trying to wrench free. "As long as it still hurts and the skin around my wrists is still burning and bleeding, I'm still alive." That is an extremely concrete and good example of an unfinished experience. The 'unfinished business' here consists of the consciousness of this personality, the slave, who still believes he's chained to those oars. The eczema around his wrists attest to the condition he was in at the end. To whom? To the present-day personality of which this slave is a part. You could call that slave a sub-personality. In the sense of representing an important fragment of life force that has not (yet) been released. An old drama can be relived in a therapeutic session so that one realizes someone died there by paying special attention to the level of consciousness of the wrists. His wrists no longer must experience the pain of wrenching free anymore, death is an established fact. The experience is finished. Because he doesn't have to hold on anymore and can detach himself from that event, there is no longer any reason for the consciousness of the wrists to produce eczema. And so that disappears. The program no longer serves a purpose. The story of the slave in the sunken galley ship is the setting of a human life in which more and deeper themes are present that, along with the surrender to death, are also released. The slave's life force can now integrate into the current day personality. A theme that has a deeper effect on the slave, for instance, is an ingrained notion of having never really been free from an oppressor, a ruler. Or that 'being a man' is associated with 'captivity'. An experience of continuous bondage.

THE LOGIC OF THE SOUL DETERMINES THE ROUTE

It appears to be an uninterrupted process that continually takes place on the deeper layers of our consciousness. So all-encompassing for our capacity to understand that any overview can easily be lost. If you don't overexert yourself trying to take it all in, insight commonly occurs. It is the logic of the soul that determines the route here, not our limited thinking. It is good to reconcile ourselves to this.

How easily do certain symptoms allow themselves to be explained when the listener does not jump to conclusions and is able to remain genuinely curious? A skin condition can indicate the burnt skin of someone in agony in a house going up in flames. Agoraphobia can refer to the moment when someone is crossing a square in a previous life and is suddenly recognized as a Jew by German soldiers and then arrested and deported. This example illustrates the belief that: "If I am spotted on the street, I get arrested and killed.' Conclusion: crossing a street is life-threatening.

Everyone is familiar with drastic events in one's present life. They are the experiences that really leave a mark on our existence, shaping our life in a certain way. They carry echoes of events from previous lives, with very clear characteristics. That is, for those who see it. And the things that happen to all of us are enormously diverse. What is considered a disaster for one person, such as having their tonsils removed at the age of four, leaves the next person cold. When ten different people have lost a parent at a very young age, that is experienced in ten different ways. Therefore, from a therapeutic standpoint, it is advisable not to fill in how you assume that must have been for someone else.

Everyone has been through something. Just look at yourself, your friends or family members. Threats, extreme expectations, aggression, separation, bullying, dependency relationships, accidents, operations, loss of loved ones, illnesses, sexual excesses, addictions, suicide, pride, complications with inheritances, family breakdown, crime, abuse. In essence, specific symptoms of previous traumatic events manifest themselves here. Scenes and circumstances that at the time, in past lives resulted in estrangement and often in death. These underlying experiences are brought up to date again in the present life, recalled to current perception of the environment. For instance, someone who was bullied a lot at school, and because of this, unconsciously at first, starts to remember how he was once excluded by the community and labeled as 'worthless', owing to, for example, Dutch National Socialist (NSB)* activities, followed by his execution. Now the updated event, which thanks to the bullying has now become a new experience, thematically offers you the opportunity of a second chance with identical ingredients. For example, to stand up for yourself, or make different decisions than you did back then. History only repeats itself to a degree because the outcome wants to be experienced differently. In this way, old wounds can be healed.

In short, when something drastic has happened to you, it carries a reverberation from an earlier time. It usually happens beyond our conscious perception, but it is recognizable because of a feeling that something ineffably deep inside you has been touched.

AGGRESSIVE AND UNPREDICTABLE

Another example. Suppose as a woman, in a previous existence you had a relationship that was based on power and violence. You never stood up for yourself. You submitted to your husband's aggression and threats. You lost your self-esteem and your natural sense of the right to be who you are. In the end, after being sexually assaulted, you were strangled to death. In your current life, again as a woman, you have an older brother who is very aggressive and unpredictable. During your childhood he roughly gropes your private parts and wants you to satisfy him under a threat of violence. Once he even grabs you by the throat, making you mortally afraid at that moment. An important part of your life is colored by these events with your brother. You don't have good relationships, you keep attracting the 'wrong men', you frequently feel unsafe, you cannot enjoy sexuality and you especially feel inferior to men. You can even develop thyroid problems that relate to the strangled throat coupled with your inability to express your own anger. This is a current reality that on a deeper level is based on the unprocessed situation from a past life. And those unequal relational conditions at the time were also the result of something that preceded it.

At soul level, it is about regaining your original power. And that is why you are brought back time and time again in these old patterns. However, this time you break the pattern with your brother. Whether or not with the help of therapy you relive the fear from yesteryear, including the humiliation, the disgust at the sexual acts and dying. You release old fears. This helps you learn to express your anger. One fine day you give your brother a serious warning. You stand tall where once you would have yielded. You tell it like it is, nothing more, and remain true to yourself. You feel a power unfolding inside you that tells you that you will never end up in a subordinate role ever again. An old pattern has been broken and released. This also causes the weight of a previous life to fall away. As a result, you react differently to men, to relationships and intimacy. And this also enables your thyroid to heal too. Karmically, you have managed to break through something very fundamental, thanks to your brother in this life.

WEIGHT OF THE PAST AWAKENED BY CHARACTERISTIC COMPONENTS OF AN EVENT

Yet another set of examples. When a baby falls from the changing table, causing it to stop breathing, an event is brought to the present concerning a knight who died in battle. Or even more detailed: a baby tumbles off the sink because his mother picks up the phone. He hits his forehead on the tip of the washing machine halfway down to the ground, where his mother finds him a little later bleeding and hypothermic. She is struck by the thought, oh my God, I'm too late, I should never have left him alone. This client experiences having been a knight in a past life, totally caught up in a pointless fight. He is detached from himself and his feelings. He doesn't understand what he's doing and loses his balance. He falls from his horse and during his fall is stabbed in the forehead by a sword. He then dies sprawled on the ground, bleeding, wet and hypothermic. The last thing on his mind before dying is a longing to be with his mother but he thinks, I am too late.

When a child experiences a serious accident with his bicycle, it can be the update of a fatal accident during the war. When a baby is choked by the umbilical cord during labor it is a reminder of a hanging because of a conviction in a previous life. When two brothers pelt each other with stones in the garden during a fight that has got out of hand, memories of a real fight are reawakened in which one of the two was fatally injured by a large boulder on his head. When someone is violently pulled out of the birth canal with forceps, it updates a fatal accident involving a person whose arms, head and torso were pulled into a rotating agricultural machine. When a child loses its father at the age of three, which makes him feel like the ground has been swept away from under his feet, that experience bears the same inner despair he felt when his tribe turned out to have been massacred. When a mother has a few drinks every day during pregnancy, it reminds the baby of a previous life with alcohol dependency. When a mother is no longer able to breastfeed, because she doesn't have the strength anymore after her seventh child, this recalls the period of the Hunger Winter, when someone became ill and died due to a shortage of food. When someone is caught shoplifting in their teens and it is reported to the police, the memory of a much more serious offense reawakens – one that had landed someone in prison for years. When a mother of a two-year-old-child loses a sister or brother, the child is confronted with an energy of sadness and loneliness that can bring back the memory of a great loss from a previous life. In other words, the most characteristic components of an event are always present with enough power just to be able to reawaken the old weight of past fear and panic.

Sometimes I wish it were farfetched, because then there would still be a human brain behind it. But these connections bubble to the surface from the deep layers of the mind of those who regress before they can even consider it for themselves. It's so refined and sophisticated. The person in his present incarnation attracts events from which he once turned away. From which he once felt cut off. And yet it appears necessary to bring about that reunification, to prevent someone from turning away forever from an event that was too painful. Apparently, that is not something the soul accepts. A soul is incapable of thriving in any form of separation. And now we see that those separated aspects of ourselves can be found again. That's how we can be unified again.

Some clients are very sensitive to trance. Then the stringing together of souls with their inherent logic can be retrieved, almost detail by detail. This gives an even more accurate sketch of the connection between old traumas and current life events, as we see in the following practical example.

CASE EXAMPLES OF BODIES BLOWN TO PIECES

A female client suffers from chronic migraine. In addition, she has problematic relationships with men. In my practice she goes back to previous lives. In the runup to the First World War she is a soldier who rapidly rises through the military ranks and who is authorized to issue orders and commands. In the madness of war, he finds himself in a situation where there is virtually no one left to obey those orders. His men have been killed, wounded, lost, or missing in action. All the misery had driven him insane. When he finds a group of lost soldiers from the same army, he feels like he is someone again. Because of his higher rank he presents himself as their leader and starts giving them orders. But none of these men respond. Stunned, dazed, exhausted, and wounded, they are no longer receptive to military orders. "They don't fucking do what I tell them to." Like a crazy madman he takes out his anger at them by randomly shooting some of them. With this he forces the other soldiers to subordinate themselves to him. Inwardly torn apart, the consequences of his insane act sink in, whereby the few seconds in which he saw what he had wrought were just enough to imprint these horrific images on his mind. He sees bodies shot to pieces, some even with the head separated from the torso. The insanity of this event drives him to a new act of despair. In his own mind he justifies his depraved behavior with the thought, 'I must shoot myself to pieces too'. On an impulse he acts upon his words blowing his brains out with pistols on either side of his head.

In a subsequent incarnation he ends up in a German family, shortly after the First World War. The family is completely broken in bits. His father was already 'shot to pieces' when he was still in his mother's womb. The same goes for his mother's father, and her brothers too. Mother kills herself because she cannot cope with all her loss and the family being torn apart. So, her son very quickly becomes disconnected from his parents and any family life. "I'm already in bits before I even leave the house."

In the run-up to World War II, he is a draftee soldier who is ordered to "shoot the enemy to smithereens." He doesn't want to get caught up (again) in the violence of war. His revulsion is based on his previous war experiences on a deeper level. He refuses to serve and helps not only injured colleagues but also enemies. His behavior is seen as unacceptable. Following military protocol, he is charged with desertion. That's why he is executed. He is shot in the head. The experience that goes with it is that he has completely lost himself, no longer feels connected to anything, feels no power of attraction whatsoever for an earthly life and cannot experience any love for himself. At the same time, he somehow feels satisfaction from being shot dead, instead of having killed himself, as compensation for his previous behavior.

CHRONIC MIGRAINE

Prior to his current incarnation, i.e., after his life from the period of the Second World War, he has yet another short life as a little boy with hydrocephalus. "I have a splitting headache." This refers to two previous death experiences where he was shot in the head. This hydrocephalic boy has a loving bond with his brother. A brother who never judges him because of his disability. The hydrocephalic boy dies at the age of 6. He then incarnates some fifteen years later in the same family, now as the daughter of his former brother. She will now be his, er...her father, knowing he will never judge her. The decision to incarnate this time as a woman (my current client) is preceded by several essential, conscious considerations. Firstly, that women cannot be conscripted and secondly that he/she hopes to reconnect with his/her feelings and earthly life.

As a woman my client is going to attract men, and with that the challenge again of being able to connect with men in general, and ultimately with the man she herself was. Her life of course is characterized by problematic relations with men. It is the representation of her own inability to connect with the man inside her. "I keep attracting unpredictable, angry men." She also has chronic migraines. First several sessions help to release her from the pain in her head as the 'hydrocephalic boy', because we live through his death again. This also releases the pain of his former incarnation into that family – especially in the relationship to her father, who lost his little brother with hydrocephalus at a young age and could never come to terms with it. The session results in there being more understanding and contact with her father, taking an essential first step in an improved relationship with men in general.

The former lives in the First and Second World War pass in revue during therapy. The bewilderment at being capable of such hideous acts of desperation, ruthlessly taking one's own life and ultimately not ascribing herself an ounce of the right to be who she is, gradually transforms into acceptance. Underlying it she experiences a deep longing to be able to live without that compulsion, as if her current existence carries with it the potential to truly reconcile with itself. To transform from 'broken' into 'whole'.

Parallel to these intense life experiences of this 'poor soul', the question arises to what extent his victimhood in the war, also as a perpetrator, is part of a natural process of consciousness development. Even though it also extends through several lives. Anyone studying the real causes of the outbreak of these global conflicts, soon discovers that there are conscious forces in the background fueling these wars and theaters of aggression. Just as in 2020 when a corona social climate was created with all the associated fears, tensions and uncertainties that will inevitably take their toll on many. This will suck in millions of souls who become involved in this form of warfare. And will result in a stringing together of multiple lives, which are thematically connected to former miseries of war. Thus, a picture unfolds in my mind's eye that charts the many layers on which many are still sick of waging war. However, the Cycle of Reincarnation does offer a solution. It is a law of nature to confront people again and again with their unfinished aspects, so that they can move on. The sooner we can look at ourselves and our themes in this context, the sooner we can create other incarnation impulses for our new lives. What would human life look like if it were no longer driven or colored by historical bloodshed or oppression?

CHAPTER 5

Organ Donation

Organs, like any other body part, carry soul consciousness. Life experiences are stored at cell level. This is also known as the cellular memory phenomenon. If someone once hit his thumb very hard with a hammer, he will immediately make a link to his thumb every time he picks one up. The memory awakens, to prevent it from happening again. When an organ transplant takes place, information from the deceased is transferred to the new owner. That information can also contain painful life experiences and cause unprocessed trauma. The organs that need to be replaced are charged with information. If the old organ is removed, the energetic coding attached to it simply remains in existence. It will now be mixed with the information introduced from the donor. This leads to all kinds of complications in the recipient, such as rejection symptoms or a restless state of mind. Many stories are known about recipients of organs who have taken over certain character traits from the donor. With the help of reincarnation therapy, rejection symptoms can be significantly decreased. Separate from the discussion about the complications at soul level and medical conflicts of interest, the transplant should be co-supervised by someone who is able to work within the invisible realm of the soul. Where possible, processes should be guided in that direction. Unfortunately, this is not yet the case.

The government bases its decision-making on scientific research, which is why the medical sector excludes the existence of a soul or spirit in its methods of treatment. After all, the soul has not been proven to exist. Anyone who thinks they can prove it is a pseudoscientist at best and such people have absolutely no voice in the discussion around organ donation or 'brain death'.

As a reincarnation therapist, I am not concerned with demonstrating or proving the existence of a soul. Rather, it is a starting point. And I'd rather work with what lives in people, than only being concerned with the materials which make up a person. I work with body consciousness, so also with the consciousness of organs, which in some cases come from another owner. An owner who is scheduled to die after those organs have been removed from him.

Progressive insight opens new visions. The debate here surrounding organ donation might well be a tricky one. If it ever turns out that there is indeed a soul that is conscious, and that the removal and insertion of organs has a profound impact on the being of both the donor and recipient, what are the implications? Anyone who then dares to go back the way they have come must be able to bear the painful consequence that the whole spiritual aspect has simply been ignored.

Persons who qualify as donors are almost always victims of an accident or stroke. One case involved a suicide that is discovered 'in time'. Sudden traumatic circumstances, where the future donor is in shock, and his (conscious) awareness is enormously restricted. In more than 40% of the cases, all medical procedures must take place before the donor dies, so it is urgent. In other cases, there is a degree of cardiac arrest and medical treatment must also be speedily rendered. The extent to which consciousness can register what happens depends to a degree on the severity of the event. Varying from the (near) fatal fall from a staircase to a traffic accident. That registration takes place in fragmented form. The soul can in fact already withdraw itself from the body in stages, while the body is still trying to survive under the resulting conditions. Confusion arises in the minds of those involved on various inner levels of awareness. So many menacing impulses and circumstances are taking place simultaneously, so many unexpected things are happening in, with, and around the body, that not all of it can be perceived with any coherency. Anyone in such a life-threatening situation is hardly, if at all, able to realize what is taking place. Likewise, the soul of a newly deceased 'cannot understand' that it has died. As a result, it remains in a daze, still attached to the earthly situation in which it found itself and to the persons with whom it is associated. In a kind of timelessness.

KEPT ARTIFICALLY BRAIN DEAD

When organs are removed in the final stages before actual death, the soul is certainly still attached to the body. Physically, death takes place no more than a few minutes after the last heartbeat. Until then, the person is either kept artificially brain dead or an attempt is made to remove the organs as soon as possible after the final beat of the heart. In the latter case, the kidneys, pancreas, and liver are eligible for transplantation, but the heart is unusable. Brain death is an extremely misleading term, as Ger Lodewick demonstrates in his book *Wat men over orgaan donatie zou moeten weten* (What One Should Know about Organ Donation), because many bodily functions are still active, with all the associated energetic and physically perceptible life streams. In both cases, but especially in a brain-death situation, the soul is in an extraordinarily intense, instinctual, survival mode and tries in every possible way to hold onto the earthly life, and thus to the body.

The dying process concerns a kind of rarefied procedure in which there is process-oriented detachment of the soul from its physical shell, the body. Leading up to and ending after that moment. The energy of consciousness, or life force, with the soul at its core, is interwoven throughout the entire body down to the smallest molecules. Even with our DNA. There is a process by which the life force withdraws itself from the physical reality, the body, and the accompanying personality. However, during a sudden and unexpected death there is little or no opportunity for this to happen somewhat harmoniously. By definition, a donor is therefore in a state of shock with the associated energetic short circuits. The phenomenon of phantom pain is a good example of this. One still experiences the sensations of an amputated limb because at the energetic level the process of processing and therefore acceptance of the disconnection from that body part has still not taken place.

In addition to the vital functions known to us, organs have, as previously stated, soul consciousness. When an organ has been injured by violence, for example, it remembers that in an encrypted form. In its physical manifestation it is usually a contraction of the tissue, or the damage caused by a particular effect. Think of being torn, getting stuck, being pinched or constricted, or of being stabbed by sharp objects such as bullets, knives, or spears. But also, being exposed year after year to insecurity, anger, fear, or sadness, shapes the texture of our organs. Chemicals and other unnatural substances also have an influence. This coding now determines the flow, the vibrational level of the life force through an organ. This effect can, in the long run, destroy the organ. When an organ eventually malfunctions, it is therefore important to realize that the origin of this lies in the history of one's life experiences. The physical manifestation, the disease, is basically a manifestation of an energetic charge. For example, due to great loss in childhood, the consequences of an accident, of (sexual) abuse, violence, oppression, or hopelessness. Events from previous lives naturally continue to have a strong effect. Seen in this way you could say that an organ is a specific carrier of information. It constantly remembers what once took place because it was never really released. If the organ is removed, without understanding the cause of the disorder that has taken place at soul level, the connection with it is literally broken and fundamentally complicated. Especially if it is replaced by an organ of someone with a very different energetic constitution and very different frequencies and information, or 'story history'. From a donor still caught up in all kinds of consciousness complications due to his recent death and with little or no realization that this has even happened at all.

In short, the organ of both donor and recipient is disconnected from the rest of the body. Subsequently, an organ with a foreign consciousness vibration is inserted and connected there. The donor then dies as planned, in the absence of awareness about the actual life-threatening event, accident, stroke or otherwise. His arranged death is caused by him being taken off the ventilator after one or more organs have been removed, which were not primarily the cause of his death. The consciousness of the heart, as the carrier of the most ultimate vital function for every human being, is the one most confused about its incomprehensible, last-minute transfer of owner. For a rational person, the term "follow your heart " is already a tricky one, but following someone else's heart is an even trickier, a practically hopeless challenge. The dying process stagnates in such a fundamental way. The receiver remains unintentionally dependent on the donor so long as there is no clarity about what happened. I call that soul entanglement.

SETTING FREE FROM THE TERESSTRIAL SPHERE

During a therapeutic session, quite some clarity can emerge regarding all these entanglements. First, the donor's story must be relived via the recipient so that awareness and processing take place about dying. After that the recipient must get some clarity about the stress that led to the malfunctioning of his own organ. Subsequently, a rite of transfer needs to be conducted from soul to soul. The donor, now fully aware, gives permission to the recipient to continue with what once belonged to him. The recipient body, and specifically the old organ, must then proceed to accept the foreign organ. Only then can the soul energy of the recipient flow into the new, released, organ with a degree of acceptance. The soul of the donor now extracts the last traces of his life energy that were left in the organ, which makes him complete again as a soul. As part of the process, he can now free himself from the terrestrial sphere. He must also let go of his loved ones, which is part of his (and their) processing of emotions.

Experience from the practice of reincarnation therapy indicates that rejection symptoms decrease significantly, and the recipient's state of mind subsequently comes into calmer waters.

This exposition is not an argument for or against organ donation. It just shows that the matter of the soul is largely absent from this whole question. Insofar as we as human beings can comprehend such a concept as soul entanglements, these are indeed applicable in the case of organ donation. Fortunately, there are also ways to do effective work when it does apply.

It is also important to emphasize here that this statement also applies when someone receives an organ from a friend or relative, as a gift. There is of course an advantage in this case that there is no death experience in between, although the organ of this donor does indeed undergo a dying process, no matter how well-intentioned and lovingly the gesture is meant. In this kind of situations, it is advisable for the more aware person to involve someone capable of guiding the spiritual aspect of organ transport. People who donate their organs for financial reasons, forced or otherwise, usually have no idea what they are doing to themselves at soul level. This is something that has repercussions. They must discover the karmic consequences of what they have created. Also remember here that undergoing the removal of an organ may well be part of the aftermath of a previous life. All those involved in performing such acts, depending on their real intentions, are also confronted at times with the results of their actions, interests, or beliefs.

I was allowed to do various sessions with people who had received an organ or tissue from a donor. A liver, a kidney (from a father), a pancreas, eye tissue, a bone marrow transplant (from a sister's marrow) and a transplant from the same body, from pelvic bone to a shattered kneecap. My client told me about a serious motorbike accident she had had at the age of sixteen in which, in addition to many other complications, her knee was shattered. During an operation, where she nearly died, tissue was moved from the pelvic bone to her knee. Which of course in itself is an enormous feat. She is now an adult woman in her fifties. She told me that she had increasingly lost the ability to move her knee freely, it had become a real handicap. During a session we made contact with the circumstance of the accident, whereby we communicated with the consciousness of the pelvic tissue that did not understand it was now a knee. There are also other programs for that. Together with experiencing it emotionally and raising awareness about the internal tissue transplant, that also entailed saying goodbye to all the knee splinters that could no longer perform their task. A kind of basic connection was reestablished with these deep layers of the body. The session resulted in this client subsequently being able to move her knee more easily.

LIVER TRANSPLANTATION AND EXCESSIVE USE OF ALCOHOL

During several sessions with a man in his thirties who had undergone a liver transplant, and had subsequently suffered severe rejection symptoms, we discovered a past life of a German SS officer. His outrageous behavior at the time was accompanied by excessive use of alcohol. When the outcome of the war became clear, it was no longer possible for him to live with the reality of all his actions. After downing a bottle of hard liquor, he shot himself in the head with his Walther P38. Having relived this dramatic ending, and after exploring the further journey of his soul, we discovered the logic behind all kinds of conflicts in its current incarnation in relation to World War II. His obsessive fascination with the war, especially the German elite troops, his extreme alcohol consumption at an early age, and his judgmental nature towards "wimps and individuals who have no clear focus in their lives", were striking aspects of this. By his mid-twenties his liver function was already seriously deteriorating. He was not even thirty when the decision was made for a transplantation.

During another session, we made contact with the donor's soul. He had died after an accident in which he hit a tree with his car. He was registered as a donor. His liver, kidneys and heart were transferred. We learned more about the donor's life through my client, the recipient of the liver. He was suicidal and the accident wasn't really an accident. He was constantly terrified of being a failure as a person, but also as a father of two young children. He felt he couldn't measure up to anything. Under the influence of alcohol, he forced an accident by yanking the steering wheel hard to the right while driving his car at high speed. We relived the accident and focused on the most important emotional aspects of his life, where his unfinished fatherhood and the sense of guilt towards his wife were central. Then came the awareness of the situation in which he was kept in a coma while having his organs removed. Let me choose my words carefully – those are extremely emotional and devastating scenes. However, giving due attention to these matters I orchestrated a conscious meeting on a soul level, in which the donor and the receiver, in this case of his liver, came face to face. I also involved the recipients of the other organs. That is possible on a soul level. Soul service, so to speak. The transfer of the organ took place with the corresponding message from donor to recipient. "Do something beautiful with it in your life." Yet another poignant moment for the recipient. From that point on, the rejection symptoms noticeably decreased, and life became a lot more acceptable.

Making people aware of all the interactions that take place on a soul level seems crucial in this field of organ donation. As previously stated, every transplant should be accompanied by someone capable of working in the invisible realm of the soul to manage processes there, where possible. It is also appropriate here to emphasize that most indigenous peoples are aware of the importance of guiding a soul from earthly reality to the spiritual world, although organ donation as such is an unknown concept for them.

PREVENTING ORGAN DONATION

During the break of a lecture about organ donation in Zeijen in Drenthe, which I shared with Ger Lodewick, I was approached by a 73-year-old man, named Sake. He was touched by a statement I had made, saying that dysfunctional kidneys often refer to extremely sad, very repressed events, usually with a kind unprocessed loss. Sake told me his kidneys were only functioning at about twenty percent capacity, putting him on the list to be eligible for donor kidneys. He therefore wanted to familiarize himself further and delve more deeply into the subject, and so decided to come to this lecture. At the same time, he told me, he couldn't remember a single sad event of significance, which made him unable to understand what the relationship could be with the poor functioning of his kidneys. A few months later he came to my practice. Sake really wanted to go for it. While seeking information about the biographical background of his family, we made some remarkable discoveries. First, that his kidneys had deteriorated remarkably since the death of his mother in 2003. Sake told me that a girl had been born before him who had only lived for a few hours. And after Sake's birth another girl had been a stillbirth. "It was never talked about," he stressed. As we zoomed in deeper, Sake began to realize his immense sadness, and even to feel that his mother must have suffered from the loss of two daughters, and that his life actually began in the midst of these events. Sake's mother made great claims on him, right up to the day of her death. "We always had a kind of symbiotic relationship, I felt what she felt and vice versa." We discovered even more about Sake's mother having experienced deep sorrow.

In 1939 his mother had lost her favorite younger brother who was then 21 years old, followed by her father who died from the effects of rheumatism at the age of 57 in 1940, at the beginning of the war.

A succession of deaths then followed in 1939 (brother), 1940 (father), 1941 (daughter) and 1945 (daughter) – all shortly before Sake's birth. He began to realize how he had absorbed his mother's great sorrow right from the beginning. How the death of his sisters must have triggered the loss of her brother and father again. Sake cried and cried and that brought relief. As to my question: "How much of mother's grief do you think you've borne throughout your life?" Sake replied, "Ninety percent". Sake felt the pain of his kidneys in his back and sides, and the realization that they had become overburdened penetrated him even deeper. And, that he had clung to the memory of his mother enormously ever since she died. "I can't imagine what it's like not to be with her." Sake was stunned that all his life he had not realized how much impact all those experiences of death must have had on his mother, and via her on him. I asked Sake to put into words how he had experienced it himself and how the effect of the session had been for him. He writes:

"For the past two years I have suffered quite a bit from inflammation in the knee, or ankle, or big toe. It turned out to be gout and a blood test showed that my kidneys functioned just over twenty percent. There is no history of kidney disease in my family, the doctor said that the cause was probably high blood pressure. I was still concerned about it. In November 2018 I attended a lecture in Zeyen about organ donation and regression therapy. The last topic was handled by Maarten Oversier, in which he explained that our kidneys are a kind of storehouse of grief. And not only grief that you yourself have experienced consciously or unconsciously, but, for example, also the grief that your mother carried with her during pregnancy. In my case it concerned the loss of her father and a younger brother at a young age, and her stillborn daughter. This was something she experienced a few years before I was born. And that grief also lodges in the kidneys of the fetus that has resulted after all those years in reduced functioning.

During the session with Maarten, I was made aware of the deeper causes of my mother's grief. That already evoked a lot of emotion in me, especially when I realized that my mother thought I should have been a girl. And that when I turned out to be a boy, I actually wanted to allay her disappointment by bearing her grief in order to be of value to her in this way. As Maarten was talking to me, I was in tears and my body shook with all the sadness that rose to the surface from within. He also involved my mother in this conversation. He literally started speaking to her.

Throughout the entire session I felt huge tension in my body that diminished over time. Simultaneously, I also experienced understanding for how my mother reacted towards me. When I finally came to myself again, I had the feeling of being reborn. A month after the session, I had a check-up in the hospital. It turned out that my kidney function had increased from just above 20 to 30 percent."

Nearly a year later, Sake writes:

"It's been about a year since that session took place, and the first few days afterwards were quite emotional. When I looked at a childhood photo big tears started to fall. The more I began to understand my mother, the more I also understood myself and everything started to calm down again. And now I feel quite well. I can stay close to myself and be myself more and more, and that gives me inner peace.

As for my kidney function, it is still rising and is now between 33 and 35 per cent. The urologist is very satisfied, for someone my age it's a very nice and special development. I now have to go to the hospital every four months for a check-up, whereas it used to be every three months. Research showed that my kidneys are a bit smaller and have become less swollen. This is what I can tell you and I have the fullest trust that it will remain stable. Organ donation is no longer an option for me."

CASE HISTORY RENATE GREINERT

Give your life or you end life?

It is February 5, 1985. A day that I will never forget is indelibly etched in my body. It is the day my son Christian didn't come home from school. Instead, two police officers came to my door. Christian is seriously injured and is taken by air ambulance and flown to the nearest university medical center. 'Will he make it?' They don't answer. When we arrive at the hospital, we find Christian in the intensive care unit. He is on a ventilator and appears to be fast asleep. All the monitors next to his bed are active, they register the oscillations of his life.

As far as I can judge Christian is not seriously injured. A cut on his upper lip, some scratches on his cheekbone and forehead. His leg is broken and rests in some kind of plastic tub. His torso is bare. The whole situation leaves me feeling as if I'm frozen. A pouch, attached at the bedside, fills with urine. A nurse later replaces this with a bucket. Christian is hooked up to several IVs.

We take turns staying at his bedside, watching him, and trying to support him with prayers. I try to negotiate with God: "Please give him back to me. I'll give you everything, everything I think I can't do without." There is no answer. I have to leave the room because the doctors still want to run a brain test. "It will take twenty minutes." After waiting an hour and a half another doctor comes who I have not seen before. "Your son is dead. Now is the time to consider donating an organ." That's all. He sends us back to a room that is only illuminated from the outside by the streetlamps. We stay where we are, frozen in a deep state of shock, unable to think. I feel like I'm caught between two walls that come closer and closer towards me, depriving me of air. Another doctor: “Christian was definitely a people person!” Was he? I do not know. He is an almost 16-year-old boy. Terrific, intelligent, in love for the first time, but he could fight so hard with his siblings over a piece of chocolate. I don’t remember anything. For me there is nothing other than my dead son. “There are other mothers who sit beside their child’s bed who are urgently in need of an organ. You could help these children, otherwise they will die.” I already cannot bear the death of my son, I don’t want a child to die, but now they hold me responsible for the death of another child, if we don’t do it. “If we could help someone,” I hear my husband’s voice say. “What will the doctors take out? We don’t know, maybe the heart or the liver or the kidneys, maybe cartilage tissue.” Doctors urge us to leave now. A very short goodbye to my deceased son, far too short for an eternal goodbye. Christian is still on a ventilator; all the monitors around his bed are active. They want us to go. Deep in my body I hear alarm bells go off. What does this mean? I’m so tired. I stop fighting, my son is dead.’

I SHOULD HAVE HEARD HIS SILENT CRY FOR HELP

What I have had to accept after years of research: doctors need living organs for a transplant. Someone needs to be on a ventilator right up to when they have to remove the organs from the body. You cannot ventilate a dead man; he will swell up and burst if you don’t stop. An organ donor is therefore still alive. It’s so painful to live with this knowledge. A burden on my shoulders weighs me down. I feel responsible for the organ donation because I didn’t stop it. As a mother I should have heard his silent cry for help. People say I should stop my research, that I should put my grief aside, but I can’t. My first thought in the morning and my last thought in the evening are about my son. I try to find words for what happened, but they don’t exist in our language. So, I try to create them.

Years later I encountered reincarnation therapy. We investigate my family tree and immediately notice that all the women are divorced. My mother, father’s mother, my daughter, and myself. My father was born in 1914. He did not fight in World War II. My father was raised by his mother who ran a retirement home. Everyone loved him dearly. He became a rather spoiled child. His mother adored him and although she was very strict and rigid, she was incapable of worshipping and loving anyone else in the same way. Her husband had left her, I don’t know when, and was living in China. My father became the director of a large steel company. Shortly afterwards he died in a car accident.

Maarten guides me back along my family line to my father, to the point where he died. I close my eyes and focus on the accident. I take on the role of my father. I am no longer aware of anyone else present. I hear Maarten’s voice and follow his words. I answer. “A car, a Porsche, is driving very fast on my side of the road. It hits my car and ploughs into my Mercedes. I feel the steering wheel in my chest. It crushes my lungs and heart, that is, my father's. I'm bleeding terribly. I feel myself to the last drop of blood, I see my body in the damaged car, and finally I am free."

Maarten: "Do you feel connected to someone?"

"With my daughter."

"Do you want to do something for her?"

"Yes, I will give her a feeling that there is a connection between our hearts."

Maarten: "Your father came back to you in the form of your son.
I treated my son the same way my grandmother treated her son, my father. My father left her and died and when my son reached puberty and I was so close to him, he left me too. It saddens me that that I did not get the connection between my father and my son, although in hindsight Christian looked exactly like his grandfather. I always had a vague suspicion that there was a connection between my father and my son but didn't dare trust my intuition. But what was very clear to me was that it was my responsibility to stop the accidents and that I am connected to and am part of everything and everyone.

During a session, in a teaching setting with a group of people, we make contact with Christian's soul that is still totally bewildered. With Maarten, I discover that the death of my son was predestined. And so, on February 5, 1985, he was hit by a car while crossing the street on his bicycle. With Maarten's encouragement I concentrate on his accident, as if I am now experiencing it on Christiaan's behalf.

THEY KILLED ME

"I'm trying to die at the scene of the accident, but they won't allow it. They push me back in my body. They want my organs."

I experience how I am kept artificially alive, and at the same time I am aware of everything. "They extract different organs from my body and put them on a table. I see it all now. They keep me alive until they finally take my heart out too."

Then I panic.

"Only now am I going to die."

Maarten speaks to all the organs, and he also involves the persons to whom they will be going. About six or seven of them.

"My organs must continue to live in their bodies."

"Heart, what's the most important thing you don't understand?" Maarten asks.

"I do not understand what they are doing. I stop my heart beating because the doctors want me to stop."

I learn to see that my life force is still in my organs as they are being extracted.

"The life energy of Christian, what happens after they take the organs?"

"I'm still alive."

"And what happened to the recipient's life energy when his heart was removed?"

"It was thrown away."

Somehow, I'm starting to realize what has happened to me. In my imagination, Maarten calls on all the new 'owners' and confronts them with me, the donor, so that they become aware of the exchange of these organs. It's kind of a soul-to-soul transference ritual. I feel how the recipients have been touched. And me too.

"Christian, what should be done now? Will you let them go or will you hold onto them?"

"I don't know, but I now realize I don't need these parts anymore. I also feel anger. The doctors shouldn't have taken the organs, I was still alive. They have killed me. I would like to say to my parents: let me go now."

"Go to the boy who got my heart, give him permission to live with it. What do you wish for him?"

I feel deep emotion and give in.

"Make the best of it", I tell him.

And then it calms down.

The exchange of questions and answers has made me realize that Christiaan has held on to his enormous confusion of consciousness since the accident, through me, his mother. I have always felt that anxiety in myself, with the various associated pains all around my body. I too was in shock and unconsciously kept in touch with him in this way. In the period after the session, for the first time, I experience a deep relaxation, and surrender into my body. Only now do I feel have really been able to say goodbye to him. It is over.

Since 1985 Renate Greinert (1943) from Germany has been committed to clearing up issues concerning organ donation, brain death and the view of humanity associated with it. She exposes sensitive issues from the daily practice of transplantation medicine and has been supported for years by critical doctors, theologians, and lawyers. Renate is president of the association *Kritische Aufklärung über Organtransplantation*. This was founded by parents who had allowed their children to donate organs, without exactly knowing enough about the background at the time, and who regret their decision. The Dutch edition of Renate's book *Unversehrt sterben! (Dying undisturbed), a broader view of organ donation* was published in 2009. It has an extensive preface by the well-known cardiologist Pim van Lommel, who has been researching near-death experiences (NDE) of patients who survived heart attacks. He published about this in the renowned journal *The Lancet* and wrote the 2007 bestseller *Eindeloos bewustzijn* (Consciousness Beyond Life), which was translated into several languages.

"Without a shred of information about what the consequences of removing organs would be for the dying donor and his family, I allowed myself to be manipulated by the transplant doctors. In deep shock and totally unable to make such an important decision, I agreed to have my 15-year-old son's organs removed. The sight of my emptied child both hurt and infuriated me deeply. Everyone needs to know clearly for themselves whether he believes that someone with living organs is already dead or in the process of dying and so still alive."

CHAPTER 6

Incarnating and Getting Lost

"Who has fully realized that history is not contained in thick books but lives in our very blood?"
– Carl Gustav Jung

Souls incarnate from a realm of souls to the earthly, material world. Once here, as a human, you can get seriously disoriented. You have lost a huge number of memories and there are hardly any signs showing you which way to turn. Memories of the origin of your soul and past lives are quickly lost or meet with no response. In its growth from infant to toddler a baby has a keen sense of which parent is most attuned to spiritual and magical connections. When there is no room for those connections, the child also then learns to close him/herself off from the world. Moreover, most information about life on earth, which is thrown at us from the beginning, turns out to be misleading. Why do we forget everything so spontaneously? Why, and especially by whom, is sand being thrown in our eyes? And what do primitive peoples say about this?

Once here on Earth, the incarnated person comes into reality, and the memory of the origin of his soul rapidly fades. To an increasing extent the person also comes into a medical, clinical environment, under fluorescent lighting, or even worse, LED lighting. The greatest difference between the immaterial state and the terrestrial, and in addition the greatest shock to the soul's perception of the world, is that the soul comes from a unitary world, while here on earth everything takes place between two poles. Rob Bontenbal, an old teacher of mine, called this 'the primal trauma'. To be surrounded by and interlaced with duality, yin and yang, masculine and feminine and the associated limitations, is an insanely intense reality to surrender to. Two ears, two eyes, two kidneys, two legs, two lungs, two hemispheres of the brain, two arms, you name it. But it's all part of it. We are now part of the biodynamic cycle in which we felt tempted to create a human adventure. And we have, in preparation, been allowed to spend about nine months in the maternal womb.

What could be an even more shocking discovery is that from the very beginning, we have been consciously doused by buckets of untruths, dogmas, and misleading information. About terrestrial laws, our nature, the climate, evolution, historical events, about who, or what we really are as humans. By whom? By those among our ranks who already set the tone before we arrived and continue to believe that they are in control. Karmic patterns at these levels are also transferable over generations.

Down the centuries, all kinds of power elites have constantly manufactured, and influenced, and exercised control over the political climate through governments, cabinets, leaders, and boards. Embedded in our history is a need for power and domination by the few, but it is the population who suffers. It's no different today, but unfortunately we often discover it too late. The hallmarks are always political correctness, obedience to authority, power, and the continuous amendment of laws from a working environment dominated by suits and ties. Within its ranks, people bombard one another in front of an audience with complicated sentence constructions and all kinds of arguments pulled out of a top hat that, on balance, don't mean much. They are supposed to give the unsuspecting, docile citizen the impression that a public airing of differences of opinion really means they care about the people. Anyone managing to get a platform within these parties, and not be under anyone's thumb, so not controlled by official institutions, is given a rough time, and bullied out of their position by political correctness. Depending on the era, the country's political structure and the (hidden) interests that were at stake, this happened either heavy-handedly or with great finesse.

History is full of malicious forms of government that instigated penal systems where everyone ended up who disagreed with them. New definitions are constantly stuck on existing concepts causing the passionate seeker of truth who is following the trail of recorded facts, to constantly get bogged down, and eventually draw conclusions that are not in line with the truth. That was why eight hundred years ago it was impossible for an ordinary citizen to discover who the real agent was behind the inquisition and ecclesiastical power and who organized it. Nor was it possible to gain access to the real facts behind battles, famines, pandemics, and civil wars. For example, those citizens of the world, still traceable in our photo albums in the form of our very own ancestors, had no notion of the extent to which the mega chemical multinational IG Farben influenced the origin of World War II. And to this very day people are still not allowed to see what preparations precede claims about a killer virus, or a self-manufactured menace to our climate, terrorist attack or life-threatening condition, in which the whole of society is deliberately held in an artificial stranglehold. It is a covert enemy offensive launched by the world's exploiters, as they see themselves, who wish to bend this world to their will at every conceivable level.

Again, by whom? Let me limit myself here by talking about an elite who likes to operate behind the scenes in secret societies, some of which do not even bear a name, so that they are difficult to trace. The colloquial word often used to refer to them is 'Illuminati'. A term that for many is associated with conspiracy theories, which suits this elite. The members consider themselves as direct descendants of the pharaohs, hence their working methods are organized in a pyramid, in which they wish to place themselves at the top, as being the 'all-seeing eye'. Their ultimate objective is a new world order.

The elite consists of a few powerful, astronomically rich, and thus influential families within which psychopathic personality traits thrive. These groups are also beset with the customary discord and are subsequently controlled by demonic powers that are not visible to humans, called archons, who present themselves as gods. Many a world event was, and is orchestrated by them through a step-by-step plan with an underlying agenda, as described in the Protocols of the Elders of Zion, to ultimately achieve world domination. These influences and worlds are not easily defined, let alone traceable. Fortunately, there are plenty of publications that go into much greater detail on this matter. In this book I prefer to focus mainly on the effects of this influence. They do not need to be proven, they are quite clearly observable and traceable through the complaints the people have who visit my practice. Whether the cause of all injuries stems from a gigantic conspiracy or not, is not really relevant to a therapist. This is however, to share this suspicion, after having seen so many clues. We are fed a pack of lies and even quite a few of our own parents parrot back what they were told, in which they involuntarily share in being part of an artificially fabricated system that passes down disinformation unnoticed from generation to generation. What is true or not true, is of course a difficult discussion. It is up to everyone to find out and investigate that for themselves. But as soon as people tap into their subconscious resources, during sessions, it simply seems that this is the only place where indisputable truth is produced. Just like in dreams. Lies do not exist in those regions either. The fact we learn nothing about those sources makes you wonder.

FORGETING HAS A FUNCTION

Forgetting has a function during the descent into an incarnation. It might be required and logical on all kinds of intricate karmic levels. It makes sense that if you were to really remember everything from previous lives, it could cause such a paralyzing shock effect that you would now wander around in an apathetic daze. After all, you would be fully aware of everything you did to someone, or vice versa, while it is precisely that person who plays an important role for you in your new life.

Because of this functional forgetfulness we can gain new experiences about old, unprocessed themes, relationships, and events, without being disturbed too much by memories of things which are still too overwhelming in nature. Little by little, old situations can be reconciled and so we resolve old karmic conflicts. After which you can broaden your horizon and can shift your life focus to areas of interest and adventures with less or even no significant karmic charge. What I see, is that 'getting to the point' with yourself becomes exceedingly difficult if we are discouraged from seeking answers within ourselves and as long as we are kept from knowing about our spiritual nature. As soon as we get snarled up in something and seek regular care, we generally face approaches and methods of treatment that are more likely to bog us down than support our quest. Methods of treatment where the question remains as to whether they are still a natural part of the confrontation necessary to liberate ourselves from old patterns.

What cannot be verified in scientific models and research methods, does not form a substantial part of our world. Nor of our worldly perceptions and social awareness. At least not consciously. Meanwhile things have gotten so out of hand that governments around the world base their decision-making solely based on those models, and "the people" must acquiesce to them under a growing threat of measures. From that angle not a single appeal is made to our spiritual essence, driven by brainwashed leaders who don't know any better or, if they do, have become so entangled in conflicts of interest that they cannot extricate themselves from them.

Native peoples tell us that we are here to give hands and feet to the Creator, so that he can experience his own creation. We are not truth seekers led by imposed standards and conditions. If we are sometimes misled in this way, then we want to do our utmost to regain ourselves until everything about us is true again. As a newcomer to native communities – currently called "indigenous" – that are not dominated by scientific doctrines, you were valued and recognized by your immediate family according to your unique, spiritual origin. Even your name was based on that, as confirmation. That was the starting point and a constant power of resilience behind an earthly existence.

CYCLE OF SECOND CHANCES

We continue to be extremely receptive and gullible as beginners. Our most vulnerable period concerns the period from the first cell division until well into childhood. Like sponges, we soak up atmospheres and outside influences as information. In this way we become partly filled with energetic ballast. The extent to which this happens depends on the extent to which you can remain connected to your essence. To a certain degree it is also important to let in influences from the environment, to finally learn to distinguish between what really suits you and what does not. To recover your own truth that you previously lost, you must first immerse yourself again in all kinds of distractions. Sometimes we do it so deeply, that we now accept even the most misleading ideas from our environment to be the guiding principle of life. And if we don't free ourselves of it, we pass it on to our children, so that the task falls on to them.

Is the task of finding the way back out of this jungle of trickery and deceit natural? I wonder. And, how entangled can we get? In any case, we now know that not everyone succeeds in doing this in one lifetime. In fact, during some lives you stray even more to be able to understand it even better later. It might take several lives for someone steeped in the doctrine that there is a hell after death to discover that this is not the true picture. On the other hand, anyone who has become convinced that there is nothing after death can take several lifetimes to discover that it isn't true.

That may be why reincarnation can be interpreted so broadly. Simply explained, it concerns a cycle of second opportunities with karma as the common thread. Karma means that our actions come back to ourselves. We are going to experience for ourselves what we once created so that we eventually learn to understand all our actions. But from a deeper perspective it is about growth of consciousness and development on a soul level, by constantly adding a new dimension to the jargon of our experience.

As became clear in previous chapters: growth of consciousness stagnates during traumatic circumstances on the earthly plane. For example, when certain events come to an abrupt and violent end, such as in a war. The shock experience creates blockages that we then energetically carry with us until they are revised, usually in the next life. The same is true of someone who dies with the assumption that he will face a lot of punishment afterwards. Those beliefs powerfully dominate the path the mortal soul takes. That makes it impossible for the healing process of letting go to take place, even though that is the desired situation.

Hence, this cycle of rebirth can also be interpreted practically: repeating to accomplish what could not be accomplished at the time. To review what was once hidden by our conditioned human comprehension. Ultimately, we come to a fuller, more holistic sense of ourselves and life. As if a greater vista unfolds before our eyes as our powers of observation increase, so that we no longer have to fall back into old patterns. We have let go of old views and concepts that we long thought were really true.

JUNK BELIEFS

Many people find it normal that children spend most of their early years going to school and are uncritically stuffed with all kinds of selective information. It is education that forms the basis of their outlook on life. It is censored information that you are not supposed to dispute, as if a new religion has infiltrated the minds of the population. Many therefore consider it normal that vaccinations protect us from scary diseases. It also goes without saying that fluorine tablets will give you strong teeth and that you will tackle physical ailments with medical treatments full of chemicals that cause side effects. The pope, the pastor, the president, our representatives, the judge and those with the most titles or influence not only know best; they also want what is best for us. That's the trend. If the doctor recommends the flu shot, you wouldn't argue with that, would you? Focusing on getting a lucrative position in the business community set up by multinationals is quite common among young people. As well as building up a good pension, putting money in a savings account and driving an electric car to help change our menacing and especially self-induced climate fluctuations. People also believe that applying sunscreen prevents skin cancer, that a microwave is safe and that you should think carefully before making any decisions.

Aspartame, flavor enhancers, glyphosate and I don't know how many chemical additions to our food and agriculture are not demonstrably harmful to our health, according to scientific research. Who still thinks it's odd to have to insure yourself against every unexpected situation? Without asking any real critical questions, everyone hangs on the internet with their 'smart' phone in a 4G and 5G WiFi field of electro-smog, like a piglet on a sow's teat. And anyone who questions reports from mainstream news sources and becomes a denier, is plotting as though it were a contagious disease. It is sometimes touching how people, when they look back at the old-fashioned propaganda methods such as those employed by Minister Goebbels, see through them with a smile on their face, while they are completely blind to their current captivity in a similar mechanism that meanwhile has become so advanced that its effectiveness and reach is many times greater.

Either way, they are assumptions that we thought were well-researched by all sorts of righteous, authorities immune to fraud. Their dominant influence leads many into a dead end without them noticing. Unfortunately, the overload and aggression of these junk beliefs are so powerful that many earthlings will only gain any awareness of it posthumously.

STORIES OF THE DEAD

I have heard stories in abundance in my practice about souls of the deceased who, due to all those deceptions, became thoroughly gridlocked during their earthly lives, which to a large degree adversely affected the quality of their life and environment. It is these astonishing stories that encouraged me to write these texts. These people continued to believe, right up to the grave what they had been told without amending anything. The energy field around Mother Earth is full of wandering, confused souls who, ironically, are still terrified of going to hell or have no idea that they are dead because their old programming is still playing tricks on them. As a result, they remain earthbound, driven by unprocessed life experiences that are "not spoken about," and that exert a disruptive influence on those who were part of their former family. We have become estranged from all the primal rituals to perform healing work here, partly under the influence of the Catholic Church. As a result, family systems weaken and are easily influenced under coercion from controlling mechanisms. Thus, salt underhandedly remains in old wounds both for the deceased and their descendants.

LAND GRAB

Things have been brutal in this world for a long time. To put it mildly, it's all about owning the earth in an aggressive way. Chief Seattle's maxim, "How can you own the Earth?" expressed his astonished indignation at the very notion of being able to own the earth at all. Nevertheless, for many it is self-evident. At all costs, flags are planted everywhere, boundaries and plots of land are demarcated, including their raw materials, brutally contested and appropriated. For centuries, land grabbing has been the core business of those in power. The greater the need to possess, the more power must be pursued. It certainly seems as if some of those incarnated want to secure their incarnations by designating Mother Earth as a property and treating it as such. They are in continuous conquest mode. As if they are afraid of losing the ground beneath their feet without that compulsion and control, and with it their right to exist.

Indigenous peoples speak of 'Father Sun' and 'Mother Earth'. Hence masculinity becomes associated with the sun and femininity with the planet Earth. Therefore, masculinity in its original form is allied to the most rarefied elements: fire (doing) and air (thinking) and femininity with the most solidified elements: water (feeling) and earth (experiencing matter). In this way, women in a general sense represent the material reality more powerfully than men, who are the bearers of the fire of life. The bridge between soul and body is most challenging for men. Seen in this way a soul is completely at the mercy of the feminine for a successful incarnation. That is, Mother Earth embodies the soul. After all, 'In-carnate' refers to *carne*, or meat. Regardless of whether you appear here as a man or as a woman, the body is the clearest evidence of this. 'Ex-carne-ren', a nice word for dying, brings us back again to the source of the soul. The meat can stay here and becomes compost for new life.

UNCONDITIONAL INCARNATIONS

Native peoples also substantiate these insights by pointing out the similarity between the nature of a human woman and Mother Earth, and thus the undeniable difference with the male: a mother feeds a child as Mother Earth does with humanity. For nine months a soul is in a dark inner world symbiotically connected with a mother before it has assumed a fully equipped physical shell for an earthly journey. Once again, it underlines its nourishing and shaping role for new incarnate life. The man in his primeval form is assigned an active and protective role in the outside world. As a guard and protector, he fends off disruptive influences during this magical process, ranging from the weather and food scarcity to people who are jealous or prying. He hunts for food, utensils and clothing and provides fire and safety. But these natural drives take on extreme forms if he no longer experiences a normal connection to himself, or rather, to his female counterpart.

Like a cornered cat, he now wants to start owning things to save his own skin. His territorial drive then pushes him to extremes. Hunting mutates into violent killing; fire becomes a destructive inferno and security becomes an obsessive control mechanism based on fear. The men at the top end up believing they are omnipotent gods, but in fact they suffer from extreme fear of incarnation. The realization that they are destroying the very ground under their own habitat no longer gets through to them. All they want to do is rise to the top. Disconnected from his emotional world, he has become a psychopath.

In suit and tie in top positions of society, where the lie factory has been established, he actively recruits human allies, who believe in him and keep everyone else in line. This is how he thinks he is still entitled to exist. His position must be safeguarded here.

The child, as an archetype, precisely symbolizes this unconditional connection between heaven and earth. The out-of-control madman appropriates children if necessary. In the most perverse ways, he quenches himself with their energy of innocence, open-mindedness, and purity. He himself is disconnected from that, which means that he cannot lead a normal human life. He can keep his vehicle going like an electric car that needs a charging station. For that reason, a bloodthirsty pedophile network exists around every excessive system of power.

ORIGINAL GUIDELINES

And us ordinary people? Are we then immaculate? Didn't we, in previous lives, also play that game, no matter in which position? Thousands of therapeutic sessions say yes, to a greater or lesser extent. Consciousness simply remembers everything. Therefore, there is no point in speculating. In the end everyone only meets their own truth. It's not 'us and them', although it makes sense to stay alert about what you've been led to believe. We just need to face up to our own former part in it. In so doing, we can take our energetic contribution to that game out of the equation, which is much more effective than fighting it.

Indigenous peoples have preserved the original guidelines for how life is meant to be here on Earth. We should be very grateful to them for that. They can be read with the heart where our ancestors also speak to us so that their life experiences can really be understood and incorporated. In this way we clear the lines with our spiritual relationships and the newly incarnated – our children and grandchildren – do not have to reinvent the wheel again and again. We learned from those whose footsteps we followed when we incarnated. When we learn to listen and act in this way again, the magnetic field around our inner compass changes and with it the course of our life. A course that lifts the fog around erring in the jungle of trickery and deceit.

CHAPTER 7

Inferioriteit versus superioriteit

"Maybe you have to find yourself before you can be it."
– Loesje

For many centuries, a common thread throughout our history has shown us the curious phenomenon that relatively small groups of people, and in particular some individuals, feel superior to others. Entire population groups are seen by them as inferior and treated as such. Just as the ancient pharaohs even imagined themselves gods, so figures keep coming and going, who essentially experience the same motives to subjugate people, to enslave them. United in elitist societies, they always actively reign, with the masses having to conform to their needs so they can always put themselves above others. They enforce their positions of power with great violence, bloodshed, oppression, and manipulation. It's as if their lives depended on it. More in-depth knowledge of this phenomenon is important in the context of the right to be, and what all this oppression brings about for those who, in whatever role, must deal with it. Since it is mainly indigenous peoples who were victimized by these violent people who set out the course of things, we zoom in on North American Indians because they are an enormous source of inspiration for my work.

From roughly 1830 to 1996, there were 145 'residential schools' in Canada alone. Some 150,000 Indian children were 'whitewashed' in these sinister prisons. "Kill the Indian, save the man" was the motto. They were no longer allowed to live their traditions and were subjected to an extremely strict, militaristic regime. Their braids were cut off, their mother tongue was banned, and their Native American name was exchanged for a number and a Bible-related name.

This is how many indigenous tribes have fared, worldwide. Why? Indians, or better yet indigenous peoples, were seen as inferior races. They were unpredictable, unbelieving, savage men with inferior life values. A threat to the Roman Catholic Church and the feudal royal houses, who wanted to expand their empires of power like an oil slick across the continents.

On top of much more rigorous measures, that literally included genocide, it was thought that the Indians living in Canada, of which the Iroquois were the most populous as an umbrella name for six major tribes, must completely adapt to the 'white man's lifestyle'. Aggressive programs of indoctrination would make them able to assimilate with, and serve the civilized European. The dramatic consequences of these schools are far-ranging. The physical, emotional, and sexual abuse was huge. Countless people were displaced, committed suicide, lost themselves in alcohol and aggression, and died of diseases originating in Europe. Internally damaged to such an extent that the souls of these peoples were eventually affected. Today's Native Americans even speak of "the Indian Holocaust" (read Hitler and His Secret partners - James Pool). This is not an arbitrary comparison, because Adolf Hitler was inspired for his concentration camp plans by the design of the Indian reservations and these educational institutions. And so, another new chapter was added to the singular tendency to oppress, humiliate, or exterminate entire nations.

To this day, mass graves of abused children from these cultures are still being discovered around the residential schools. No matter how lost these children felt, their souls are never lost. As always, the truth is coming out, especially today.

THE DARK PAGES OF OURSELVES

Where does the idea of wanting to suppress or even eliminate so-called inferior races come from? And what criteria make a race inferior or superior at all? Perhaps this phenomenon has an extraterrestrial origin where non-terrestrial beings, unlike the souls known to us, fight for physical habitats in the universe such as Mother Earth. Or is this singular longing sometimes better understood if we don't look too far from ourselves for the answer? Via reincarnation, for instance.

Through the many thousands of regressions that I have been allowed to do, a picture of this has formed. Deeper connections that surface during sessions explain a lot. A great deal in fact. It's amazing that in our time, even among the more conscious people and spiritual seekers, we have little insight into the relationships with the unaccepted parts of ourselves from times gone by.

For many people the idea is quite plausible that we can literally be part of the history books according to the principle of reincarnation. It still appears difficult to accept that we sometimes also play roles in its dark pages. Reason enough to share this story too. Just to be clear, I'm basing these conclusions on regressions with people who, in past lives, didn't just encounter themselves as peasants, innocent herbalist women, or heroes. Slave drivers, murderers, executioners, church fathers who commit sexual abuse, (top) Nazis and power-hungry people also come forward, provided the working atmosphere in my practice is safe enough. All of these constitute extreme life experiences that indeed are the result of intense victimization in even earlier lives. This usually causes the pendulum to swing completely from one end to the other. It goes without saying, I share this information out of great respect for the courage of these clients. Even though the need was often great, in almost all cases it did them a world of good after these inner confrontations came to be seen in a different perspective ¬– at least different from how it had been impassively stored in the subconscious until now. Typically isolated in shame and guilt and condemnation of 'the self'. The request for help with which they initially reported to my practice can be taken as quite serious. And on a physical level as well.

THREE WISE MEN

As curious souls who in- and excarnate, due to various circumstances during many lifetimes, we can develop good qualities of the soul. But also, maladies of the soul. Though normally speaking of course, a soul cannot have a malady, but the term indicates that something can be deeply ingrained, and with which we can identity down to our deepest, most unfathomable levels. Think of profoundly etched karmic disorders, such as delusions of pride or serious undervaluation of ourselves. Disorders that arise when we explore ultimate and extreme life experiences during certain incarnations. We too are then capable of eagerly indulging in evil temptations and satanic power plays. After all, that is also a part of the unlimited possibilities of our universe.

Then, after leading such a bizarre life, when we physically die, we feel our conscience starting to trouble us. The scope of which is simply too big to allow at that moment. A conscience that can only be denied now but will continue to impact subsequent incarnations. Still, a realization simultaneously awakens in the deepest recesses of that conscience. That is where we feel shame, scandal, and guilt. These "Three Wise men" tell us when we have broken cosmic laws. This happens when we play God ourselves without complying with or respecting the original creation. Then we literally go against our own nature. And then? What goes around comes...

We have now become victims of a gigantic judgment we have created ourselves. A judgment with the same potential as the acts we perform. As a result, we feel our very existence is in jeopardy. We say to ourselves: 'I am bad and have no right to exist anymore.' Pretty much turning ourselves into cosmically homeless people in the process. We have now become inferior beings ourselves. The one who then takes us in again and offers us shelter is, of course, the devil himself. As the CEO of an immense galactic asylum for the homeless, his success depends on the influx of wandering souls who have lost themselves by having gone completely beyond the pale in one of the many brutal scenarios orchestrated by Mr. Devil himself. After all, against his better judgment, he wants to generate his own creation and there is no turning back for him.

He now helps them forget their shortcomings, offering false recognition through all kinds of medals and awards, giving them a new kind of right to exist. Under one condition, of course. You must sell your soul to him and continue to play his game from then on, namely, combatting inferiority. In other words, fighting against ourselves by obsessively pursuing a perfectly organized society. A New World Order, for example, as an improved version of the creation already in existence. One in which a great deal of technology, artificial intelligence, robotics, gene manipulation, and extremely advanced control systems prevail. And the latter is the most important because Mr. Devil realizes, of course, that no one can ever really become satisfied and happy in such a world, and therefore always keeps looking for how things used to be. So, it's a vicious circle. And guess what makes a reincarnation therapy session successful? When a client discovers his own dark side, processes the deeds associated with it and then begins to release himself (more) from his contract with Mr. Devil and his henchmen. Until then, he can only do two things: either deny that he was (once) like that and so placing and combating evil outside himself or continue being a part of it. This exercise gets increasingly harder, however, because countless souls feel from deep within that a great transition is underway, and that the opportunity to free themselves from such "tar and feather pasts" is now up for grabs.

So, the battle of inferiority versus superiority essentially takes place within us. We fight against ourselves, but we look for external adversaries. Those adversaries basically have the same characteristics we once had ourselves. For some, they are gays, the disabled, the vulnerable, the slothful, the dumbos or the refugees. For others the authorities, the power-hungry or the untouchables. Or more literally? Sometimes the Jew, other times the German soldier, sometimes the rapist, other times his victim, sometimes the slave, other times the slavedriver. These are real stories from real people. I wish I had imagined them, so that we could at least sit idly by and watch.

PART II

IINFLUENCE OF ANCESTORS

CHAPTER 8

Integration of ancestral awareness

"To forget one's ancestors, is like a river without a source. Or a tree without roots."
– Chinese proverb

We could simply divide the life experiences that our ancestors went through into completed and unfinished experiences. Something that has been lived through leaves 'medicine' in the terminology of the Native Americans. The repressed, unfinished events retain the need to be completed. For the newly incarnated, their (grand)children, both are important.

When our (ancestors) parents have completed their life experiences, they form a fertile foundation. They are stored in energetic form and every new family member can and may use them. What our (ancestors) parents could not live through themselves, become triggers in our lives. Their unfinished experiences awaken in the lives of the new generations. So, it can seem as if we are burdened with their remains. That is in fact the case, but they do have their function and are based on a conscious choice. It sounds a bit practical and from that perspective it may well be. The soul always makes it clear that it cannot deal with broken experiences.

The history of mankind spans an endless chain of generations. Where and how it ever began is a question I do not wish to venture into, although I have serious doubts about Darwin's theory of evolution that humans are descended from apes. It is clear however that a great deal is transferred in the succession of lifetimes, family histories and traditions. Some characteristics have a high degree of continuity, others change substantially over the course of decades. In addition to genetic information, parents also impart a socio-cultural legacy. They look after their children, as well as influence people who do likewise with their offspring. The way in which this takes place can be traced back to their own life experiences. And of these, the most painful also have the most decisive effects.

Our ancestors are our roots. As soon as we are out of touch with them, we feel uprooted. Again, when our (ancestors) parents have repressed fundamental life experiences, we are burdened with them. At the same time, this burden not only offers growth opportunities for us, but also helps to unburden our (ancestors) parents when we take up the challenge that they passed up under the circumstances that prevailed at the time. Even when they are physically long dead. Symbolically, we can fix the leaks that started with them, because we are no longer in the rainstorm. At the same time, we heal essential parts of ourselves. That's an important conclusion I can draw from all the stories I've heard from the family biographies. The present-day complaints with which clients come to my practice are always connected to their predecessors. The way their lives are entwined with ours is quite literal, and usually much closer than we see. It requires a slightly different view of (ancestors) parents than we have learned. Have a look with me through the windows of the ancestral house in this part of the book, that open out onto what is important to understand, to feel, to fathom and above all to experience from our (ancestors) parents.

INCOMPLETE INFORMATION

Usually, we know little about our grandparents, except that Grandad smoked fat cigars, was a stuffy old man and that Gramma was a good cook and liked to spoon a glass of *advocaat* in the upstairs room on Sundays after church service. Many clients don't even know how many siblings their own father or mother has, let alone how many their grandparents had. They hardly know how they really fared. In this way, a good image of their lives, their reality, their difficulties, shortcomings, and challenges was never formed. Built out of shreds of incomplete information, many of us draw all kinds of conclusions that give a very distorted picture. At the same time, I saw fruitful developments when a family member took the trouble to compile a family book, when an uncle or aunt managed to keep the stories from his or her family alive in a special way or when someone went to investigate for themselves to resurrect faded, forgotten, or repressed stories. Fertile soil on which beautiful sessions could grow. Every time someone thought they had reached a dead end during their search for important information about their ancestry, that information came suddenly from an unexpected source. It seems that providence preserves exactly what is important for one's growth process. A birth certificate, an old photo or letter, a distant relative that turns out to be still alive, a diary, diploma, certificate, scribbled notes, a pendant or ring, a newspaper article, you name it. The passionate quests of Derk Bolt in the popular Dutch TV program *Spoorloos* (Without a Trace) have much in common here. My biographical research into insights and clarifications concerning the actual events that took place in the different generations of a family are a prominent part of the initial consultation. It is an aspect of my job that I really enjoy and that makes me feel like Sherlock Holmes. In the following chapters I will elaborate on the power and logic of ancestral work.

FAMILY TREES FULL OF TABOOS

The dry reality I usually come across in my practice, is that family trees, apart from many fascinating, incredible, eccentric, and exciting stories, are full of taboos. With extremely thorny and shameful events where people, often under coercion and threat, were not allowed to be talked about. Events overloaded with reproach, judgment, and traumatic break ups. It's too simplistic to think that something like this won't affect you if you just don't think about it, talk about it, or pause to consider it. Yet that's the way it almost always happens.

Many indigenous tribes find it important to know the ancestral lines and to heal old family wounds by giving them appropriate attention. Many traumas that occurred in this past are still unprocessed and therefore misunderstood and anchored in us. Soul garbage, as it were. The person living at that time experienced these things on a personal, emotional, and physical level. Just like we do now. That this can have repercussions over time should not be underestimated.

Because everyone is part of a family, you could say that you are always in contact with other family members. However far away they may feel. All completed life experiences are preserved and accessible in the form of a power, a medicine, which every new family member can and may use. You can, as it were, tap into it. It is a source of medicine. We then say that we feel the power of grandpa or grandma and let it inspire or encourage us. Many a family tree, however, has become energetically burdened due to all kinds of circumstances and as a result, its growth has stagnated.

THE SOUL WANTS TO EXPERIENCE WHOLENESS

That which could never be integrated into the encompassing body of the soul, the primordial soul of the entire family through pain, dissociation, and death, is then passed on like a baton, from generation to generation. Waiting for new opportunities, longing for attention and recognition, looking for ways to cope and hoping for deliverance. Often the same souls very consciously incarnate in the same families for that reason, so that theoretically you could have been your own (great) grandfather or (great) grandmother. Or the reincarnation of a 3-year-old drowned brother or sister of your own father or mother, grandfather, or grandmother. Souls can also disperse and reincarnate in other family trees. This is done according to a logic of the soul that is difficult for the mind to understand but is always quite understandable and logical when explained by the person in question in a trance. For the soul, an incarnation to a completely different continent, a completely different family and culture is comparable to the impact of emigration. In this way everyone will once again seek the part of something that is unfinished. In making the choice the soul is extremely creative and efficient. It only wants to experience wholeness, and its longing for it contains irrepressibly instinctual potential. In this connection, the soul urges itself on to seek encounters with disconnected parts of itself. Or to reconnect with what once fell apart. This potential, still to be able to solve matters, is basically always present. However, the ignorance of this connection in our modern society makes it easy for us to get stuck once we have entered an earthly life again. We no longer recognize these deeper perspectives. We are influenced by powers and forces from our conception to birth and then throughout our life to death, and indeed beyond, and we are distracted from this essential knowledge. So much so that we hardly, if at all, consider taking reincarnation, the approach to our essential conflicts, seriously.

OLD EMOTIONAL ISSUES CARRY ON THROUGH GENERATIONS

It is sad that the diseases of modern humans are hardly recognized in this context anymore. This has put us in a vicious circle. For example, when a child dies in a family, the family members involved are deeply moved. It used to happen quite often. It also has an affect if a child is lost after a few months, in the form of a miscarriage, or an abortion. But certainly, also in the case of a stillbirth, if one of the twins does not make it, or in case of cot death, or because of a fatal illness, or due to a fatal accident in early childhood. The older the child or the more ardently the pregnancy was anticipated, the more bonding has already taken place. These events, among many others, appear to be deeply engraved at the level of the soul. In practice it becomes clear that these are rarely processed. One tends to think that such an event did not have much influence on those involved, because 'life goes on' or 'that happened so often in the past'. These are major pitfalls.

The fact that life also continues for the deceased is something that not everyone thinks or thought about. The impact of such a major loss lasts for generations. As I have already mentioned, it strikes me how people have such a superficial knowledge of the history of their own family. Grandfathers and grandmothers from Indonesia, (a) German or other overseas ancestor(s), a deceased or childhood love of grandfather or grandmother who never returned, hunger, inheritance conflicts, family feuds, you name it. Everything keeps on working. The event itself may be well out of date and the emotional consequences for the most part dubiously resolved, but it turns out to be very fruitful to subject these kinds of old emotional issues to further investigation.

As a reincarnation therapist, I interview clients extensively about their ancestral history. We shake the family tree together so that the hidden monkeys fall out. I have noticed that many clients feel an enormous aversion to (one of) the ancestral branches, the family from which they themselves originated no less. A common tendency is that there is a secure and an insecure parent, based on karmically determined patterns that eventually work out, but first must become recognized. The degree of insecurity you feel with one person determines the degree of dependence you feel with the other. As a result, clients have usually not been curious about the background of the insecure parent. The deeply rooted – 'we're not talking about that' – has then done its job so powerfully that the newcomers copied it blindly. And so, in families, in addition to children, many lies, and half-truths were born.

Just as every era has specific characteristics, our ancestors in previous centuries often lived under difficult conditions. Hard labor, hierarchical and feudal structures, periods of famine, very often bitter poverty, social control, flooding, powerful church climate, persistent diseases and, not to mention two world wars in the previous century. All this formed the backdrop to the lives of those from whom we sprang. Thus, it could happen that seemingly innocent, repressed events left imprints far deeper than we ever thought possible. In short, great therapeutic treasures can be found in the catacombs of the family chronicles. There it becomes apparent that old emotional wounds that were hidden away, quite simply continue to affect subsequent generations.

HEALTHY GENERATION TRANSFER

We have old entanglements to unravel. It literally concerns (step) fathers, (step) mothers, grandfathers and grandmothers, brothers or sisters who continue to exercise their influence after their physical death. To do the untangling we have to make contact with them and fortunately that is possible. We can "download" our ancestors or other people closely related to us. In other words, let us drain away the unexpressed emotions of our ancestors through the present descendants. While the client is in a light trance, the ancestors can be reached and are receptive to fruitful interaction. It is always useful to do this in cases when there was never room to talk things out when they were still here in the flesh, due to all kinds of family tragedies and areas of conflict. It is a must. Old misunderstandings, tenacious conflicts of loyalty, skewed relationships, imploded anger, or frozen grief. This can and will all be explored and dispelled.

The desired completion of these sessions concerns the final release of the descendant from his ancestor. I want to emphasize that this does not mean the populist 'sending into the light'. With this letting go, in which there is therefore also no 'severing or breaking', a natural integration of ancestral awareness takes place. That's basically what it all entails. That is what peace, healing and deep acceptance brings about. As a result, nothing needs to be severed.

When it comes to matters of dying, there is always a degree of gradualness. The ultimate act of letting go is an automatic consequence of this integration. Souls here experience very intensely being peacefully absorbed into spheres of light. Spheres that reveal themselves to them when those exchanges with their loved ones left behind on earth (who, incidentally, were not always so beloved in life itself) were there in reality. This release is preceded by many tearful "I'm sorry' s," "I love you' s' " "forgive me 's," or "live your own life's." Extremely moving. But again, that can only happen when essential information has been exchanged, the emotions that go with them have been felt, and new insights and understanding have landed.

It is the safeguarding of the soul connections in the family tree, the importance of which indigenous peoples always emphasized in their traditions. In this way, connections with family predecessors remain energetically healthy and with it the well-being of the entire family system. In that way they remained autonomous, powerful, and self-sufficient, also for future generations. That's what Native Americans have often told me: when you make a big decision in your life, realize that it will reverberate for at least seven generations.

THE RELAY BATON

I think a nice metaphor for this, is handing over the baton during a reconnaissance run or obstacle course. Each participant, representing one generation, symbolically transfers his life experiences to the next. With the help of the baton, which he has carried during his part of the journey, that transfer becomes a fact. The baton here is the bearer of life experiences, like a kind of energetic USB stick that can be plugged into the new generation, which thus experiences a basic knowledge of predecessors on which it can build. The baton here has an encouraging effect, is a driving force, produced by kindred spirits who carry the same kind of life motivation to want to complete the journey. The baton is translated in many cultures into a 'family medicine bundle'. In the form of symbols and objects, the history of their ancestors is preserved in their meaning, maintained in their value. The most important milestones become revalued, such as in the wampum belts of the Iroquois.

This bundle appeared during certain important ceremonies. It passed from hand to hand, and the various objects were unpacked and displayed. In this way, 'the medicine' of the ancestors was awakened again from memory and the connection with them was confirmed. All this in support of the current progeny leading an earthly existence. As mediums, the shamans or seers of these communities were able to observe the presence of the ancestors and to interact with them. Where necessary, certain messages about specific events were adjusted and passed on.

A somewhat weaker variant of this medicine bundle, but somehow comparable, are our old photo or family albums. If you really sit down to have a good look and let the various images work on you, connection and recognition with your ancestors will also happen. When you do that very consciously, just notice how many symbolic messages are hidden in old photos. Certain facial expressions, disguises, settings, body language. Photos are overflowing with valuable information.

CHAPTER 9

Embracing ancestors

"Every generation blames the one before, and all of their frustrations, come beating on your door."'
– The Living Years – Mike and the Mechanics

Everyone is thematically connected to their immediate ancestors and to the events that deeply marked and shaped their lives. For example, sometimes the root of your problems with relationships stems from the fact that your grandmother lost her favorite brother as a teenager.

In addition to ancestors, another beautiful designation is family tree relationships. This indicates more clearly that it is not just about family members who have already died. The specific relationship of a person in the present with his ancestors is echoed from the previous generations. And it is different for everyone. My brother is much more attuned in his life to business entrepreneurship and the fascination for mechanical and technical matters than I am. Our father and especially our grandfather, who was a progressive entrepreneur, both clearly had this in their blood. I am more attuned to emotional matters, deeper mystical themes, and the spiritual side of existence. Our father also had an element of that in him, as was later confirmed to me in a conversation with an 88-year-old favorite niece of his. But in his life, it was hardly given any right to exist, he was unable to develop it. There was no breeding ground for it, even though it was there latently. Just like our mother, by the way. She had powerful magnetic gifts. However, this never took any serious form because of her world that was dominated by church and rationality. Everything that even had a whiff of extrasensory perception was already brushed aside before it was accorded the slightest value. Apparently, I continued to further embroider and develop that. Obviously because I was already working on this in previous lives.

IN THEMATIC TERMS, PROGRAMS REMAIN ACTIVE

The ancestral database can be seen as a thick power cable that consists of many separate intertwined wires. They all have varying colors that represent countless different themes and allow for combinations. In the areas of intelligence, spirituality, willpower, perseverance, expectation, creativity, self-esteem, body, emotion, talent – and on a social level – and so it goes on. Most of those threads are stimulated by interactions with family members. After all, everyone undergoes radical processes to a greater or lesser extent in his life in relation to family members. You can easily check that for yourself. It has an important meaning if you felt insecure with a parent or very dependent on another. Or if you always felt inferior to your brother or sister or superior and highly valued.

The consequences of those circumstances and associated events are dealt with in therapy on a regular basis. They expressly demand attention. Many clients have had no contact with certain family members for many years for all sorts of unexplained reasons. It reflects a damaged past. With divorced parents, for example, you often see that one child is loyal to the father and the other to the mother. At a later age this can degenerate into a new separation in the contact between a brother and sister. This secondary separation is based on the unprocessed separation of the parents. They are thematic programs that are still active, which in turn create new separation situations. And then the divorce of the parents is again the result of situations from the life of the grandparents. This probably brings us to the period where the crux of this theme can be found in war and/or the influence of the church. I don't mean to say that divorce issues dominate here. It is about detecting the real causes behind situations of conflict, which otherwise permeate through generations.

It is remarkable how often clients report that after sessions quite miraculous situations arose with the persons in question, who had been out of the picture for years. Such contact then quite coincidentally and spontaneously takes place in the most unforeseen ways and moments. The energetic interlinking that was unblocked during a session turns out to offer space again for a new flow and a new connection. This space is always accompanied by a fundamental insight that up to that point remained veiled and turned out to be the cause of the separation.

Suppose your grandmother loses her only brother in 1943, at the age of 15, because he was executed for his work in the resistance. Grandma marries Grandpa years later, but her unprocessed grief runs deep and continues to trouble her. She loved her brother dearly. When she has a son, she names him after her deceased brother. Her son is bestowed an honorary role. So much so that Grandpa becomes jealous of the bond his wife has with their son. He (the son) gets taken in by his mother so much he feels guilty about the prospect of having another woman come into his life when he gets married. Grandma puts this marriage under pressure. Although the son marries, he feels that he is abandoning his mother. And now a gap is created between his parents because their son goes his own way. Both parents are now thrown back on each other and have the same feeling that no matter what they do, it is never right. This leads to a divorce. When these parents are yours, this becomes your mirror to the phenomenon of relationships. Grandmother's executed brother has literally and figuratively disappeared from the picture, while the sad end of life is in fact the reason for the emergence of a theme of divorce in this family tree.

CASE STUDY, RICHARD'S AGGRESSIVE FATHER

Richard, a middle-aged man, has had an incredibly painful childhood because of the aggression of his father, John. John was a father who drank a lot, was unpredictable, hit first and asked questions later and thus created a continuous climate of insecurity. Obviously, this childhood profoundly and painfully determined Richard's later life. When we study the biography of his father, we see that he is the second son after two older sisters.

Father's older brother Ian, the third child and thus the first son, has Down syndrome. Ian's life expectancy, it is said, is seven to eight years at most. But he will reach the age of 47 and will therefore have a strong presence in the family for a long time. It is also important to mention that Ian is the first child born after the Second World War.

Grandma, the mother of Ian and John, originally comes from a very wealthy English family. At the age of twelve she had to go to the Netherlands as an au pair and to a boarding school. She appears to find this so terrible that she has gradually learned to transcend her own emotions, as a kind of survival mechanism. Her 'high society' parents are, apart from being (influential) rich, are very judgmental. Someone only amounts to something if achievement and status are associated with it. In old age, grandma becomes a cold woman. Her favorite brother, who she intensely shares her childhood with, dies as a soldier during the war. Subsequently, after giving birth to two daughters, grandmother becomes pregnant with her first son. This child symbolizes hope and new life in a battered Europe. She wants to name the child, if it becomes a boy, after her recently deceased brother. Grandma (and Grandpa) are enormously disappointed when their first son turns out to be different, mentally disabled. The naming of the boy after her brother is reserved for the next male child. You're not going to associate a favorite brother with a Mongoloid son by name. A sledgehammer blow for the atmosphere at home. The next born, Richard's father John, arrives in a household bristling with expectancy. He must and will compensate for Ian's disappointment and from childhood he learns how achieving, meeting very high expectations, and maintaining yourself in a straitjacket, is rewarded by his father and especially his mother. On top of that, his parents brag about John's qualities and abilities to the outside world from every conceivable angle.

An extremely dualistic and at the same time symbiotic fraternal entanglement. John must literally make up for Ian's shortcomings all the time. John also learns that there is constantly someone in the family who "isn't good enough", resulting in his parents expecting John to overachieve without them having to say a word. These become life programs: as soon as John reaches maturity, and has dealings with a new someone, he automatically experiences a need to show his surroundings that he can do better.

ENGERGETIC BALLAST

Father John can never really be himself because of this. He learns, or better yet, is programmed with the knowledge that a meaningful life can only be achieved if you meet sky-high standards. It yields him a damaged and twisted personality. He lapses into aggression, drunkenness, and unpredictable erratic behavior when he becomes a father himself. All a result of his youthful frustration of never being able to 'just be good'. He projects all this energetic ballast mainly on his first son, Richard, through the blurring pair of glasses with which he also sees Ian in his son. Still in need of his mother's acknowledgment, John is stuck in his old patterns in a new era. Son Richard must always bear the brunt. For John, the internalized programs continue to remain active. He belittles Richard, has to constantly trump him by doing everything better.

There are a lot more connections that could be mentioned in this story. The point is that Richard, through the exposition we generate in my practice, had never realized before what the consequences of his father's life have been on his own life and behavior. "That part of my father's life never dawned on me. I never really realized what an impact his brother Ian's life had on him, and therefore on me. And I never consciously knew how haughty Grandma was, but also that she missed her parental home intensely from the age of twelve, and how decisive the death of her brother has been in the whole family." It is quite apparent that the consequences of the war once again played a crucial role in this family.

As you can see, past lives do not even come into in this setting, although their influence has of course written the script of these lives. Still, the result of such research and reflective insightful work is that Richard's life subsequently underwent a pleasant change. For the first time he experienced recognition, understanding and love from and for his father, who incidentally has has been dead for years.

FAMILY TREE RESEARCH

It is always meaningful and exciting to consider doing some deeper family research on your own. You really don't always need to consult a therapist for this. Direct your attention through your search with love and respect. You will notice tears welling up, things falling into place. You can feel your heart asking for your own forgiveness. Or that your heart asks you to do that to (one of) your parents or ancestors.

Here are some themes to keep in mind. They may be able to help you keep the right focus when conducting a bit of family tree research. The list below is a selection of the stories I often come across that can act as guidelines to better understand and embrace your ancestors.

•illegitimate children •rapes by soldiers •amateur abortions (such as with knitting needles) •deceased (nameless and/or unbaptized) children: shortly before, during or shortly after birth. (When these took place in strict religious families, this is almost always seen as God's punishment). Because of this Grandpas and (especially) grandmas became terribly afraid of dying for fear of going to hell •adopting the church blindly as an authority and life guide •NSB(Dutch National Socialist) grandparent(s) •World

War II secrets in a general sense •suicide •sexual, physical and/or mental abuse •'vague' accidents (often intentional or where suicide was involved) •homosexuality •egotism •inheritance conflicts •grandfathers or grandmothers who died young, resulting in 'second choice marriages' •grandfathers sent into forced labor, including grandmothers being left alone (who out of misery often secretly sought intimacy from others) •food shortages •extreme patterns of expectation •a family with mentally handicapped children •grandparents who ended up in an insane asylum and/or were mentally ill for a long time •children who had to take the place of a deceased father or mother •children (usually women) who were not allowed to study because they were needed in the household.

CHAPTER 10

Hereditary burden

"Only when we are brave enough to explore the darkness, will we discover the infinite power of our light."
– Brené Brown

There is a world to be gained if mainstream medicine, especially mental health care, would understand more about the spiritual and energetic logic behind many alternative treatment methods and therapies. A teenage girl suffering from an eating disorder would not need years of behavioral therapy if she were to discover and relive that she died in a previous existence during the Hunger Winter of 1945. Heredity plays an important role in this, but in a completely different concept than we have now. Her eating disorder and the scenario it entails in which it remained unresolved, becoming stuck in her etheric body at the time, has been reactivated in this life. Specific genetic codes of her (ancestors) parents ensure this. Her grandparents, for example, had been extreme victims of hunger and malnutrition in their own lives. This left its mark in the form of DNA structures that continued to carry these experiences. Not so much because it should not be forgotten, but because it is still in need of healing. That has nothing to do with coincidence, it was a conscious choice of this teenager when she incarnated in this family. She still had something substantial from this earlier life on the theme of nutrition. A groundbreaking insight.

This is why we are hereditarily burdened by our parents and ancestors. Our parents, in their specific living environment, initially remind us of those themes and burdens that we left unresolved from previous lives. Through them, those patterns are updated again in our current personality. You will find a palette of how things could develop in every conception. Each brimming with themes and subject matter. It is our soul that drives us to connect with them. To embark on new adventures, to undergo new development and to incarnate again and again. The themes and patterns that are important for the growth of the soul are simply contained in frequencies that carry information, stored in our family system. The DNA of this is the visible database, which is formed from (to the naked eye) invisible information.

As people become more aware, the knowledge that everything is connected grows. The realization that every material manifestation is an expression of a spiritual origin is gaining ground. After all, everything from a flower to a serious illness, from a fairy to a bully, are all creations. This realization makes us uncontrollably curious, like a child wanting to know where babies come from. And so, in every age, life continues to challenge us to push our limits, longing for deeper, more substantial answers. Wouldn't everything just stay the same otherwise? Wouldn't we then stop evolving? That would be against our nature, being part of a creation that is constantly moving, changing, and expanding on the waves of a growing consciousness. Those who wake up and rub the sleep out of their eyes see more and more.

BECOMING CURED FROM CONDITIONS CONSIDERED INCURABLE

What spiritual causes are there for our physical or mental ailments, our blockages, and impediments? And can we attach a meaning to them that sheds a different light on our current, often limited observations? These are big questions that we all must deal with. And if answers do indeed exist, who would want to ignore them? Even when unhealthy, malevolent forces are busy blocking spiritual growth with all kinds of distracting, controlling and manipulative systems, natural laws ultimately do not let themselves be messed with. As an old Toltec wisdom keeper, Grandfather Tlakaelel once said:

"*Whoever fights against the laws of The Creator has lost in advance.*"

GRANDFATHER TLAKAELEL, TOLTEC MEDICINE MAN, AND GRANDMOTHER SARAH SMITH, MOHAWK, MY SPIRITUAL GRANDPARENTS WHO ENSURE SUPPORT FOR *THE RIGHT TO BE* FROM THE SPIRITUAL WORLD.

That we can all randomly fall prey to some or other hereditary condition through our ancestors' gene bank has become an assumption we no longer critically examine. An unclearly defined assumption, born of all kinds of probability calculations and statistics, like a cloned child of father Evidence and mother Based. A you-are-your-brain couple, disconnected from the emotional world, who do not realize they are cut off from spiritual input. Seen in this way, it would be a godsend if we could simply edit, cut and paste unwanted DNA structures, which would prevent us from developing diseases and related complications. That an elementary cosmic law of nature is manipulated in this way, and that the processed DNA will then manifest itself elsewhere, must again be discovered empirically.

Heredity. What has not been said and written about this? Has our understanding of this actually progressed over the years? I do not think so. In fact, I think that we are consciously deprived of essential insights in this regard. The multi-billion-dollar industry that thrives on the benefits of progressive insight could otherwise be in serious jeopardy. It seems clear to me that we have a predisposition for all kinds of things that are genetically anchored in a family tree. The question remains, of course, which factors determine why, whether, when and to what extent someone works out hereditary information in his own life. It is known that the composition of a gene, the genome, of a person's chromosomes ensures the development of blue, green, or brown eyes, a large or small nose. But who or what determines that composition? A probability calculation? Chance? That a so-called disease-causing DNA program, where one speaks of a defective gene, can change, is evidenced by the countless cases of people who are cured of diseases that are considered incurable. And what we know about those people is that in tandem with that healing, they underwent a profound inner transformation to which they ascribe their cure. To a greater or lesser extent consciously and with or without the help of guidance, therapy, or because of major transcendental life events. In any case in such a way that they apparently restructured their own software without anyone from outside tinkering with it.

SURGERY AND THE HALF-KNOWLEDGE OF HEALING

That regular health care has to do with surgery is a half-truth. I don't mean that cynically. Anyone who has studied the Native American Indian Medicine Wheel, or the Eastern yin-yang symbol will quickly learn that one half is the visible half of a creature and the other the invisible. Half-knowledge would therefore be better, to quote Marcel Messing. Finally, conventional medicine focuses only on the physically observable. But what if there is indeed another half that should be taken seriously if we want to understand our own creation? A half where a completely different law is in charge than we thought until now. That would give a radically different view of the whole. Even the most holistic theories then need to supplement the statement that 'we are what we think we are'. The insight then becomes – that unprocessed trauma produces the thoughts from which our disorders arise. If causation is to be found there and the effect in the visible half, then a plethora of confusing conclusions regarding the origin of our diseases must be reviewed. In that case the insight does not just progress, it sprints ahead.

Better cooperation between the representatives of both fields of health care, alternative and regular, would of course be an extremely welcome development. For years, many self-respecting doctors and women have underlined such an initiative. But isn't it a fairy-tale idea? Over the years, the 'big pharma' factory has grown into a global authoritarian network through which tsunamis of money, lobbies, and interests flow, and through which many last words are spoken. Words that are furthermore put into the mouths of our representatives with appropriate force and are subsequently touted as proof into our living rooms, with the help of the mainstream media in deluded and complicated terms. "And that's the way it is," to use the words of the late Walter Cronkite.

The pharmaceutical world and politics largely determine who has a voice there. Dr. Matthias Rath gives clear explanations in several YouTube videos about what you really wouldn't want to know. Namely, how the powers and forces are distributed in these worlds and what is really intended, which is certainly not human well-being. It's not a joke; our primordial chemical elements, bestowed upon us by Mother Earth's natural world, can turn into someone's private property in our time. In the pharmaceutical world, these are predatorially appropriated with the aid of patents. It is subsequently manipulated, resulting in creations that are alien to nature, which, when used, in turn lead to reactions alien to nature. And anyone who has read Dr. Hans Moolenburgh's book *De Nieuwe Watergeuzen* (The New Sea Beggars) can not only be stunned by the basis on which our health regulations are determined, but also by the consequences they have on our health in general. So yes, should we wait for the mainstream and the alternative to embrace each other in brotherly love, or will we conduct our own research for our own benefit? Without wishing to dismiss the one, I certainly advocate the latter. Attention to our ills from both worlds sometimes seems inescapable, but the monopoly position that the mainstream scientific field has appropriated often strikes me as menacing.

FUSION OF RIGID LOGIC AND NEW INSIGHTS

Reincarnation therapy is perhaps the most alternative of all alternative therapies. At least, in investigating patterns of consciousness that underlie our blockages. Reincarnation therapy has been put on the map as a mature discipline. Countless publications and documentaries, yes, even scientifically based satisfaction research such as that done by Dr. Ronald van der Maesen, who obtained his doctorate in reincarnation therapy, demonstrate the efficacy of this form of therapy. When we address issues surrounding heredity and our well-being in general, it is therefore extremely useful to investigate the history of a particular predisposition or condition. In reincarnation therapy the invisible part of our being manifests and expresses itself in surprising ways in the visible part of our ourselves, namely our bodies. This world is quite easily accessible with the help of trance. Valuable insights and explanations about where our diseases and ailments come from are then accessible. And that is quite new for people who were used to looking for causes in only the physical aspect. For those who are open to this, it also requires a measure of flexibility in their mindset. After all, laws apply here that need to be understood slightly differently than the rigid logic we are fed at the university. The convergence of the laws of both worlds will have to gain momentum in the process. It depends on our willingness to let go of the old but retain the good parts and to connect them to the insights from these spiritual worlds. A merger that promises exponential growth and opportunities. That all sorts of miracles may not immediately be up for grabs here for everyone is understandable. After all, homeopathy and acupuncture were not put on the map in a single day.

Reincarnation therapy is also based on views that must act upon us and sufficiently marinate our consciousness to become more receptive to the sessions that generally have a potent effect. To the old-fashioned quack, accepting the existence of energetic meridians is still an obstacle, or the possibility that an endlessly diluted and thereby potentiated agent could bring about healing. That idea simply doesn't fit into his conditioned paradigm. However, hereditary predisposition is the basis for our disorders that are fixed in percentage terms and must therefore be fought aggressively – and in that capacity. Accepting effects from previous lives will take him a while, perhaps even lives. However, the willingness of people who are awakening to open themselves to this approach will no doubt play a part in the pace at which reincarnation therapy will become even more accessible to the wider public.

ZYCLON-B

Classical homeopath Ewald Stöteler has acquired an impressive international reputation in his field. He rewrote the homeopathy bible of Samuel Hahnemann (1755-1843), the founder of homeopathy, in such a way he could have been the founder himself. It is a real pleasure to exchange ideas with him about how such disciplines as homeopathy and reincarnation therapy might beneficially complement one other. Just consider that, the homeopathic remedy *Hydrocyanicum Acidum*, among others, called 'Zyclon-B' by the Germans, which countless people were gassed with during World War II, could play an incredibly supportive, unblocking role for people who experience being gassed in a reincarnation therapy session. Or that Aurum (gold) can be used as a homeopathic remedy if someone discovers that they committed suicide in a hopeless past life during the Second World War. Gold is seen by some native tribes as a materialized form of the sun, the bringer of life force and vitality, which they worship for that reason. Life force in solid form, as it were. Perhaps that is why gold is being pursued at so many levels. People who suffer from severe depression and hopelessness and who no longer have any meaning in life can therefore be prescribed Aurum. Obviously, such a drug prescription requires the specific knowledge of an expert. A visit to a classical homeopath is therefore highly recommended.

CHAPTER 11

Private James' Kidney

"Why should we look to the past in order to prepare for the future? Because there is nowhere else to look."
– James Burke

"When Private James dies after his kidney was destroyed during World War I, his soul will reincarnate in a family where kidney problems are hereditary." This was the penetrating statement made by the American Dr. Morris Netherton, arguably the most famous past-life regression therapist in the world. I will never forget it. He did so in the Netherlands in 2001 during a seminar on dying, conception and birth. It took me many years of practical experience to understand what this pioneering man had said.

Looking for a new incarnation to find himself again after a dramatically ended, unfinished life, Private James (we could call him Marc), seeks recognition in corresponding frequencies that already exist on Earth. In principle, they must be present. Already in substance materialized in the DNA of his new parents.

The goal of James' soul this time is to bring about (a piece of) healing. That kidney is of course not the only criterion, although a major one. It is a complex of conditions that an incarnate seeks in his new family depending on his new life mission. Other frequencies embedded in the DNA, as necessary ingredients for James/future Marc, of a new family system, are for example: loss of children, melancholy, migraine, visual impairment, or immobility. You can view these human experience areas as vibrational fields, present in the DNA as the blue-printed preliminary stage from which it shows itself to the naked eye (under the microscope) as genetically fixed material. As I also pointed out in the previous chapter: unprocessed events from a previous life carry the script for (part of) the new DNA in energetically coded vibrations. That is energetically preserved and held together on a soul level because it could not be released before.

SOLVING DEFECTS

If we look for meaning in the word defect as in "defective gene," the defect would refer to the absence of elemental awareness from a previous experience. As a result, it could never be properly understood in its entirety. That absence is also characterized by a vibration, a tremor. The soul, as you have already read in previous chapters, wants to solve the defect so that it no longer forms an obstruction for the whole.

If we link these hereditary codes to Private James, remember that in 1917 this man never again saw his two children, who were at home in England with his wife (loss of children), and that partly because of this he had been suffering from depression for a long time (melancholy), and furthermore because his two older brothers were already dead in the same war. Also remember that at some point during the battle he fell on a stone and from that moment on had a stabbing headache (migraine), his eyesight was severely damaged due to a gas attack (visual impairment) and he broke his leg when a grenade exploded nearby, which had prevented him from walking normally ever since (immobility). Finally, a shell fragment punctured him in the side and kidney, which was the very last thing he felt of his body before dying.

It is very important to see that all these physical pains and injuries continue to connect the soldier to life. The attachment to these miserable circumstances gives James the illusory (desperate) hope of being able to come home, get out of the war and reunite with his loved ones. What is really happening, is that his consciousness is dissociating from his distressing physical reality on the battlefield. It splits off from the gross and shocking reality of dying. As a result, he misses a crucial part of the total experience at that moment, and life can therefore not let go at all levels of being. In other words, he does not die completely on all levels of consciousness, even though his heart has stopped beating.

DEEPLY INGRAINED INJURIES ARE STILL AMONG US

If you visit the World War I-themed *In Flanders Fields* Museum in Ypres, Belgium, you'll see countless archive photos showing how soldiers were mauled. You can see that my random list of conditions is not so farfetched. Every victim who dies collects his unprocessed, traumatic cargoes as energetic information on a personal database. In this way he remains connected to it on a deep level.

As you could read in Chapter 5, every organ, every part of the body, from a kidney to a little toe, remembers the damage or stress that once happened to it. Of interest here is the richly illustrated book by Ian Stevenson, *Bewijzen van Reincarnatie* (Evidence of Reincarnation), in which all kinds of inexplicable physical imperfections and stigmas of mainly young people are related to past lives.

Anyone looking at the shocking photos from the 1924 anti-war propaganda book *Krieg dem Kriege! Guerre à la Guerre! War against War! Oorlog aan den Oorlog!* by Ernst Friedrich, with texts in German, French, English and Dutch, and banned by Adolf Hitler, and therefore quite rare, would have to wonder where all those deeply engraved wounds have gone. The answer may be staggering, but at the same time very logical, and above all close to home: among us!

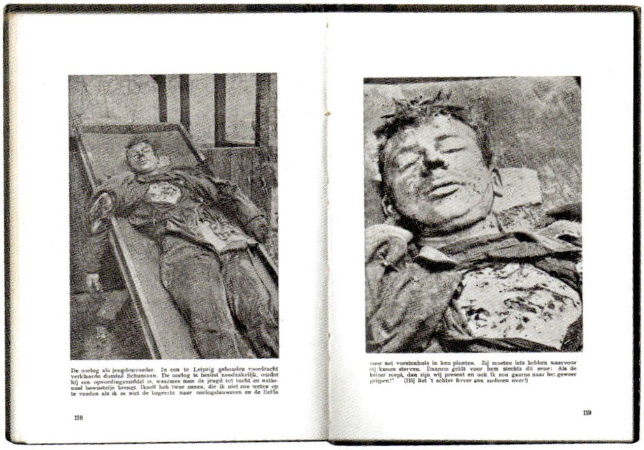

WAR AGAINST WAR
BY ERNST FRIEDRICH

The war as an educator of young people. In a lecture delivered in Leipzig, Rev. Schumann declared: "War is absolutely necessary because it is a means of education by which the youth is inculcated with discipline and national consciousness. I have two sons myself whom I would not be able to raise if I could not instill in them the desire for the laurels of war and the love of the royal house. They must have something to die for. Therefore, the only thing that applies to him is this: "When the Emperor calls, we will be present, and I too would gladly take up arms!" (He preferred, however, to leave it to others.)

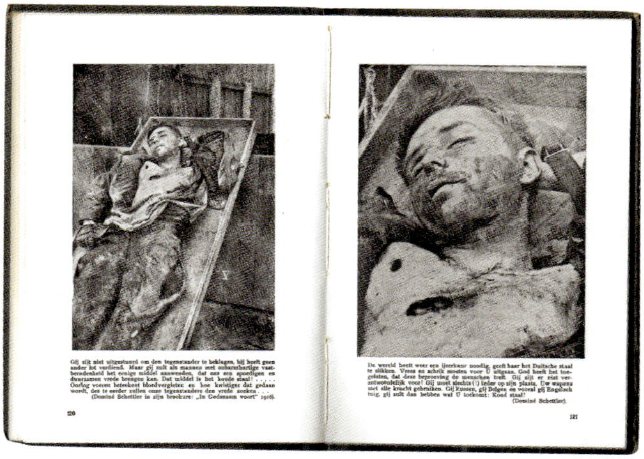

THE PROMOTION OF WAGING WAR
BY RELIGIOUS AUTHORITIES.

"Thou art not sent out to pity the adversary, he deserved no other fate. But you, as men, will use with unmerciful determination the only means that can bring us speedy and lasting peace. That remedy is the cold steel! To wage war means to shed blood, and the more lavishly it is done, the sooner our adversaries will seek peace..."
– Dominé Schettler in his brochure *Onward In God's Name* 1916.

"The world needs another iron cure, give it the German steel to swallow. Fear and terror must go before you. God has permitted this affliction to come upon men. You are not responsible for it! You must only (!) each in his place, use Your weapons with all your might. You Russians, you Belgians, and above all you English scum, you will then have what is due to you: Cold Steel!"
– Reverend Schettler

A soul who is not incarnated lacks a grip on matter, therefore it can commit itself to it by taking on a new earthly life. Or to reincarnate. As mentioned, in the energetic field of the DNA of its new parents, it now seeks – or better yet searches for – itself in terms of the most essential unprocessed matters. It goes without saying, that heredity also includes all desirable powerful qualities, such as talents and abilities, a solid physical constitution, spiritual awareness, optimism, perseverance, or emotional flexibility. Powerful characteristics that for the benefit of the development of a new life can be replicated, can vibrate freely, and be internalized in the current personality. If a soul could think, it does so in possibilities, not in impossibilities.

That the incarnating soul used to be part of the same family is also not uncommon. That would then entail extra sensitive and characteristic bonds with specific people, while the relationships with others are more neutral. Subsequently, the soul worms its soul energy into its new body and life during conception, pregnancy, and the birth process. You could say that the cell division and formation process of the body is driven by the life force of the soul. A film that shows this beautifully is *Enter the Void*, a psychedelic melodrama from 2009 by Gaspar Noé. The impression it gives is heavy and specific to the incarnation process of the main character, but it is very clear. Gradually, through various events that take place in his life, the person will now begin to remember, mainly unconsciously, his previous existence as the English soldier James, along with other relevant issues that want to be addressed this time around. His complaints, (physical) idiosyncrasies and conflicts, or indeed powers of attraction or repulsion with certain new family members or social circles, are therefore not isolated. They carry a resounding echo from a past existence that is recognized on a subconscious level and produces a trigger effect ranging from being In love to disgust.

AWAKENED MEMORY

For example, when the new mother of Private James, now called Marc, falls down the stairs during her pregnancy and hits her head violently, it activates the memory in the unborn child of the fall he made on the battlefield. Or when the mother's brother dies during pregnancy, it updates the grief of the loss of his two brothers from the First World War. In other words, his former depression is awakened thanks to mother's fall. When a leg gets tangled in the umbilical cord during birth, it awakens the memory of a leg that fell off (think of a club foot). And when, as a toddler, he was confronted with a huge display of fireworks on New Year's Eve, this fueled the terror of the 1917 shell explosion, which then reactivates the mortal fear from that time into the present and, basically, causes his kidney problems. In medical terms it is said that he has a congenital kidney defect, and this brings a deeper vision into the picture. And all that while his present-day brother and sister have no problem with the same fireworks because they don't attach any consequences to it. They have a different past history. It is also plausible that his former children will be born again with his former wife, who is now his partner again. The deep desire for fatherhood, which is of course also part of his unfinished business, will be fulfilled this time. It means that Marc's new family does not have significant hereditary issues concerning fertility, and that he will get the wind in his sails in the domain of 'family life' without insurmountable setbacks.

Meanwhile, the new personality called Marc is forming. He no longer consciously remembers his past lives. It could be that as a child Marc experienced a fascination for war and soldiers. He learns from an early age to deal with pain and above all not to give up. Marc regularly plays war wearing Grandpa's soldier's cap. Grandpa fought in World War I. Marc and his brother like to playfully shoot each other with wooden guns and come back to life after ten seconds. He now also has whole new plans for his current life. Like a flower gradually sprouting from its bud, Marc's new adventures unfold in his future that will take him in a different direction. At a deeper level, however, there is an understanding that these 'World War I pieces of unfinished business will demand attention. In fact, to achieve his new life goals, that is even a condition.

In reincarnation therapy the term used for this old soldier James in a new guise as Marc, is known as 'partial personality'. How much more literal can you get? As soon as the kidney acts up in the present tense due to pain or disease, framed by the complaints referred to earlier, we simply say: 'it runs in the family'. We forget that with that specific condition, an old English soldier knocks on your door and is basically asking you to process an almost forgotten, painful chapter from the book of your life (lives). Now the energy of the soul that was once frozen can finally melt, be released, and completely integrate into the whole, current person. This will make it feel more complete or healed. It is also nice to stop and think about the word healing.

POSTHUMOUS CARE FOR THE DYING

Helping an old personality die is at the core of reincarnation therapy. Posthumous care for the dying would be a better way of putting it. Anyone who goes through this during a session also experiences something quite profound to be transformed to the core. In that sense, I can relate to what Buddhists say. That it is good to die a little bit every day of your life, so that when actual physical death comes, it is no longer so insurmountable. That is why, as a human being you can end up in a situation where it feels 'as if something is dying'. This concerns updates of old events that were never brought to a successful conclusion. How valuable would it be if we learned to recognize it as such?

Incidentally, this is again comparable to a basic principle of classical homeopathy, that a minimum amount of energy is required from the substance that originally caused the pain to activate yourself, your system, into healing. In this discipline, it is referred to as 'miasma'. It represents the agents of the hereditary infections that can always awaken certain themes from generation to generation.

"All the answers are within you," says every wise person. As a therapist, I am simply sitting next to a gold mine: my client. Isn't it remarkable that most clients have never delved into reincarnation (therapy) and yet turn out to contain all kinds of essential information and backgrounds about their situations? We, and certainly most of our parents and (great) grandparents, have become deeply confused by the disinformation with which education systems, science and religions have poisoned our outlook on life. And so it may be in the present day that during his entire life, Mr. Pieterse never realizes that the death of his mother's favorite brother, while he himself was still in her womb, plays a causal role for him in his persistent depressions. He has been on prescription medication for his heart for years because he has assumed that 'it runs in the family', without making a deeper connection here, let alone going through a process of acceptance on this matter.

Some more practical examples? Someone with severe psoriasis, with numerous spots spread all over the body, died because of a mustard gas attack during the First World War, an example that is discussed in detail in this book. A client with severe lung disease died in a gas chamber. A person with chronic neck complaints was hanged. Someone with eczema died in a bombed, burning house. A woman with a uteritis underwent an amateur abortion with knitting needles because she had become pregnant by a German soldier. A client with a tumor in his head was executed (and shot in the head). A person with a spastic gut did not survive the Hunger Winter. A person with migraines was undergoing medical experiments. A woman with a breast disease sees that in a previous life her large breasts were the cause of rape and thinks, I would have been better off without breasts.

RESTRICTIVE CONVICTIONS

Fortunately, in recent decades a large amount of information has become accessible about all kinds of pathogenic external influences on our well-being. Chemical junk in our food, air, clothing, fillings in molars and in our water. As well as, genetic manipulation, weather influencing, electro smog through 4G and 5G networks and the subliminal messages meant to distract us from our real nature. All are frequencies that affect our immune system and bring us out of balance. What all these things have in common is that it has not been scientifically proven that they can be harmful. In the increasing amount of knowledge on offer about all this, I often miss the most important factor: our restrictive inner convictions that we have unintentionally created ourselves. Convictions about ourselves, about men, women, children, the world, life, sexuality, races, birth, death, struggle, equality, religion, health and so on. These convictions do not just come out of nowhere and are not genetically determined. They arose due to actual human events in the lives that we consider to be past.

Reincarnation therapy makes visible the logic behind the universal laws for the cycle of the soul, or karma. Karma manifests itself quite differently than is often imagined. Perhaps most importantly, by learning to understand and live through its history of existence, it changes itself. How refreshing is it to experience that fortunately we can still have control over this ourselves?

The initiation of conflict after conflict, of war after war, generates enough food for the round belly of the power elite. They live, enjoy, and depend on our encapsulated trauma energy. Our ignorance about this is vital to them. The fact that processing automatically gives our self-healing mechanism new impulses and restores our autonomy is a fact that often goes hand in hand with tears of happiness. And those tears immerse our DNA in other forms that reconnect us to our loving core. The core in which the Great Spirit lives. Don't take my word for it just because of my beautiful blue eyes, which I don't have because my parent's genes provided me with brown ones but do your own research. Improve the world, start with yourself!

CHAPTER 12

Infant mortality

"What follows is always related to what preceded it."
– Marcus Aurelius

When a child, baby or fetus dies in a family, the family members concerned are touched to their souls. Regardless of the cause of death, whether it's an accident, disease, miscarriage or abortion, the impact of such a great loss works through generations. Sometimes that doesn't seem to be the case at first glance, but appearances are deceptive. They are experiences that have profoundly colored the lives of many people and are rarely processed or accepted. And it was very common.

The emptiness that departed little ones leave behind leads to frantic reactions. The void was filled with all kinds of remarkable characteristics and behaviors. Dead children are often fictitiously kept alive. How? In various forms. Shrouded in all kinds of moods, people still experience being connected to the dead. Depression, chronic despair, unfulfillable expectations, isolated feelings of guilt, intoxication with alcohol or medication, aggressive or unpredictable behavior, or zones of reality that ignore what is earthly acceptable, thus acquire a function. New states of mind are born this way in a family, obviously not without consequences for the other children or for the children who have yet to be born. It became a transferable loss, the consequences of which the new generations, sometimes many decades later, are still experiencing. "We don't talk about that," was usually the cure. Unfortunately, this afforded the event a repressed place in the psyche. Anyone beginning to fathom the connection between cause-effect relationships, and karma, knows that this is not the end of the matter. The offspring, usually with one person at the center, forms itself into that of a deceased toddler, without realizing it.

Countless children lie buried with no name under a stone in the farmyard or under a weeping willow. Flushed down the toilet or disappeared in a hospital waste basket, they have been forgotten. Many babies and toddlers died of intractable diseases, were killed, or mysteriously disappeared. Countless newborns, who in turn had to fill the gap, were named after them, and therefore born with enormous expectations from the parents. Or with great disappointment because this time the gender was different than hoped for. Sometimes surrounded by the anger and defeat, or by the grief of those involved who did not process the death of a previously born person, and thus projected it onto the new child. And those people could easily be your father or mother. What is also possible is that you are the child that has been looked forward to for a long time, after a child had died previously in your grandparents' generation, after which your grandmother almost compulsively took on the task of being a mother, at the expense of your bond with your own mother. In any case, all these lives are characterized by, to put it mildly, major discomforts.

To gain a better understanding of how deceased children passed through generations, I tell the special story of one of my clients, Anne.

ANNE'S MEDDLESOME MOTHER

Anne is 48 years old, married to René and mother of three children, Willemijn (22), Jeanne (19) and Wouter (16). Anne is so insecure and afraid of making mistakes that she decides to undergo regression therapy. She feels distant towards her husband and has always focused disproportionately on her children. As a result, other matters in her life have hardly received any attention. It has demanded a lot from her that her son Wouter is a troubled child. He has ADHD, is asthmatic and has had constipation problems since birth.

Anne tells how her mother always kept an stern eye on her from childhood and compulsively never left anything to chance. It still feels that way even now six years after her mother's death. Her mother disagreeably imposed herself as a babysitter for Anne's children, interfering especially in the upbringing of her grandson, Wouter. "She was like an octopus towards our Wouter," said Anne. "She just shoved me aside. "I've always had the feeling that's why I fell short as a mother. There was always a tense atmosphere when she was around."

We decide to investigate the ancestral line of her mother, Truus (1945). On the one hand, we do this by retrieving the already known biographical information and organizing it into a complete picture. On the other hand, I put Anne in a trance, so that she can easily make contact with the various people in her family. This is what Anne sees.

On a farm, somewhere in the Dutch countryside, in the mid-1950s, the daily activity follows a routine. The many children of the farming family are each given their share of responsibility that must serve the interests of the business as well as possible. The eldest brothers already do much of the heavy farm work in the stables and on the land. The sisters take care of house-keeping chores. A hierarchy that adapts to the needs of the busy parents.

The harsh conditions of the war years has not exactly made life any happier. Although the family is not directly involved in the war, fate strikes when Nico, the eldest son, is killed by a grenade explosion during a bike ride to the village.

Mother (Anne's grandmother), who is pregnant practically all the time, makes an urgent appeal to her eldest daughter Sjaan, who over the years has taken on the role of mother. Mother has become chronically fatigued by all the life she helped bring into the world. Because she has distanced herself from the household over time, she loses her grip on the logistics of everyday activity. She barely realizes the extent of all her outsourcing. Sjaan becomes swamped but does not admit it. Her dear daughter does what she can and then orders her younger sisters around at her discretion.

Three-year-old Nico is the eleventh and therefore youngest member of the family. He is named after his deceased eldest brother, so the family experienced a vague sense of consolation when he arrived. Nico is placed under the care of his two-year older sister, Truusje. Sjaan urges her to take good care of Nico.

GRUESOME DISCOVERY IN THE CESSPIT

One pitch-black day, everything changes. Nico is nowhere to be found. When a thorough search of the entire farmyard yields nothing, panic really breaks out. Truusje silently implodes. In a childlike way, she is perfectly aware of her responsibility yet does not realize how disproportionally great it is. And no one has ever told her. Truusje isolates herself, adjusts and makes herself invisible. She dreams night after night about her dear little brother speaking sweet words to her, which confuses her when she wakes up.

Truusje feels like her mom and dad have turned their backs on her and, more importantly, Sjaan, who represents her mother. Sjaan also feels guilty but doesn't know what to do with it. She understands that she can't put all the responsibility on Truusje, but she also doesn't know how to explain it. This leads to vague and nasty mutual recriminations cropping up everywhere. The days pass. After the meadows and ditches in the surrounding area have been combed out several times, the false hope also disappears. Gloomy despair creeps in as the farm demands tasks be done to ensure its continued existence.

As time passes and there is still no sign of Nico even after months, it suddenly dawns on the farmer like a devilish bolt from the blue: the cesspit! And yes, when it is emptied, he makes a gruesome discovery. The remains of his youngest kid are submerged in a stinking cesspool. It's a new sledgehammer blow to the family consciousness. Like it was yesterday, the farmer remembers how, a few months before Nico's mysterious disappearance, he had called all his children together and gathered them at the cesspit. The lid of the pit that can easily be pushed to one side reveals a bubbling and fermenting sludge of cow manure, the source of the smell that always pervades the farm. Father says in a surly and menacing tone of voice: "If you end up in here, you enter another world. Forever! You have been warned."

In a childlike way, Nico, with the help of sister Truus, registers and interprets these words. His fledging life is not very exciting. No one pays attention to him, and mom and dad feel miles away. The only time he is distracted from his ever-increasing loneliness is when he is playing with Truusje. One day his curiosity about 'that other world' becomes so inexplicably great that he is drawn to it like a magnet. He fantasizes about a world other than his own at home, and hopes to find more pals, warmth, and fun. He does not realize what the term 'forever' means. At an unguarded moment, his clogs carry him to the scene of the disaster and Nico 'stumbles' irreversibly, accidentally on purpose. Even though it is only a brief moment from the fall to the choking, to death, it is fraught with the panic of not being able to breath because of the ammonia.

And so, Nico loses his young life. His spirit is released, confused, while his body is swallowed and dissolves into the slurry. As usual, he, at least his soul that is, clusters around his sister in shock. He takes for granted that the contact now feels a bit strange and that Truusje no longer reacts as before. Nico feels Truusje's guilt and sadness. He tries to soothe her mind by constantly letting her know that he is with her, and he promises never to leave her alone again. A small consolation that Truusje in the long run will subconsciously cherish her entire life.

When Truus is 20 years old and latches on to a bashful boy she met through the local skating club, it does not take long before she gets pregnant herself. She has become a reserved and hard-to-reach woman. No one knows the turmoil that is going on inside her. The worst thing that can happen to her is doing something wrong, and that leads her to become passive and practically incapable of taking any initiative. She feels safe behind the back of her robust, young husband. As the pregnancy progresses, she secretly hopes that it will be a boy. She would call him Nico, she fantasizes. Her mother dies of grief over the loss of her two Nico's, a few years before Truus leaves the parental home. Father, who turns out to be a tough old man, continues to concern himself with the farm that has now been taken over by his second son. Truus' eldest sister, Sjaan, never left the parental home. She never went beyond the border of the province.

NEVER FREE FROM MOTHER'S SPHERE OF INFLUENCE

When Truus gives birth, she looks into her daughter's eyes with veiled disappointment. They call her Anne, just like Truus' mother. So, it's not a boy. And she doesn't look a thing like her brother, she concludes, while her body is still exhausted from giving birth. Her second child is also a girl and when the child, an afterthought, comes into the world many years later, Nico is still welcomed with open arms, although Truus is now in her late thirties. Mother Truus is practically focused on Anne all the time. She overloads her with all kinds of tasks and work, while her younger brother is treated like a prince and put on a pedestal. She continues to correct Anne compulsively, trying to save her from 'the mistake' she made herself when she was five. At the same time, she arbitrarily punishes Anne for everything she considers herself guilty of. And so, Anne becomes her pet project and is still the little daughter who never got out from under her mother's yoke.

Mother Truus cannot deal with it when Anne marries and has her own children. She fights tooth and nail against the fact that Anne now threatens to lead her own family life. This freedom her very own daughter is claiming, which she herself never had, is something she virulently opposes. Whenever she doesn't get the chance to intrude on

Anne's life, she forces the issue and constantly points out Anne's so-called shortcomings. When Wouter is born, grandma Truus seems to get a new project. She thrusts herself into the family even more firmly and mothers her grandson, who becomes the apple of her eye. He is spoiled, while she hardly pays any attention to her granddaughters, Willemijn and Jeanne. Unlike her own son, she sees her dead brother in Wouter, and she wants to prevent something bad from happening to him at all costs. Anne, who was already insecure, never leaves her mother's sphere of influence. Not even after Truus dies.

Several sessions, during which, among other things, we address the soul of Truus, Anne's deceased mother, help Anne to extricate this highly charged event from the morass of her family. Or perhaps I should say, from the cesspool. Mother Truus has now not only gained awareness about her unjustified feelings of guilt, which arose in her early childhood because of the death of her brother, but also about the complicated division of roles in her family. Truus was still attached, with her spirit, to her 'brother-who-was-now-Wouter' after her death and thus forced all sorts of things on him. That this created confusion in the bond with Wouter's real mother, Anne, and that his restless nature relates to that, quickly becomes clear.

Nico's soul who once fell into the cesspit and has undergone a new incarnation in the form of Wouter, has finally been able to process an old trauma – choking to death in the pit –through his new mother Anne. Thanks to this clarification, Anne has been able to resume her original role as a mother. First, she has seen herself for who she really is, separate from her mother's permanent sphere of influence. Second, for the first time, she experienced real recognition from her own mother. She finally understands her mother's excessive behavior which has brought her huge relief. Anne's obsessive fear of making mistakes, the kernel of which in fact lay with her mother, has completely disappeared.

Miraculously, Wouter has also become much calmer at home and his bowel movement problems have also disappeared. Anne explains: "I think he went into such shock at the idea of poop or pooping, because he associates that smell with dying, that he put the brakes on himself. And that asthma is related to the suffocation." I think it's a nice conclusion, which we will leave open.

Anyone who discovers connections between old, unfinished family events and current life situations has a great advantage: they can connect the dots. For example, by shaking your own family tree. Ask the members who are still with us about certain events, such as the death of children. Don't be fobbed off with such platitudes tossed at you as: 'that used to be very common', or 'that's not something you talked about'. You may have to brave some hurdles and emotions, but you will see that movements toward healing are naturally set into motion. So-called time barred issues that have been put to one side are revived and the subsequent coincidences, which will arise as a result in and around the family, will surprise you. About what? As to the question of whether it is indeed all so coincidental that we just happened to be born into our own family. Each family has its unique events, and you get to shine your light on yours.

PART III

INFLUENCE OF WAR

CHAPTER 13

The war isn't over

"After thousands and thousands of dreams, we awaken. After thousands and thousands of births, we are born. This, the end, is only the beginning."
– Dr. Brian Weiss

Wars have a gigantic and heavily underestimated impact on the state of mind and well-being of the current population. On the one hand because countless people had one or more past lives in those periods, and on the other because most of our (ancestors) parents literally experienced the war and are therefore still living carriers of the experiences and consequences thereof. What happened in the First and Second World Wars and how the influence of these events is transferred, differs from country to country, from people to people, from region to region. The specific history of a nation plays a decisive role in this. The effect of the war on the population of, for example, Germany or Italy is substantially different from the effect on the people in the Netherlands or England. Because, for example, Germany, and indirectly Italy were regarded as the aggressors, the aftermath of the war leaves substantially different popular themes particularly for the German population. Guilt and shame complexes almost collectively take root in the ranks here. Even an excessive need for chauvinism can be an expression of a deeper layer of doubt about your own right to exist, which must be suppressed. After all, everyone wants to be proud of their homeland, and rightly so. And when those foundations are shaken, one must set something against that. It is actually an expression of uncertainty.

But whatever those differences, in the end it is always the lack of freedom, the disruption of family systems and the loss of loved ones, values and self-esteem that determine the tenor of the new families. The consequences of the Second World War are perhaps the most clearly perceptible on this continent and therefore the easiest to explain.

Countless dramatic events and circumstances at the time could not be lived through or changed by our immediate ancestors or others who were there. Associated feelings and sensations of fear, sadness, and anger experienced by those involved remained congealed because processing rarely occurred. There was no room for that. Not only were effective forms of therapy or other methods hardly available, but there was also on average little awareness about the importance of processing. And even then, people were so immersed in the harsh reality of everyday life that they couldn't see the forest for the trees anyway. Their main concern was to put food on the table and find gainful employment. One had to get through the days, reorganize and work on reconstruction where possible. It was more common that bottled-up feelings were dragged along during the rest of their lives like frozen emotions. Often even to the grave.

These blocked emotional worlds are transferred as energetic charges to the new generations – as discussed in the chapters about the ancestors. In short, because they still wanted to be worked out.

Practical experience shows something quite remarkable: that new generations are abundantly manned by those who lost their lives shortly before, during or (shortly) after the war. In other words, as souls they entered new incarnations after they somehow experienced the war in a different form, in a previous personality. These rebirths also took place regularly in the same family lines. Specific events often tied them to specific persons. Such as, for example, the two brothers from the following practical example.

THE FOXHOLE

Two brothers are both in the army during World War II. The oldest feels responsible for the youngest. He proudly promised his parents to keep a close eye on his younger brother. However, as so often in a war, the inevitable occurs. The youngest brother gets a serious shrapnel wound in his shoulder. Not a medic or aid station in sight. The wound is provisionally bandaged with torn, filthy rags. Tenaciously, they continue walking for nearly two more days, all the time goading and encouraging each other to keep moving. Giving up is not an option. The oldest gives the youngest physical support, as he can hardly walk any more. The festering wound finally takes its toll on the young soldier's weakened body. Due to exhaustion and pain, he cannot go any further. Somewhere in a chilly foxhole, he is left desperately behind against his will after his older brother promised to come back with help and medication. He is just able to hear him cry out "Hold on!" as night falls. Desperate and left to his own devices, the younger brother eventually dies of blood poisoning a day later.

Anyone witnessing this scene would have seen a collapsed young man with a colorless face and clammy forehead. Chilled to the bone, fading away, releasing his very last breath as his chin sinks completely down onto his chest. However, in the moments leading up to his final heartbeat, a different reality takes place inside him. His inner agony is so heartfelt, almost militaristic, that at that moment he does not actually realize that he is dying. With all his willpower he resists the death that is forcing its way into him, not only because he is still expecting his brother to come back with help, but also because he does not want to disappoint him and his parents by never coming home again. In those final moments, he frantically clings to his struggle and pain. Surrounded by the violence of war, all the elements that characterize his miserable reality take on huge significance. "So long as I still feel that throbbing pain and my exhausted body, so long as I can continue to mentally resist the misery that is present in my body, I am still alive... and there is still hope." And even physically inside his body. "So long as my spleen is running at full speed in an attempt to purify the blood and heal the wound, so long as my heart is pounding heavily and my temperature is too high, I'm still here." In vain, of course. He dies.

At the level of the soul, however, the brothers remain connected to each other. The inscribed, powerful 'life and death' agreements, responsibilities and the division of roles remain and connect the two. The older brother, desperately seeking safety and help, himself dies not much later, also from the effects of exhaustion and infection. He feels that he has abandoned his brother, that he has not kept his word and is therefore unreliable. In addition, he is gnawed by a huge feeling of having failed in the eyes of his parents. Meanwhile, the younger brother blames himself for not resisting long enough to have persevered against the painful reality in his body. The consciousness of his spleen is still hyperactively running through its functions. The spleen had wanted to heal the wound, as the source of the life-threatening infection.

THERE IS HOPE AS LONG AS THE WOUND IS NOT HEALED

These souls are inevitablygoing to meet again in a new incarnation. Moreover, the old patterns will reveal themselves to them once again with the object of still reaching a process of letting go and acceptance. Let's see what that looks like now, in new lives. One of them, José, I speak to during a workshop in Spain. He is in his late thirties with (again) an older brother and (again) both are soldiers. This time professional soldiers, in contrast to the previous life, because then it was a question of compulsory military service.

José has just returned from a five-month mission in Afghanistan. There he saw several colleagues go back home in a coffin. From an early age, both brothers had a penchant for soldiering, for military situations, ranks and positions. José says he has had a condition in his spleen that causes his wounds to heal very badly ever since he was young. For him, there is a constantly threatening undertone about which he has not been completely honest at various medical examinations. In addition, he has a chronic pain in his right shoulder, medically explained as a recurring infection around his shoulder blade. When he was 7 years old, it turned out that his one-year-older brother had a form of leukemia. Their parents brought him to a hospital a few times a week for treatment and then stayed away all day and evening. After that José's spleen problems started to develop. Whenever he was left alone by his parents and brother, it unwittingly brought back memories identical to his situation in the foxhole after his brother left in the previous life never to return. There, too, he believed his brother would be with their parents. Albeit subconsciously now, but quite actively from that perspective. His survival mode was reactivated in this childhood. In essence: "If my brother and parents leave, I will be left alone, and I will die."

At the same time, the same strategies are being reused with which he thought he could prevent death at the time. A lonely, inner struggle in the throes of death where his shoulder pain crept in again as a reminder of an old reality under similar circumstances.

And then, more interestingly, an overproduction of cells in his blood from the spleen that is supposed to reverse inflammation. An overactive spleen that also does this when there is no need for it this time. At that time it wasn't successful at healing the wound, there is no awareness about dying and so old programs keep on running. In short: "As long as the wound has not healed, it hurts and feels unsafe, there is still hope that my brother will come back, and I will be saved." This explains his spleen disorder in a deeper way than is rationally possible. Because we now make these connections during a session, in which we guide him as a soldier in the foxhole in his process of dying. Now that he goes through it again in a re-experience, he can distance himself from it. José's first reaction, about four weeks after the session, is that he feels quite well. He feels liberated. He experiences that he has ended up in a process of profound inner change. A medical examination, two months later, indicates his blood values appear to have changed. He still can't believe it yet.

THE FEELING THAT AN OLD THREAT IS STILL RELEVANT

In summary, the souls of people who died under dramatic circumstances often become the (great- or grand) children, brothers, or sisters of their own children at the time. Depending on many factors and considerations, a place is determined in a family system. And that while they are still immersed in the circumstances of their former death with their penultimate personality. Circumstances carrying with them desolation, confusion, insecurity, a fighting spirit, or feelings of hatred, in determined secrecy or – as in the above examples – trapped in the sorrow over the loss of a loved one.

Many never consciously experienced the end of the war because they died before that time, often under terrible circumstances. In those situations, parts of a person's consciousness may be under the assumption that a war is still going on, whereas they were born after that time. In a new incarnation, these people may always feel that a threat of war is still relevant. However, they do not see that it is a projection of the war they have never left behind. In the following chapters many more practical examples pass in review because it is precisely in wartime that so many people die or disappear abruptly. That's why it makes a lot of sense to know the history of your ancestors from this period.

FIGURES FROM THE WORLD WAR

Ten million bodies! Ten million people have come to the end of their lives. The flowing blood from these ten million murdered people – forty million liters of steaming human blood – could replace the huge body of water of Niagara Falls for a whole day, and by its power provide the electric current for a metropolis. All the equipment of the Prussian railways would not be enough just to transport the hacked off heads of these ten million murdered all at the same time.

Civilization! ..... Imagine the fantastically long train: The first car is already in Munich, the last one still in Berlin, and all are filled with bloody human heads. Civilization! .... The ten million murdered people are laid head-to-head, toe to toe, that makes a sixteen thousand kilometer – not meter – long grave, which spans all of Europe, Sixteen thousand kilometers of corpses. Civilization...

From Leonhard Frank – "Der mensch is gut"

Know ye,

That at the moment annual expenditure for armament amounts to 120000, 000.00 guilders.

That this is a stack of guilders 25000 KM high.

That this is twice the distance from Amsterdam to Batavia.

That in the world war German soldiers died a martyr's death in barbed wire supplied by the Magdeburger Draht und Kabelwerke.

That Krupp invented the tank with which Germany is conquered.

That the ignition heads of the English grenades, with which the German soldiers were killed, were the trademark of Krupp.

That the English soldiers were torn apart by German projectiles, the belt feeders of which are supplied by English firms.

That the German army supplier Stolzenberg used Sulphur dust in France during the world war. This French sulfur substance came back as a German phosgene in the lungs of the French soldiers.

That the world war cost 854,000,000,000 guilders.

That is 50,000 guilders per hour since the birth of Christ.

That the cost of killing each of the 10,000,000 is 80,000 guilders a head.

That about half of this flowed as pure profit into the coffers of the arms industry.

That the arms industry earned more than 40,000 guilders from every hero who died for the fatherland.

That the solemn "Mort pour la patrie" (fallen for the fatherland) that adorns thousands of crosses on graves is a tragic lie which should be replaced by "Mort pour la industrie" (died for industry.)

Publication Hilversumse Vredeskring:
Secr. D. F. Veldkamp, Huygenstraat 22

THE HIDDEN FACTS AT A GLANCE

CHAPTER 14

Hunger, uprootedness, and shame

"The natural wisdom of a child is too often buried by the wisdom tricks of human education."

There are many war-related fields and areas of interest the specific characteristics of which need to be studied therapeutically. Think, for example, of victimization, perpetration, experiences of witnessing unpleasant events, hunger, insecurity, fear, forced lying, loss and uncertainty about victims who have not returned, unspoken secrets or secrets passed on to succeeding generations. By practically dividing the war period into special events and episodes and then linking them to their current forms of expression, more insight and understanding is created. This understanding is necessary to ask the right questions during sessions.

A client told me that in her childhood, in the early nineteen seventies, her parents only allowed her and her two brothers and a sister to share a single boiled egg between them on Sundays. They looked forward to it all week. For the rest of the week there was hardly any food, it was tasteless and always never enough to go around. Going to bed feeling hungry was the rule rather than the exception.

These typical stories usually refer very directly to the Hunger Winter that their parents had experienced. I constantly get that confirmed by requesting the family history and naturally, after a while, all those connections are no longer a coincidence. However, no one makes the link between that time and current complaints. This example of the egg sounds innocent but remember, if you are raised at a time when there is always 'too little' your experience of freedom is hugely affected. As if you always begrudge yourself, and later your environment, some abundance or prosperity.

It is not necessarily the case that these parents still have to live with shortages after the war in a literal sense. However, there is a constricting of the flow of food and food supply in general, arising from an extreme period of hunger associated with harsh conditions and restrictive thoughts. These tendencies, stemming from wartime are still maintained so that food, as a phenomenon, permanently bears this burden and is constantly associated with a sense of lack.

Along this line, think of the Hunger Winter as the cause of countless eating disorders such as bulimia and anorexia, spastic intestines, or all kinds of digestive disorders. Or as a cause of more expansive themes such as fear of shortages in a broader sense of the word, exhaustion disorders that can disrupt the function of the adrenal glands in a new life. The fear of cold seasons or cold in general, excessive fear of poverty, savings, and an obsession with hamstering and so on.

Cow's milk allergies later in life can find their cause in problematic breastfeeding. On a deeper level, there can be a fear of losing the connection with mother in 'accepting' the substitute of alternative baby food for cow's milk. Mother, in turn, may experience a feeling of 'never having enough' due to direct or indirect influences of the Hunger Winter, causing breastfeeding to stagnate. Or the opposite, her breasts are bulging with a richly overflowing cornucopia of food with which mother unduly binds her child to herself so as not to have to feel an old loss from her parents' generation. Later in life, her child may develop eating habits in which that abundance must always be experienced by overindulging in too much (fatty) food. Incidentally, in the meantime a mother can emaciate herself by her desire to give. So long as there is someone who needs her and whom she can feed, she experiences the feeling of being meaningful. As soon as such dependency relationships stop, before experiencing being liberated from them, a mother can also undergo a serious dip and even get sick. A necessary process to free herself of fixed themes.

UPROOTING OF HOUSE AND HOME

Because of the bombing of large cities during the war families had to uproot house and home and relocate. In the Netherlands, families, or some of their members, were accommodated in the relatively less affected northern provinces, for safety reasons and because there was more food. Often, they learned weeks later that the father or son who stayed behind had been arrested or had died from the bombardments. The consequences of this are manifested in people living today who are unable to feel at home anywhere. For example, they always experience a need to move the moment they have settled. They are still haunted with a belief that the phenomenon of 'coming home', goes hand in hand with intense sadness, emptiness, and loss.

In Germany, entire populations have been uprooted. Families, living in villages or on a farm near a city, were completely torn apart. Think of Germany's Sudetenland, divided into four occupation zones because of the war, or of people separated during the Cold War or by the Berlin Wall between East and West Germany. So many never saw each other again, or only after decades. How many gaps has that caused in the flow of communication in family systems? And then the most destructive consequence of the war for the German people, to which affected many people: the uprooting of the right to exist, to be.

When the outcome of the war becomes clear and Germany is blamed internationally, millions of people feel pangs of conscience simply because of their nationality. Towards life, towards others, towards themselves, even to the air they breathe and the water they drink. To protect themselves somewhat, to keep themselves in alignment with a sense of neutrality, they must disconnect emotionally from their ancestry. After all, everywhere they looked there were fathers and (great) grandfathers who had shot people when they were soldiers. This uprooting literally results in shallowness in new lives. Shallow, because there is no need to stir up deep emotions. So long as life is mentally feasible, well organized, and practically effective, there is no need to feel and experience more deeply. Because that's where many people find a layer of (self)condemnation.

Can you imagine how displaced someone could be if it was common knowledge that the person has an aggressive SS grandfather who was responsible for atrocities? The gulf that this role has caused with his daughter, who in turn is the mother of a client, means that, this client has not built up a fruitful connection with his mother. A single example out of millions. These patterns are etched infinitely deep. And at the same time, all those broken connections need healing and attention, and will manifest themselves again and again in the hope of being recognized.

No pen can describe what happens to the resilience of family systems after they were once forced to leave their homeland or, according to authorities, could no longer claim it. Every human being attaches great value to the place where he came into the world.

Dutch families with a German grandfather or grandmother, mostly families who lived near the German border, were looked down on by their fellow citizens during and after the war. Yet another underestimated fact. The resulting unnatural patterns of behavior caused discord, ambiguity in ways of dealing with one another and all kinds of miscommunication in families.

Regarding the outside world, one had to adapt and behave according to all kinds of standards, but behind closed doors there was an atmosphere of frustration and of pent-up emotions that were vented on each other.

The dramatic circumstances in which hundreds of thousands of sons and young men, who later became our grandfathers, were forced to work, often in gloomy camps, caused deep distrust of life. The life force of these people was poisoned. With just as many mothers and grandmothers left behind in fear and uncertainty. Also, the numerous families that fell apart shortly after the war because many, especially sons, went to try their luck in the land of the liberators, Canada or the USA. This caused deep familial disruptions. Not only because the family members left the home front behind, but also because they did not play a full role in the period of emotional recovery for the wounds that their families suffered. The consequences of this were then powerfully downplayed. After all, the war was over, and in the land of milk and honey everything gets better. Many sisters, little brothers and mothers saw their older (favorite) brother or sons leave, but due to the circumstances could not give any expression to their pain about it. The emptiness that ensued following their departure had to be confronted by those left behind. There was plenty to reconstruct. For sisters and mothers, this had irrevocable consequences for later relationships with their husbands or partners. Either because they were never good enough (the deeply felt void of the absence of a brother or son was never satisfactorily filled), or because there was again fear of another departure with the resulting bonding conflicts.

A list like this deserves a hopeful counterpart, because of course it is not my intention to just emphasize all this misery without any perspective. First, it is good to realize that for you, as a reader, only your own family history is important. No matter how much pain it contains, you have the strength to be able to look at it and to face it where necessary. Charting so much world suffering is only intended to provide insight and most importantly to make this area accessible again, because for so many it has been left unfinished. And what is most hopeful is that healing is always possible with proper attention.

"MY GRANDFATHER WAS A FUCKING NAZI"

My daughter and I visited a powwow in Canada a few years ago. These are breathtaking traditional festive Indian gatherings, where dance, drum and song are central. In colorful, ceremonial clothing full of symbols and meaning, following the trail of the ancestors, there is exuberant dancing around the tree of life to a powerful drumming rhythm that represents 'the heartbeat of Mother Earth'. The original culture and tradition of these peoples is kept alive and propagated in this way so that the new generations can connect with it. The powwow was held in Golden Lake, Northern Ontario, the original habitat of the Ojibwe Indians. At the end of the day, we were honored by several locals with an invitation to join the festive meal.

There was roasted venison with various and sundry side dishes for about two to three hundred people. Everyone was waiting in a long line after a long day (of dancing). Two Indian ladies of around thirty, both dark blond, who looked somewhat European but also with Indian features, stood behind us. They asked if we were speaking Dutch or German to each other. They recognized the accent from their own family and told us that their great-grandparents were from Germany but had moved to Canada. I reckoned that must have been shortly after the war.

Their grandchildren, these ladies' fathers or mothers developed a relationship with Native Americans that now gave them a Native American identity. "Our native communities are full of people with these histories," said one of the women. Behind them was a bear of a guy in his forties. He stood out in the line because, like me, he was a head taller than everyone else present. His long blonde braids reached down to his midriff. The piercing blue eyes in his Germanic looking face contrasted strangely with his many earrings and numerous tattoos with Native American symbols on his arms and calves. One tattoo spoke plain language: Proud to be Ojibwe, in a brightly colored medicine wheel with a diameter of more than fifteen centimeters. It pretty much took up the entire width of his upper arm. He was one of the powwow dancers. The remnants of his dance regalia still hung from his stocky, sweaty body. He followed our conversation and said out of the blue: "My grandfather was a fucking Nazi, and his son is my father. They fled from Germany after the war. It's a shame, the bloody Nazi's." It was a wonderful exchange, somehow so transparent, but also valuable to see, in a broader context, the course that so many descendants took. A man with a wholly Germanic appearance who is proud of his Native American origins because his father, full of shame about his own father, left for the other side of the world and married a Native American woman. He detached himself from the ties of his biographical bloodlines through the new Native American identity he acquired, and one that he lived deeply as a powwow dancer. And yet, one day, this man also comes to realize that the broken connection in his disintegrated family wants to be included in the dance of life. "He was a fucking Nazi, it's a shame" then turns into: "My grandfather did things that he could not forgive himself for, but I love him." Obviously, I thought he was the man himself and that he bears the broken connection with his father's father. This time disguised in an Indian appearance. Not yet integrated in this life, but on the way to being himself and with the possibility of reconnecting with original life values, in the beautiful way the Indian culture provides.

KRAUT WHORES AND TRAITORS

I notice when I look at the many biographies I have requested that a striking number of grandfathers and grandmothers became ill relatively shortly after the war and died young. All the impressions sustained because of violent and merciless events took their toll. The consequences of very serious conditions such as treason, the loss of sons, or daughters who were called kraut whores, are not resolved in the same life. Kraut whores or traitors in a family are violently condemned and such a family member is denied a place in the family tree by the others out of shame and dishonor. Such designations often manifest themselves in new families because of a tendency to believe that a scapegoat must always be found for something, someone who can be designated as the cause for all kinds of problems. In that way the finger pointer can always continue to wash his hands in innocence. His/her own part in this oppressive condemnation does not have to be faced.

How many grandmothers stopped their daughters from becoming wives? How many grandfathers condemned the natural beauty and bodily curves of their (grand) daughters before they became physically visible during puberty? Recovering families thus faced new setbacks by the truckload in the post-war decades.

The causes of all these disorders are only sporadically associated with what actually happened. They weren't talked about, one had to 'look ahead now and be positive'. They rarely received the recognition they were due, and people seldom truly let go of all sorts of despair they had accumulated and still carried quite vividly inside.

Meanwhile, I hope to have sufficiently fluffed the pillows so that you yourself can also recognize similar situations in your own bloodlines. It may cause confusion when you read these texts, perhaps causing tears to well up or other such emotions as dismay and it is very likely that at this moment someone from the unseen world is hopefully knocking on your door. Take a second and think about it. Perhaps it is a sensation where you feel goosebumps or a tingling, are a bit dreamy, or an image suddenly appears before your mind's eye. Just be kind and understanding, it's ultimately more about the opening than the explanation. It was a really bad time for many, and any chance to understand and re-assess will be gratefully embraced. Finally, an impressive case history, written by my client Rinus, 58 years old, from Germany.

CASE HISTORY – CONCENTRATION CAMP

My entire adult life I have felt insecure, sensitive, and unstable. I had little self-confidence, suffered from depression, and always had the horrible feeling that I was no good. I often felt desperate. In my profession I always set high goals that I usually could not achieve. I have been fired more than once, and more than once I had to find a new direction for my life. I needed psychotherapy for decades, a total of six multi-year treatments. Poverty is an issue for me, I have always been afraid that something would go wrong with my company. To escape the specter of poverty that was haunting me, I worked long and hard. Much more than was good for me. I could not stick to a reasonable limit. When I sought out Maarten, I was chronically exhausted.

For some years now, I have noticed a particular sensitivity to themes such as German fascism and World War II. This war was waged by Germany as a war of extermination. Terror was also systematically used within its own ranks. Fear forced obedience from one's own army and the population. The atrocities committed on behalf of the Nazi regime are numerous. The descriptions of the inhuman sadism in the extermination or concentration camps had a special effect on me. One day when I was working in the kitchen and heard a news item on the radio about the umpteenth liberation day of the Auschwitz concentration camp, something happened to me. I was overwhelmed by a wave of deep sadness, a huge outburst of tears and could no longer stand on my feet. I didn't understand that at the time, but I didn't do anything with it and a short time later I forgot about it. However, in the months that followed I was again confronted with this theme by a book, film, and the radio, also in other contexts, and again it caused a very sensitive reaction. Of course, I started thinking about it, but I couldn't explain it. I am not Jewish; my parents were children during the Second World War and my grandparents were not in concentration camps either. Then it suddenly occurred to me that a few years earlier I had seen a film set during World War II in which German SS soldiers do utterly horrific things to Jewish civilians. I couldn't watch the rest of that movie because I found the violence intolerable. The film touched me deeply. I was confused and numb and noticed huge tension in my arms. It felt like I was in a horrible déjà vu, as if I had seen something real instead of a movie. The line between fiction and reality had been erased. Have I ever really experienced such things? That's how it suddenly felt. Every year on January 27th, the liberation day of Auschwitz in 1945, I was overcome with a great sadness.

During a family visit in the Netherlands – I live in Germany myself and am slowly beginning to understand why – I heard about a lecture by a certain Maarten Oversier. The theme was: How war experiences of parents and grandparents affect the younger generations. This is my chance to shed light into the darkness, I thought, and I immediately contacted Maarten.

I tell Maarten my story and that I feel both the desire and the fear of discovering the real reasons for my enigmatic involvement with the victims in concentration camps. He looks at me calmly and tells me that it is quite possible that I have been there. Then he says, "Just close your eyes and you'll see what it was like there." So, I'm embarking on a dream journey into an earlier life. Almost immediately I see everything in front of me. I can start speaking, the words gush out of me.

I am lying alone in a dark cell, there is no chair and no bed. It is a space of roughly one and a half square meters, about the size of a toilet. I am lying on the ground that is stone cold and I am thinly dressed. I am wearing the hated striped uniform made of cotton, like all prisoners. I lie in my own excrement; I am dirty and wet and terribly cold. I am very weak and feel like I have been starving for months. In the corner is a feeding bowl with slops in which I could recognize cabbage stalk, peels and sawdust, boiled compost. It tastes and smells so disgusting that I wouldn't even feed it to the pigs.

I am desperate and furious. Furious at the inhumane treatment and injustice I experience, furious at Nazi Germany and furious at the commander who had me locked up here. I am also furious with myself because I have made a fatal mistake. Maarten asks what kind of mistake I made and why I am locked up here. I know the answer. I am innocent. Maybe I had picked up something like an apple and immediately popped it in my mouth. I had been assigned to the transport detail. I transported stuff with a cart and went practically everywhere in the camp. I assume that I also transported food and that an apple or something similar fell off my cart. Precisely because all the prisoners were suffering from such immense hunger, there were terrible penalties for stealing food. That was my mistake, I couldn't control myself. Hunger in the concentration camp means life.

Back in the cell. I feel numb and am going crazy with hunger, cold and misery. I can't think straight anymore. I'm totally exhausted now. And then it becomes clear to me that I will not come out of this alive. Maarten confirms my thought and suddenly he is sitting next to me and tells me that we are now going to the end. He asks if I can see myself dying. I can go to that moment, and I can describe how my strength is increasingly diminishing. Maarten now presses his fingers on my throat. I can hardly breath. Then comes my last breath, a sigh and I'm dead. Maarten indicates that we are not ready yet, I am still going to bury myself. I lift myself up, I don't weigh much anymore and carry myself out of the camp. I find a place on the edge of a forest; I dig a grave among the trees.

Over a period of two years, I had four sessions with Maarten. The sessions had a clear effect, I quickly had a feeling of getting better. A year after the last session, I can quite plainly say that I have become more emotionally stable. I am no longer distraught; I no longer cry, and I feel calmer and more satisfied. When I look back on my former life, it's like I've shaken off a bad dream. The strong pressure I used to feel, the heaviness and fear of failure have decreased considerably. My fear of becoming poor has slowly disappeared, my fanatism has passed. I can feel when I need a break and because I'm taking them now, the burnouts and depressions stay away.

CHAPTER 15

There where blood flowed

"Peace is more than the absence of war."
– Thomas

Every war, worldwide, has shaped our ancestors through a series of dark and deeply etched experiences. Whether it is about experiencing events yourself or living in a society disrupted by war. Each country or area has its own historical characteristics that must be considered when looking for the true causes of complaint patterns in family lines.

PRACTICAL EXAMPLE – THE BOMBING OF WESTKAPELLE, ZEELAND

When he was a teenager my client's father had to go with his father (client's grandfather) to flooded houses near Westkapelle, Zeeland. The flooding was deliberately carried out by the Allies in October 1944. The dikes were bombed to pieces to weaken German positions. Grandpa was a rural policeman and was expected to check out the affected areas. Many residents were trapped under the rubble and could not get away.

Once when he was there with his thirteen-year-old son who had to help, (children's) corpses were floating in and between the houses. The many animal carcasses among the floating household belongings completed the gruesome spectacle. The impact of witnessing this horror scenario has profoundly affected this young man's life. Out of self-protection, he has numbed his emotional world. His confidence in life vanished to an absolute low point. As he got older, he never talked about it. My client has never seen his father uninhibited or cheerful in any way. He took it to heart himself, as if he did not meet the expectations made on him as a son. His father's eternally melancholic aura has greatly influenced his own life. Stronger than he could have imagined, he discovers. It's a huge relief when matters are released during a session and can be put into perspective. Parents and grandparents, regardless of whether they are still alive, always need to express their repressed and sometimes terrible life experiences. Their descendants recover when they also get to know about them. In this way, my client finally learned to let go and no longer feel burdened by his now deceased father. This, after he had felt what his father's childhood had been like.

LINK BETWEEN TORTURE AND HAZING RITUALS

Every country, every city, every village, and every hamlet has its own history; an indelible imprint is left where blood has flowed. The themes that correspond to them remain topical for those who were involved, in no matter what capacity. Often barely recognized by the present-day generations.

Rotterdam was taken in one week – the powerful beating heart of this dynamic port city ripped out in the blink of an eye. In Groningen, the Scholtenhuis on the *Grote Markt* was confiscated by the Nazis. It became the SS headquarters from where the seizure of the Netherlands was supervised and controlled. 'The pub', the clubhouse of the current elite Vindicat student fraternity, is currently located where it used to be. Although the original building was demolished several years ago, the new clubhouse is in the exact same location. Vindicat is notorious for its hierarchies and hazing rituals. Could there be a connection to a period of perverse torture, humiliation, and arrogant abuse of power by those declaring themselves superior during World War II? With bizarre pride and an extreme need for rank and position?

In Den Hoorn, five Dutchmen were publicly executed in 1944 as a reprisal measure for the death of an SS officer. Joost Schrikx made an impressive film about this, *De oorlog van mijn vader* (My Father's War). He shows how this event leaves its mark on the current inhabitants, including his father who was a teenager at the time. You see how a village was affected by a horrific act for a long time. A contagion sneakily surged its way through the population and the witnesses can see no clear connection this has now with their dejected or joyless state of mind. In the end, no one remembers 'how it ever came about'. Witnesses are interviewed in the film. They were children at the time. All of them tell what they saw from their own vantage point, in an alley, behind a wall or sitting on a fence. They watched as five healthy young people, in the prime of their lives, just slumped over lifeless against a church wall.

It was the dictator Franco and his regime whose actions were decisive in causing the trials and tribulations of the grandparent's lives in the family systems of almost all my students in the classes I gave in Catalonia. The emotionally charged experiences of that time came to the surface clearly when we delved into the family histories of the participants. The learning setting made it possible to map out quite a few extra details of what happened. The therapists who received lessons from me conducted very specific and in-depth research into the connections between then and now. Many seemingly insignificant details even told a story and they recognized how the ways of dealing with one another today and their actions had been affected. The insights gained, not only made the big picture increasingly clear, but also the scope of the effect of history. Both supporters and opponents of Franco's regime derived identity, status, and self-worth from their position, no matter how shaky it was. Usually with the advantage of being able to survive, after which you then publicly associated yourself with such a system. In the same life, it is then nearly impossible to look at yourself in a mirror and see any other person than the one who made the best of things under the circumstances. Later, your children reminded you of the identity you had assumed, without them having the awareness of the underlying fear and misery that caused you to take the position you did.

Among the Native Americans in Canada and the U.S., or closer to home the Sami (an indigenous reindeer herder people in northern Scandinavia, which you may know from Armanda Kernell's 2018 film 'Sami Blood'), it is the reformatories that dehumanized the original population. The soul of these peoples is still extremely affected by this; the present generations suffer from the violence inflicted on their ancestors. The enormous wealth of spiritual knowledge is therefore kept alive with difficulty, while that is precisely the source of the people's existence: the medicine of your ancestors. Anyone who wants to detect the true cause of current patterns of complaint must take into account that each country or area has its own historical characteristics.

GERMANY'S KARMIC BALLAST

Extra attention in ancestral work must be paid particularly to Germany's karmic ballast. The role of an oppressor collectively produces heavier layers of shame, dishonor, and guilt. It brings an extra receptivity to (forms of) (self) condemnation, and therefore also an extra need for self-defense or increased difficulty in accepting criticism. Creating a safe space should therefore be given top priority; it is indispensable to be free of judgment and genuinely curious in this challenging field of activity.

Feelings were already running high during a training session in Bavaria, Germany dedicated to the relationship between complaints among the current population and the unresolved, extremely traumatic experiences from the war. Starting an active exchange with ancestors, simply asking directly for facts from the life of grandpa Kurt, grandpa Günther, grandma Sophia or grandma Maria, already set so much in motion that in no time a noisy, palpable energetic whirlwind ran through the workspace. The power of simply naming names and circumstances and then not attaching any value judgment to them is huge. By tuning into these people, a certain potential is now being generated within which enormously desired transformations of old residual tensions can take place. Some of those present in my group were their direct descendants, the others their grandchildren. As a result, they all literally have a family tree connection. An alignment with the innermost feelings of those truly involved ancestors from the war is quickly made with the help of some exercises and focused, exploratory questions. The process of dealing with them can begin via the (grand) children.

CASE HISTORY ANGELIKA

Angelika's mother was one of identical twins. Angelika said the twins were taken to a playground by their mother (Angelika's grandmother) in Dresden, where they lived. It was February 1945. The twins must have been about three years old. Mother urged her daughters to stay there until they were picked up again. Bombs were falling. After a while

Angelika's mother, still just a toddler, walked off to look for her mother, leaving her sister behind, despite this insistent instruction. Shortly afterwards, she witnessed a stray bomb hitting the playground and leaving nothing left of her twin sister. Angelika was later named after this sister, her aunt, and had a symbiotic relationship with her grandmother, who died in old age. As a result, her own mother had always remained at a distance, resulting in her feeling neglected by her.

Grandma had wrapped herself around her granddaughter like an octopus. She had never gotten over Angelika, not even after her death. Her granddaughter filled the gap of her daughter's absence as well as the hole of guilt for leaving her girls in the playground. She has never been able to process the untold pain. It was still there between them. By paying attention in a session now to this still very emotional event – admittedly out of date – a process of letting go could finally take place. Grandma has let go of her granddaughter, to Angelika's great relief. This was followed by a period in which Angelika was able to breathe new life into the bond with her own mother. Angelika's mother's life had an undertone of her 'not mattering' and 'not being important', so she always put herself in the background. Deep down, she continued to bear the burden of being conflicted about having left her sister alone. This contained a conviction: 'If I leave and follow my intuition, someone will die.' An attitude that weakened her autonomy as a mother, making it possible for her mother to penetrate far too deeply into the life of her daughter. Angelika suddenly wondered if she might not have been her mother's twin sister in her previous life, but the answer came naturally to her mind. That could explain her deep loneliness, the feeling of losing a part of herself, and her continually shifting physical pains. And at the same time the frustration that she had never felt able to connect with her mother. An example out of thousands.

CHAPTER 16

Seed carriers for the new Reich

Napoleon: "What shall we do with this soldier, Giuseppe? Everything he says is wrong."
Giuseppe: "Make him a general, Your Excellency, and then everything he says will be right."
– George Bernard Shaw

German soldiers made impressive appearances in many ways during World War II. The usually well-built, athletic, blond, young men not only instilled awe in the enemy, but they were also extremely attractive to many women. The uniforms of the high-ranking soldiers were designed by none other than couturier Hugo Boss and fit like a glove. Pride radiated from the men, and they looked immaculate, well-fed, and dangerously sexy with their fresh and well-trimmed heads.

National Socialism and the totalitarian fascist regime elevated the young male body to a symbol of vitality and fertility. The seed carriers for the New Reich. Their appearance was seductive, invincible, and charismatic. They paraded hypnotically in sync through the streets of the occupied cities. And perhaps because it was not done as a patriotic and ecclesiastically raised wife of an occupied land to openly respond to these sensual stimuli, that the attraction was even more irresistible. But women who collaborated with the enemy had their heads shaved bald, were pulled on a cart with a swastika daubed on their foreheads and paraded before jeering people. Citizens expressed their contempt with horror on their faces, so that the women felt rejected to the core. Normal participation in the once familiar society came to an end for good. Undoubtedly, every sexual relationship between a German soldier and a non-German woman had sweeping consequences. For them, the war continued while for everyone else it was over.

With a degree of innocence at first, it just happened that a country daughter was seduced by the charms of a young soldier. She didn't really see the seriousness and extent of what was to come. Can you picture it before your eyes? The young girl, aroused by her natural curiosity and longing to break the daily routine of the farming family, naively and dreamily falls into the arms of the far-from-home soldier who is on patrol in the village on that day. Fiery adolescent passions and scrupulous loss of virginity are the order of the day. Many women feel helplessly seduced, confused, and sucked into irreversible processes or seriously abused and stripped of self-worth. Many fathers are furious and powerless. Spouses, boyfriends, or brothers feel betrayed, jealous, or abandoned. Families and relationships are torn apart.

IMPRISONED BY PROPAGANDA AND MASS HYPNOSIS

The army is a man's world and needs square as time passes and victories are won. As violence increases dramatically, sex becomes the ultimate flight from mortality. Death links itself to orgasm, to madness. Whoever kills, according to natural laws, gets the urge to reproduce.

The urge to reproduce with excessive display of power. Romance, gentleness, and equality give way to an unprecedented diabolical compulsion fraught with perversity and aggressive oppression. The genie is out of the bottle. Hand in hand with the bottle, all morals are numbed and rape and killing become daily activities. If any sober realization comes into play, it is immediately quashed. After all, the seriousness of the deeds has reached such proportions that no one wants or is able to stop and think about it.

Feelings and emotions are radically eliminated, as well as the causes that appeal to them, such as wailing victims or children with empty, teary eyes and huge question marks on their faces. As soon as the alcohol begins to wear off and the production of adrenaline, constantly fueled by the war machine, is toned down for even a moment, feelings of guilt, dishonor, and shame immediately creep up. But cunningly held captive by propaganda and mass hypnosis, from which a dark voice tells you how invincible and wonderful you are by working so hard for your homeland, every wrongdoing is justified. This ensures the future birth of countless people suffering from borderline personality disorders.

Amateurishly conducted abortions are the order of the day and if children are born, their lives are dominated by disapproval because the father is a German soldier. Pregnant girls are forever excluded or cursed by their parents in front of all family members. And so countless young women are psychologically battered and left to their own devices. From 1940 to 1945 our polar world found itself existing between extremes.

GETTING AROUND KARMA

The explanation provided here shows the reality in which millions of people experienced life during the Second World War. It is a realistic sketch of the many stories that reincarnation therapists must deal with on a weekly basis. Few realize that all these events have a considerable effect on the present across the generations. The wet blanket of war still lies over a large part of the European population, in an energetic form. I would go so far as to shout from the rooftops that countless souls who gained indelible impressions during this dark period have reincarnated and are among us in large numbers. According to my estimates, there is a great chance this includes you. But at the same time the chance of this being recognized is quite small because we have not been brought up with these connections. And certainly not with the possibilities to heal old wounds at this level. Even people who are familiar with esotericism, doing energetic work, practicing meditation or reiki, have learned to think positively, are philosophers or have studied life extensively in other ways, may be deprived of the knowledge that the influences of these fresh past lives are still there. These layers lie dormant deep in one's consciousness, and the experiences stored there are so repugnant that locking them away serves a clear purpose: "Never again this pain." It is a hard place to reach. However, as the understanding of reincarnation and its connection to cause and effect increases, so too does our ability increase to recognize ourselves and others and to learn to forgive. I believe that this world will then open more and more so that the trapped pain can come out, instead of it continuing to play itself out below the belt of our understanding. Incidentally, that is played out to the great pleasure of the pharmaceutical industry, which is getting rich from people who want to regulate their pain with the help of chemicals. But also, expensive forms of therapy to regulate behavior often skate over the ice under which the active area is located.

Seen from a much greater perspective, you could say that these two major wars, the years 1914 to 1918 and 1939 to 1945, still 'had' to take place in the previous century. Had to, because the great transformations among humanity, predicted by countless seers and indigenous peoples, such as the Mayas with the well-known 2012 story, could not otherwise take place. Fed by emotional charges from earlier eras where violent theaters of war were far from finished. And what has not sufficiently run its course cannot really transform into new forms of consciousness. Karmic laws are based on cause and effect, on action-reaction. This means that the essence of every action that someone once performed, ultimately wants to be experienced in its fullness. By one and the same person, that is, where the truth lies literally in the middle. If you shout nasty things at someone, you are mainly connected to the experience of the shouter, not to the person on the receiving end. But to understand what the effect of shouting is, you will also have to put yourself in the receiver's shoes. The initial reluctance to assume that position also causes someone, driven by a decision of the soul, to take on that role himself. In another life, for example. Without qualifying it as good or bad. Giving someone a helping hand or slapping someone in the face with the same hand are both actions, subjected to the same law. In this way, the experience becomes complete for you, and you can reach a conclusion internally based on your own actions so that your consciousness about a certain event becomes complete, becomes one. This applies both to large-scale events, such as war or a pandemic, as on an individual level, although the scale and impact of large-scale events are in fact determined by the diverse experiences of the individual. The individuals are the building blocks of the total event. So, without any filters, everyone eventually gets to know the consequences of his actions and that makes growth of consciousness possible. A trajectory that may take lives because one human life is not sufficient to accommodate all the divisions of roles that are necessary to understand the whole.

History, meanwhile, has been written by the victor for centuries. Those are a few words for a gigantic insight with mega implications. A winner can only be a winner if there is a loser and at the same time, both form the opposites of the whole. The irony is that both poles are needed to arrive at the total awareness necessary for real change. Thanks to his acquired power, the winner always knows how to maneuver himself into positions, always focusing on having his actions turn out in his favor. He cunningly cleans up his traces of blood for the naked eye of future generations. In this way, the truth of the original event is constantly kept hidden, piloted from hiding place to hiding place. In other words, one is constantly disconnected from the consequence of one's actions. And the condition for this is that the loser continues to suffer under the power of the winner so that the real truth, the original event, does not come to light. Anyone being led down the garden path and who does not realize it, has no insight into the actual making of wars and disasters. And yet, for many reasons, these major events have been accorded nourishment and the right to exist.

You could therefore say that in the intensity of the battle in terms of karma still existed at a much too high level among the great stream of in- and excarnating souls. Many became deeply intertwined and have become attached to the stubborn forces of the Ages of Pisces. Many energetic wounds in the aura of Mother Earth have remained open as a result. Wounds that arose around the last days of Atlantis, about 13,000 years ago. During countless wars, slavery, the systematic oppression and slaughter of peoples and populations, epidemics, the excesses of many world religions and so on, these wounds have had salt rubbed in them again and again, making real healing impossible. A macabre journey through 13,000 years of human history in which the lava of the unprocessed painfully moves through the generations and is ignited again and again in a different form, but with the same underlying themes.

Huge excesses of all these pent-up charges manifested themselves during roughly five hundred years of Roman oppression. It is not difficult to see the similarities between the Roman and German armies. In addition to an almost flawlessly tight, uniform organization, both powers appropriated the strength of the – for indigenous peoples so sacred – Eagle as a symbol of power. Both powers were seized by a gigantic sense of imperiousness and superiority. Everything that did not belong in their vision had to be destroyed. Even the tight movement of the hand to salute the leader is the same where *'ave and heil'* both substantively and energetically, have the same empowering effect.

Everything that cannot be settled at one time or another always seeks a suitable star under which to still do it anyway. As mentioned, history repeats itself. At an individual and group level. Similarly, mega events, such as wars, are energetically orchestrated by those involved who need to be able to experience it at some level. Those who have ever been intensely humiliated and trampled on can create a need to emerge victorious in battle, attracting them to incarnate in eras where wars are about to take place.

Those existing under oppression as inferior beings all their lives have an irresistible need to experience what it is like to be superior and to have other people's lives at their disposal. A war about to happen is then a godsend. Wars can break out, with the help of any kind of manipulation, if there are sufficient conditions for it. In theory, no one has to put on a helmet or follow orders. Isn't it a beautiful quip by the Dutch cartoonist* Loesje: "Suppose war breaks out and nobody shows up...?"

In the 20th century, the "mother of all wars" broke out, where everything that had built up over many centuries began to fester. Almost everyone was involved in every conceivable role imaginable. 'There was no escape' is only partly true because no one was forced to incarnate at that time.

ESSENTIAL TIPPING POINT THAT LEADS TO HEALING

A small group of power-hungry people used the oil they had already controlled to throw on the political fires they had also created themselves. Many a war was drawn up this way including the First and Second World Wars. In the process they took advantage of the forgetfulness of many people regarding their past lives. Latent in that oblivion are the factors that still dominate. They stem from myriad unresolved miseries created by war, including having been both a victim and perpetrator of aggression and even extreme psychopathic behavior. The thousands of clients I have been able to guide over the years have shown me that it can indeed be put in such black and white terms. Countless war victims from the Second World War met in the German oppressor that part of themselves that once had to be banished forever. For example, a ruthless Roman centurion who once decided to become untouchable forever. Or a hypocritical priest who converted people while molesting children. That makes your dark side, about which so much is written, indeed quite concrete! And it also makes it clear why many people find it so difficult to fully accept themselves.

Now that people fear a third world war and no one really knows which way things are going, a focused exploration in your own underworld is quite useful. You cannot escape your own karma, no matter how many beautiful healing forms are out there. Certainly not by only focusing on 'the Higher' while 'the Lower' is still packed with sub-personalities craving attention. Anyone who truly heals from any disease or disorder has discovered somewhere that nothing human is foreign to him. And how enormously confronting that discovery can be. But there is an essential tipping point after which you will withdraw from the power of attraction to any battlefield, refrain from making judgments and the lost Love for yourself will awaken.

Characteristic of the average German soldier, but of course also of the soldiers of other nationalities, is that they are low on being critical and highly receptive to following orders by their superiors. They feel strong so long as they can function in a hierarchically structured, medal-revering group, where ranks and positions and clearly formulated rules, norms and values are in charge. Individuality is subordinate to the collective. Together you are someone. The idea of being able to do something for the world and therefore 'doing it right' plays a major role. At home, most of these soldiers were already praised by dominant fathers for their achievements as men, while mothers played subordinate roles and therefore the development of female intuition remained far below par. Self-esteem is measured by performance and the success of desired behavior, which means that the original self-esteem has already been seriously undermined in previous lives.

AGE OF AQUARIUS

These world wars had to take place before 2012. The consciousness, that with the onset of the Age of Aquarius is increasingly flowing around the Earth and among people and permeated with much more awareness, will make warfare increasingly difficult in the future. A force that will crack the toughest nut of popular beliefs: "That's the way it's always been, and it will always be like that." Half a century from now, anyone still openly admitting to being a war monger will be a curiosity. Those who still broadcast too much hate will no longer get a tit for tat answer. By then people on average will be more forgiving so that the hateful person in question must either go to another planet to work out his karmic junk and/or will have to learn to love himself and his fellow man. And the latter, as is evident from many therapeutic processes, seems to be a great challenge for the time being. The most stubborn processes are about being kind to yourself.

That is why in the decades after 1940 to 1945, with an emphasis on the 1960's and 70's, many souls have returned from the war and are now part of what some haughtily call 'the overpopulation'. What can still be experienced, worked out, set straight, relived, finished, or explored now that there is still adequate war energy among the living generations? I dare say that a high level of serious illnesses, ailments and mental disorders stems from great internalized guilt, dishonor, and shame complexes that were born during the war. Supplemented with injustice, hatred, self-hatred, and enormous fears. Especially the killing and humiliation of others is food for depriving oneself of happiness in a new life. All this is quite literally based on the wisdom that what you do to another you also do to yourself: Do we need another global catastrophe before we wake up?

Fortunately, nowadays increasingly more is known about the insane practices of power cartels, which deliberately poison people by sickly manipulated and chemical food, polluted water, chemtrails, questionable vaccinations, electro-smog and a constant stream of propaganda with censored and biased news. Nevertheless, the seed for change is still within us. Even though extraterrestrials once tampered with our DNA, we will have to repair it ourselves. Here too, the following applies: "Make the world better, start with yourself."

ARCHETYPES FROM THE WAR

Archetypes from every war are primarily the perpetrator and the victim. They seem to have an inseparable connection if no forgiveness has taken place, and therefore always seek each other out. Throughout various lives. Simply put; if you were ever a perpetrator, then in a previous time you were the victim, also connected to the same souls of yesteryear. You can recognize them in your immediate environment by those who cause you excessive turmoil. Or even for whom you feel the most hatred or disgust.

On a larger scale, at the popular level, there are well-known people who trigger people *en masse*. Anders Breivik, Marc Dutroux, Joris Demmink, Queen Elizabeth, Putin, Trump and so on. Many have a favorite trigger figure, and when one disappears from the scene, a new figure emerges. The effect such a person has on enflaming someone else is much more interesting than continuing to point to the person himself. Here, too, we see how often we tend to want to reject things from ourselves. They are simplistically explained connections, but with a core of gold. Many personalities who experienced the war in a past life are among and within us. They exist as 'old personalities' in a new main character. They are like you and me.

In my practice, many people experience having been soldiers of varying calibers and of different ranks and positions. Think of pilots, tank drivers, strategists or (teenage) soldiers. Or they experience having had a different role in the war. Think of concentration camp victims, victims of sexual abuse or medical experiments, resistance fighters, NSB (Dutch National Socialist) party members, male and female farmers with people in hiding or people who lost a child because of an exploding grenade. Many were insignificant individuals from the grey masses whose fear, insecurity, hunger and cold are deeply engraved into them. And as I wrote in the previous chapter: also think of people who have witnessed from a distance, executions, secret transactions, rapes, or exploding bombs.

Many German soldiers have huge amounts of deeply concealed internalized guilt that lies like a grey veil over their enjoyment of life. Their right to be, has often been thoroughly damaged, even if their part in the war was negligible. Therefore, through overachieving or pleaser behavior, they now seek sufficient appreciation from others to live. In their lives they often still accept an authority behind which they can hide in the form of a domineering father, partner, manager, leader, or guru. Many of them still love to be active in a collective, but now preferably with 'white' objectives. The whiter the better and sometimes charities are even compulsively created to compensate for what was once destroyed. Erstwhile supporters of the Nazi regime can also regroup in a new life in aggressive fighting or fan clubs with similar beliefs and racist statements. That's also a way to linger in the war and not have to dwell on yourself for a moment.

FORMER PERPETRATOR NOW TAKES CARE OF HIS FORMER VICTIM

Without exception, those (former) victims from the camps, who were gassed, have breathing problems in the form of asthma, bronchitis, TB, or other lung diseases. For example, they are people who in their current childhood have had to endure enormous fear at summer camp or during a medical examination. People who would prefer to constantly cover their faces in public or have their super blue eyes open as wide as possible this time, because they want to convince their surroundings that they are not a Jew, so much that they get tired of it. They are people with bulimia or anorexia whose compulsively perpetuated hunger continues to bind them to their children or parents-at-the-time, because that hunger had become so familiar to them that they associate life with it.

All kinds of conflicts of authority are also unmistakably present among them. On the one hand, out of a need never to want to be dominated again, they either position themselves emphatically above others or docilely below them. In that way they protect the value of their identity, which they had let others too easily determine in the past. In remarkably many cases they come from traditional well-to-do families, sometimes Jewish again, but in any case, with strong ties, norms, and values. And, perhaps even more remarkably, I discovered that many former Jewish people in present-day life, connected with former German soldiers in real life. On a subconscious level, of course, but with very similar, understandable patterns. This time, the former perpetrator takes care of his former victim to hide his guilt while the former victim feels protected by the presence of the former soldier because it is assumed this will ensure safety.

Because many people in those wartime lives have had to deal with excessive forms of sexuality, the consequences of this are still present. Think of a disturbed balance of power in relationships with sexual excesses. Such as an active sex addiction to total passivity and shutting down. Many uterus complaints, ranging from fibroids, excessively painful menstruation periods to more serious conditions, were alleviated when a woman experienced during a session that in energetic form, there was still a child because of a rape. Or that the aggression of sexual abuse still accumulated there, so that the energetic disturbance that resulted forms the breeding ground for infections or other genital disorders. Female clients were finally able to get pregnant after trying a long time, and after painfully reliving how in a previous life they used knitting needles to remove the bloody fetus that was the result of a rape. During sessions the condemnation of such female curves as buttocks and breasts was neutralized as soon as one came to realize that it was not the fault of these body parts that they were once 'singled out'.

People who were resistance fighters in a previous life, and who were still very secretive in a new life leaving them feeling again emotionally isolated, couldn't believe that the war was really over. For them, revealing information or names, or 'expressing yourself' went hand in hand with torture, and that resulted in death. Moreover, opening oneself up to these traumas brought with it the extremely painful realization that others may have been killed, because what they said had actually taken place, was believed.

ANNE FRANK

It is understandable that we still watch so many war films and documentaries, read books about the war and why big sporting events feel more like a life-and-death struggle than a game, including the former slogans and former symbols. It is also understandable that war memorials worldwide are systematically restored and refurbished. It is understandable that commemorations and wreath-laying are an established part of society and that many people feel an unpleasant emptiness that comes bubbling to the surface when the chestnut tree in the garden of Anne Frank's house is reported to be in danger of falling over. At the same time, we keep ourselves imprisoned in what we also want to be set free from: war. The war is among us, we have lost ourselves in it and many parts of the soul are still roaming there, making it impossible for us to really let go of it. We subconsciously cherish and maintain that time with our biased outlook on life, our prejudices, political affiliations, or survival strategies. Our fear of it happening again is unconsciously fed by the thousand bombs and grenades that invade our living rooms every day via the media.

"I was there", is Bram Vermeulen's powerful message from his brilliant film *In den beginne* (In the Beginning). A statement that courageously reveals that he did take the responsibilities seriously in his current life that he once relinquished – during the First World War. Incidentally, this was shortly before he died (again). I, Maarten, was also there and gradually discovered what makes 'being in the NOW' so difficult. Fortunately, we can now be grateful for the freedom we have. A freedom that many of our ancestors who – were- sometimes-also-ourselves – lacked. A freedom that this time affords the possibility of searching for and rediscovering yourself. Because why would you look for yourself if you haven't lost anything of yourself? Like, for instance, in some war or other?

CHAPTER 17

Processing options

"A soldier does not have to care about wisdom, only through heroic deeds on the battlefield is he honored."
– Abu-al-Qasem Firdausi

The consequences of the Second World War for those who were there and for the generations that followed are unimaginably profound. Although we talk about first- and second-generation war victims within spiritual care, there is on average little awareness about the true extent of the traumatization in family systems. It is an unfathomable area. Especially for the third generation, which I generally have to deal with in my practice. The second generation was often dismissed with: "Ah, you were so small, you were just a baby, fortunately you know nothing about the war. We have experienced everything consciously, for you it is peacetime." Here lies a core conflict for this second generation, namely that the feelings of the parents count and those of the children do not when it comes to that issue. The third generation also grows up here again under the influence and upbringing of parents who learned to subordinate their own feelings and views to those of others. Healthy feelings of self-worth and self-love become disturbed and exhausted so that life becomes a difficult, sometimes even impossible task for many people. And then in a society free of war that is quite dynamic, which fosters yet another dose of misunderstanding about their inexplicable moods and complaints.

Here, the possibility that those same children, both second and third generation, may well have experienced the war in a previous life, is royally ignored, and vibrate with the themes of their (ancestors) parents based on their own experiences. Putting aside and downplaying the inner conflicts of this second (and subsequent) generation(s) thoroughly complicates their recognition and processing. After all, there is always someone who supposedly had it much worse.

That there are causal links between the Second World War and the manifestations of countless disorders on an emotional, mental, and physical level for post-war births, as we know them today, is therefore a completely neglected insight. We painfully and unconsciously bear these war burdens, as we move, alive again, through the auric field of Mother Earth. Fourth and sometimes even fifth generation 'war victims' too are absolutely no exception in my practice. As I wrote before, Native Americans speak of a time frame of seven generations, which is necessary for extreme events happening to a people such as war, mass murder or oppression to evaporate from family lines.

CASE HISTORY OF STAYING IN LINE

15-year-old Sarah visits my practice with her mother. Sarah is fifth generation. Her great-grandparents experienced the war as children. Sarah has a compulsive need to follow rules. Everything must go as prescribed, and she has an excessive fear of men who get angry. These two complaints make her socially isolated and put an enormous strain on her relationship with her mother. Sarah literally says to her mother, "If you weren't here, I wouldn't want to live anymore."

In a relived experience, she sees herself as a young mother who is separated from her two children shortly after a train journey of no less than three days and two nights. On an impulse, she decides to ignore the finger-pointing order to "walk in line with the others" and desperately runs after her children. The dogs that are unleashed are kept within an inch of biting her. With the barrel of a pistol against her forehead, she is relentlessly shouted at in a foreign language by an evil, menacing man in a uniform. She is then violently removed and ends up in the gas chamber a short time later. At that moment she is utterly convinced that if she had stayed in line and done what she was told, she would still have lived and seen her children again. She feels like a bad mother who abandoned her children because she disobeyed. Her self-image shrivels on the spot. She transfers the excruciating fear and associated thought patterns to her current life as Sarah.

Sarah's father leaves her mother while Sarah is still inside her as a slightly more than three-month-old fetus. From her perception of the world in the womb, she says: "He doesn't want to see me live." At this early stage, the seeds are already being planted for a hefty relationship of dependency on her mother, who does want her, and with whom she experiences that she is allowed to live. "He doesn't want to see me live" and "I don't mean anything to him," are the exact same words that go through her when the soldier in her previous life threatened her with his gun. And now, as a teenager, Sarah distrusts people in general, and men in particular. When she does have contact with others, she tries obsessively not to make any mistakes through adapting her behavior, to prevent someone from getting angry. "I can only live when I'm with mom." Keep in mind too that Sarah already condemns the idea of becoming a mother at a stage of her life in which that does not (yet) apply at all. These convictions might just end up coming true if she were given the opportunity to become a mother. At the end of the session, Sarah says in tears: "I did what I could, it's not my fault, I love my children, and myself too. It's that twisted war that destroys everything in people."

Some people say that the Holocaust was made up for all sorts of reasons. I feel no need to get involved in this discussion, because I do see that countless historical accounts have been stripped of their truth. It is clear to me that everything has been distorted about the facts from the period of this war, and perhaps also about the persecution of the Jews.

As I wrote before, it is mainly the winner who writes history, and then it becomes very complicated when that winner turns out to essentially have had close ties with the loser, if only because in the years leading up to the war, he supplied massive amounts of war material to Germany, a country that was still in sackcloth and ashes because of the First World War. These are downright shocking and disconcerting details, very important and useful for further research into finding the truth, but not in this book. To me, it doesn't matter whether six million Jews were killed or whether it is a different number. I don't examine those numbers anyway. Therapeutically, I focus on the patterns of complaints and the associated, repressed stories that come up and are treated during sessions, without attaching any interpretation or value judgment.

Obviously, I can't imagine that the many hundreds of clients in my practice alone over the years, who experienced dying in a gas chamber, spontaneously made up those stories because the biased history books tell that this is how it happened then. Apart from the fact that most people hated the war so much that they structurally avoided every book and every film, school assignment or conversation about it for a lifetime. And then, would anyone experience true relief and change in their daily life after sessions based on fabrications?

SECOND OR THIRD GENERATION WAR VICTIMS

War-related traumas are based on an enormously broad spectrum of origins and circumstances. From the gruesome Japanese internment camps, where deported fathers had to leave their wives and children behind, and the terrible conditions in which countless soldiers found themselves, to heroic stories of resistance fighters or high-ranking soldiers who made ultimate rescues. And in the intervening grey areas, no one really escaped the influence of aggression, oppression, hardship, temptation and the consequences of uncertainty, loss, and injury. Obviously to a greater or lesser extent. If a rural family had enough food and managed to do relatively well, there was always a brother or sister who lived in the big cities and experienced the opposite, so that there was still a feeling of guilt or an emotional gray veil shrouding it. Not to mention countless unspoken secret events, which in retrospect never really made it clear why grandpa or grandma exhibited such incomprehensible, sometimes excessive behavior.

When it comes to unspoken, secret events, the story comes to mind of a grandfather who had to pick up milk cans from surrounding farms during the war. He had just stopped by a the farm where he had a nice little chat with a child of about four or five years old who lived there and whose parents were busy working on the land. On the country road back home, he sees through the rearview mirror of his truck a stray shell or bomb explode at the front of that farm. The face of the little boy with whom he had such an amusing chat not five minutes ago, is indelibly etched in his mind. Grandpa freezes with terror, never to thaw again. He doesn't talk about it when he gets home. He projects the fear he incurred of what could have had totally unexpected fatal consequences, onto his family, mainly on his own son, who is the same age. His approach to his son becomes one of making contact and rejection. There is always a dissatisfied undertone of "At least you have a life, why don't you do anything good with it?" In saying this, the father confuses his son with the dead boy who has no life (anymore). Once grown up, this son later has a son of his own and he visits my practice as an adult. He can now trace his father's behavior. "My father was never satisfied; I could never do anything good in his eyes. As if his father, my grandfather, was constantly watching with disapproval and it was never good enough." The clarification of this event finally makes him keenly aware of and understand why there has always been such a distance between him and his father.

One may not directly recognize examples of second or third generation war victims in this, even though they of course are. Grandpa did not meet the criteria for this, because no identifiable war-related event was known. Besides that, there was always milk and they actually had it pretty good. But grandpa had become a fearful, retiring, aloof and unreachable man while no one really knew what event was at the root of his unfathomability.

READER'S REACTIONS

When my article about reincarnation and World War II appeared in *Frontier Magazine*, I received many impressive and moving responses. Reactions that ranged from readers who recognized or heard themselves in the connections that were sketched between then and now, to reactions from people who had already undergone intensive transformation processes with war scenes in the background from their current or a past life. In many cases, people at first had no notion that current complaints originated in a period that is now behind us.

Several times I was asked whether other wars have had less impact. Of course, that is not the case. Many countries, peoples or even continents have a violent history with war, oppression, or genocide in the background. The consequences are far-reaching and in an energetic sense hereditary. The setting of the Second World War concerned quite a few countries and peoples.

On November 11, 2018, the First World War of a hundred years ago became history. It was said that this war never really stopped in 1918, but that there was an armistice of about twenty years. In other words, World War II arose from the ashes of the first. There has been an energetic, thematic transfer from one to the other. What happens karmically on a personal level also takes place in the larger context. The previous history is the breeding ground for the next one. In all kinds of specific ways, from country to country, from province to province, from city to city, village to village, family to family. Old, dormant, triggers that have almost cooled down, then blaze again in a new situation, in a new era.

Publishing personal experiences of people who have already done their processing in this deeper context is therefore very valuable, encouraging and extremely instructive. With sincere thanks to those whose story or example I was allowed to use here. It is on their behalf when I say that this openness should be understood as a loving and stimulating helping hand. From man to fellow man.

RIJKE MARIA RUITER WROTE:

"I was born in 1944 and found out through dreams that I was in Auschwitz and was murdered there, I think in 1943. I was in a women's orchestra and in this life, I am a violinist again. I also had a dream that I had to go back very soon to bring a lot of things to a conclusion. The violin I play on was built by an Auschwitz survivor. The music I play on this violin is mainly Jewish (Klezmer and religious) music, and I also give lectures about it throughout the country. In this life I was born into a strict Orthodox Christian family, so it took a while before I got to my Jewish roots. Now I have made a nice connection between the Christians and being Jewish again by also giving angel workshops set with Jewish music."

GUIDO VAN MIERLO AUTHOR OF THE BOOK *CHILD OF THE WAFFEN SS* WROTE:

"The question that brought me to the reincarnation therapist was: Where does my low self-esteem come from and why do I have prostate cancer?" Maarten led me back in time, to the Second World War. My current father was a Dutch policeman at the time. I saw images of him filling out lists of Jews being transported. On one of those lists is the name of 15-year-old David.

I experience David's train journey, the arrival in the concentration camp, his parents being split up. How he desperately seeks his sister and desperately clings to a German guard. He receives a merciless blow from the guard with a rifle butt in his crotch (I can't pee anymore, my wiener is broken), which makes my member painfully contract. "Jews are not worthy to live', is David's experience. Finally, I undergo his death in the gas chamber, very physically. I literally feel shortness of breath and a burning sensation in my lungs. When the moment of death arrives, David's last thought is, 'this is my punishment'.

Under Maarten's supervision and in my imagination, my current personality is carrying David's dead white body out of the gas chamber, and I am overwhelmed by a wave of deep sorrow. The image is etched in my mind. I recognize, "This is the punishment I have been carrying with me for years. Enough is enough, it doesn't have to be like that anymore." I go home with a huge sense of relief.

A year before this session I wrote a biography, *Child of the Waffen-SS*, of a man whose father was also a member of the police during the war as well as involved in the persecution of the Jews. He never dared to ask his father about it. "At the time I did think: Gosh, my father was a policeman during the war. He never told me about that. I had no idea and now this...'

The details that came up during a session with Beitj Huismans about a young resistance fighter were so specific that I wrote them down. Name, age, place of residence, nature of the resistance activities, and finally even the exact location of the bullets in the body after being executed. A detailed description of exactly the same details of this person was found in the archives of the resistance museum in the Dutch city of Leeuwarden. He is buried in an honorary cemetery in the Netherlands and recently a fresh bouquet of flowers was placed on that grave...

CASE HISTORY OF A FLEEING SOLDIER

A fleeing soldier, loaded down with a heavy duffel bag on his back and ammunition and weapons hanging over his shoulders, is being chased by the enemy on the battlefield. His pocketknife, the still half-filled canteen, and a few hand-grenades rattle against each other with a dull jingling sound while his soaked army boots keep him staggering on course. He is in absolute survival mode and focusing with all his might on a single goal: a trench in the distance. "I'll be safe there" is the recurring thought racing through his helmeted head, compelling him forward. Adrenaline is pumping through his body and another, even more pressing thought arises. "I have to make it!" In addition, he is forced to leave tracks through a half-frozen field of mud. In all the mayhem, he hardly pays any attention to the stabbing pain that he suddenly feels in his neck and lower back. Exhausted and a bit dizzy, this poor soldier thinks he has to keep encouraging himself because deep down he knows that he must not give up. "Because?" I ask. "I won't make it otherwise...", my client replies, shivering and sweating. "And because I promised my fiancée that I would come back," he adds reluctantly with sadness.

At my request, he shifts his attention to the stabbing pain in his neck and lower back. He now breaks out into a sweat. "I'm getting hit!" he shouts angrily. "Dammit, no! They're shooting me down!" Pressing lightly with my finger in his neck, I imitate the spot where a life-threatening bullet penetrates. He then cries out and then painfully experiences how he falls, breaking his jaw on a stone and within moments dies gurgling at the mouth. While it is almost immediately followed by an intense feeling of relief, now a gentle stream of tears runs down his cheeks into his ears. "I didn't make it," he repeats sadly. "I have failed. I should have run faster to make it to that trench," he continues. We take the time to take stock of what had happened in the blink of an eye, by enlarging the moment and placing it in slow motion. The whole event now ripples effortlessly from his subconscious to the surface.

"I WANT TO FEEL MY TEARS"

My client, a man in his forties, tells how he was sent to the front in the Second World War as an inexperienced solider and ended up in an ambush with several buddies. Fraught with fear, he recklessly and insanely starts shooting in all directions to reach a safe place. He tells how in a short time he was forcefully trained by an arrogant, grim, self-proclaimed superior military apparatus, to which he unsuspectingly pledges his heart with his signature no less, to become a ruthless soldier who shows no mercy to his enemy. His fiancée, with whom he is madly in love, is waiting at home and he has promised her, against his better judgment, to have a future with children, he says with dismay. A vale of tears descends and the pillow on which his head is resting becomes more and more wet on either side, while his previous body dies bleeding on a cold and deserted battlefield. He doesn't want a tissue. "I want to feel my tears, they've been there for so long." He now experiences the process of his own death and sees his body, pale and broken, among many others. A large pool of blood in his crotch is clearly visible. The result of the first bullet that pierces his body in his lower back.

"Oh my God," he realizes. "That's why my abdomen always hurts so much and I'm always afraid I'll never be able to get it up again." The thought of 'never being a father ' runs through his mind, seconds before his physical death somewhere between the years 1939 and 1945. It took his wife from his current life, with whom he has two children, years to get pregnant, making him doubt himself all that time. The tension in his neck and shoulders also appears to have a deeper explanation than the physiotherapist could have imagined. And an even better bit to his story was about his depression and melancholy, of not coming into his own and always being in the pits. "I realize now, that at the time I was looking forward to that trench so much that it now seems like I only feel safe when I'm in a pit as it were. In short: so long as I'm in a pit, I'm safe and no one sees that I was in bad shape. My father always felt like that too," he realizes. Many pieces of the puzzle subsequently fall into place over the coming days and weeks.

CHAPTER 18

Rest in peace?

"The first death in every war is common sense."
– A. den Doolaard

The Latin *requiescat in pace*, the English 'rest in peace' or R.I.P. for short, has been engraved on many a tombstone for centuries. However, I must disappoint anyone who thinks that the countless soldiers who have fallen in a war are resting in peace. With all due respect to the next of kin. Whether it is the graves of the *Kriegsgräberstätte* in Hürtgen, where three thousand German soldiers found their final resting place, or the almost ten thousand graves in the American war cemetery behind Omaha Beach, at Colleville-sur-Mer; in peace there is rarely any rest.

That a (soldier) corpus is associated with rest and peace more likely indicates how those left behind view it, who understandably seek comfort in that idea. However, just as a ship in heavy weather that disappears before the eye on the horizon does not suddenly rest in peace, it is also not necessarily the case with people who die in war. These persons all too often undergo difficulties because the soul leaves the body in a jarring way. Because of this, their consciousness is in a state of confusion. It doesn't understand what's going on at very basic levels. Dying takes place physically, since the body is dead, but at a level of the soul that is not how it is experienced.

The existence of a soul is still questioned by many worldwide. In situations that really do call for it, such as in conditions when a dramatic death occurs, a lot of trouble could be prevented if it were considered seriously. Whereas in indigenous community relations it was the shamans, seers or other spiritual guides who were nominated to guide matters of the soul in the right direction, in our current world it is the highly educated, (and therefore) intellectually oriented people who usually have the authority to deal with these matters. Decision-making power, when it comes to essential human affairs, should depend on a proper degree of spiritual awareness. Ranging from organ donations, vaccinations, assisted dying and euthanasia issues to defense policy, genetic manipulation of food and using animals to test our medicines. Here decisions are made that absolutely do not match the real needs of the soul. With 'God rest his soul', a platitude from the church, the voice of the world of experience of a deceased person is silenced. By constantly discussing whether that soul exists at all, no attention is paid to the damage that one causes by letting everything be determined by reason. Among policy makers there is no decisive awareness of the spiritual essence that underlies our outer form as human beings.

DYING OUGHT TO GO HAND IN HAND WITH APPROPRIATE SPIRITUAL GUIDANCE

Some political campaigns are still proudly and confidently reinforced by such polarizing slogans as "Sympathize with victims, not perpetrators," as was read a few years ago on huge billboards along the highway. Political directions based on such views in fact produce division and therefore perpetrators; this is apparently not yet realized. When we also associate war and violence, that is swarming with victims and perpetrators, with reincarnation, a fascinating spectacle unfolds which we ourselves are part of.

If we could see the correlations between the years 1939-1945 with the present time from a holistic perspective and seriously involve them (victims and perpetrators) in political decision-making, then the course would be changed à la minute at crucial points in our so-called democratic policy. It is a bit of a shock to discover that the suffering that we once inflicted on someone else in the long term, so for example in a next life, in the end is directed at ourselves. In the meantime, the less awareness that has emerged concerning this, the more literally it will have to be repeated. That is how we can also be affected by the consequences of a dying experience in which no attention has been paid to the soul's perception of it. In this way we experience what that does to someone. Karma in a nutshell.

As I mentioned in an earlier chapter, most indigenous cultures do realize that every death must go hand in hand with appropriate spiritual guidance through ceremony and ritual, in order to reach the best possible conclusion, so that you protect the offspring from unnecessary energetic burdens. That unprocessed matters simply move to the next generation is traditionally known there.

Karmic laws have often been described and interpreted. Gina Cerminara's book *Living in Relationship* is highly recommended. In this book the views put forward by Edgar Cayce, 'the sleeping prophet' on contacts, circumstances, karma, and reincarnation, are exquisitely expressed in coherent detail on a subtle spiritual level. Joan Grant's book *More than One Life* also testifies to subtle insight. These stories fit best with reincarnation therapeutic practice. Especially since these authors unbiasedly put forward "war," like so many other scenarios that can play out in a country or territory, as a backdrop. A backdrop against which personal experience pertaining to the soul can be gained on many levels by players in need of it on their way to the finish line. I once read the beautiful line that our breathing is actually already a karmic consequence of incarnation in our dual reality. We are more likely to explain karma through violent conflict. And then it is unsophisticated to assume that we are eternally hot on each other's heels. First as a perpetrator, then as a victim with some 'lives in which we rest' in between. Karma is active on all levels of our lives, not just in terms of putting things right. When it come to the practice of reincarnation therapy, it mainly concerns the old wounds that translate to the present. The following practical example of a young mother is especially fascinating because it also clearly addresses physical complaints that are considered incurable according to the regular medical world. The cause turned out to be in the Second World War.

CASE HISTORY – HOLDING ON UNTIL DEATH

A woman in her early thirties, mother of two small children, tells me that she has a great and inexplicable fear of losing her children. "It controls my life and that of my children and my husband to a far too large extent," she says. Through regression therapy she hopes to gain clarity as to the origin of her complaints. The first signs of this fear arise during the pregnancy of her first daughter. I notice that the fingers of both her hands are contorted. It turns out to be rheumatism. It has never occurred to her before to make a connection between her request for help and the rheumatism in her hands.

Because body parts have their own consciousness, I ask her hands, while carefully taking them into mine and consciously not looking her in the eye, what they are doing. "I have to hold them," she hears herself say after slight hesitation. It has to do with having to hold the hands of her two children, as it turns out. As fear wells up inside her, her hands begin to palpably squeeze, which hurts her even more. "I have to hold them until they are dead," she repeats spontaneously with a face that grimaced with pain. All these sensations coming to the surface put her in a completely different scenario. She experiences herself as a Jewish woman with a small child on each hand at the gate of what turns out a little later to be a gas chamber, somewhere in a drab, grey concentration camp. As if from nowhere, the story then unfolds in detail. She breaks out in a cold sweat and there seems to be no turning back from the experience. Just like in the gas chamber. Totally cramped with fear and anxiety, she squeezes her children's hands almost to a pulp to avoid losing contact with them in the middle of all the other people. They are survival instincts that kick in, in such situations.

The strongest human bond between two people is that of mother and child. The forces that are released when a life-threatening situation presents itself are so great that the DNA becomes disturbed and rearranges itself. "The air smells strange," she says. Confused and in panic, the young mother notices that things are going completely wrong. Her breathing burns in her throat and lungs. Realizing that death is imminent, she concludes: "I want to witness the death of my children. I don't want to leave them alone. I can't die until I'm sure they're dead." Such decisions are made in a pure state of shock. As she herself tries to hold her breath until the last moment, squeezing her children's hands in her own totally clenched ones, she too then succumbs to suffocation. We now relive the whole thing again in the present and she snorts, gurgles and coughs like never before until she feels a magical silence flowing in. This time in the knowledge that she did not survive either.

In the insane daze of that moment, she no longer knows how it all ended. When we let her feel that there were no survivors, which is fraught with emotion, she experiences her body letting go of tension. When evaluating what happened, she learns to understand that there is still some kind of inherited programming inside her. So long as she kept squeezing and clenching her hands shut, she still had her children with her. In a manner of speaking, the awful awareness of the death of her children and herself, was something she kept on and on postponing.

Full of wonder, bewilderment but also recognition, she explains to herself the logic of the fact that her hands started to react from the moment she turned out to be pregnant in her current life.

"I became a mother again," she says. "As if those unconscious programs became active again when I became pregnant and from that moment on, I thought I had to hold onto them with my hands and witness the death of my children. Unbelievable." She recognized how this totally corresponded with her fear for the loss of her children.

We went through this whole concentration camp experience a few times. After the second time of reliving the experience of dying at the time twice, she noticed that her hands became more relaxed. At home, the fear of losing her children appears to have decreased remarkably, there is even some joy and room for other maternal matters. The last time, a few months after these sessions, she told me that there was virtually no pain left in her hands. She had reduced the medication on her own initiative. She said, "There's only one problem left now. How do I tell my rheumatologist this?"

THE BOND BETWEEN MOTHER AND CHILD

During a war, it is clear that one has to deal inordinately more with death, chaos, insecurity, fear, loss, despair, injuries, hunger and thirst than in quieter times. How this affects the different generations without all family members necessarily having to go through a war, is perhaps easier to understand if we consider the following again: the strongest bond between two persons is that of mother and child. Emotionally, spiritually, mentally but especially physically. Remember that as a soul we incarnate in order to experience life in a physical reality and that in every (womb) mother an incoming soul avails itself of a life vehicle. The mother is the condition for this, the supplier of a body. Every person remembers this bond internally and often unconsciously over a lifetime. Even if you later hate your mother. The DNA unfolds with the formation of the new body on numerous levels including predisposition to disease, talents, external features, and difficulties. And following this preliminary education, after which it depends on the breast for quite some time, one can then call oneself a real human child.

For nine months you are connected to mother like a fish with water. Inner and outer influences, such as that of a dad, impressions of external surroundings, domestic conditions, and energetic exchanges from that short time in the womb, determine not only how you will experience your own body, but also how later the outside world comes across to you. In short: as within, so without.

The next question that arises now is of course what criteria attracts a soul to a mother and a father of whom it is clear they have been shaped to a considerable extent by the experience of war. After all, thorough reincarnation research shows that the soul itself chooses incarnation, and with which parents, albeit in a fluctuating degree of consciousness. An incarnation with parents who emphatically carry the consequences of the war deep within also means that the incoming soul gets its specific portion of it. That is even the intention. A portion of war influence, embedded in the field of experience, DNA, from your parents, can help you in fulfilling your own life's mission. Of course, it's not just about the influence of the war, but about every influence that your parents have molded into their personality. For many the war has been the most decisive factor. Through biographical insight into your own family with, if necessary, some extra detective work, you can check for yourself whether you have anything to do with the war. What you should and actually do with it depends on your life plan, but those who dare to actively engage in exploring this field will always come out richer than they went into it.

According to some interpretations, it is attractive to assume that you needed your parents' war shit to be able to 'work your way out of it'. A nice thought perhaps, to want to transcend the dramas and unpleasantness of the parental home, but one that is quite implausible. The reality that reveals itself during sessions is often, equally as different from what was initially thought, as it is sobering. In the confrontation with your parent's pain caused by the war you may also have to deal with having to compensate for a personal experience from a past life at the time of that same war. It could even be an act which you have condemned yourself for. You may have acted out of self-defense, or you were like a rat in a trap of deception and conflicts of interest, as was often the case in NSB (Dutch National Socialist) situations.

For example, suppose you discover that it was you who shot your grandmother's brother. Or that you unintentionally took the life of another family member from the previous generation of your current family, indirectly, because you detested your brother at the time who was not with the NSB (or precisely because he was a member), after which you also died. Or, for instance, because you turned in the people who were in hiding on the farm of the person you were hopelessly in love with, but who had rejected you. Or because at dusk you shot the wrong person who turned out afterwards to be an acquaintance from the village, and no one ever knew that you did it. The emptiness thus created resulting from this can become a reason for you to want to fill it with your own, new incarnation. Many, if not all, of your qualities and life forces are then consumed in undoing the grief in your family until you become exhausted. You never get to dealing with yourself because you didn't learn to live for yourself, and to discharge emotions stemming from an old, but very defining event.

Nor is it an exception if you decided on a whim in a past life to end your life because of the hopelessness of the war. Dazed and overcome with grief, you left a loved one behind, perhaps with children. In your new life, in which you consider yourself unimportant, you now want to make everything right for your partner and / or children. You get bogged down in pleasing others at your own expense. In short: we all too often incarnate in the nest of consequences that we once already caused ourselves. The boomerang came back again from the one who once threw it away. But how honest can you be with yourself? This is a crucial question. Pride and ego prefer to dominate everything, and it remains to be seen how long this can be sustained. Are you still too impressionable because of that? In that case you probably haven't been able to get this far in the book. But for those who do have the courage to switch, it is encouraging to know that during processes of working through things, an appeal can always be made to what is the inherent forgiving and loving nature of the creation of which we are a part. A creation that makes new opportunities possible at any time.

THE LOGIC OF THE SOUL IS DIFFERENT FROM THAT OF THE MIND

Reincarnation therapy makes it possible to follow paths taken by souls that preceded the current conception. It can become clear, for instance, that a considerable amount of war stress on the future parents is actually desirable to bring to an end that which had previously stagnated. I call this the logic of the soul, a very different kind of logic from that of the mind.

For example, a former German soldier, a pilot with the Luftwaffe, incarnates as a boy into a new, current life in a Dutch, Jewish family that on his mother's side had been blown to pieces during the war by a German air raid. This is incomprehensible to the mind. His soul, however, sees it differently: it says that it is important to be keenly sensitive to and therefore understand what people experience when they constantly feel threatened and unsafe by planes flying over dropping bombs. In this family, the deeply hidden but powerful guilt about his actions at the time is now constantly fed, especially by his mother. This mother is an active member of a working group on Jewish War Victims. From the point of view of the logic of his soul he experiences this as a consummation of a 'punishment' he called upon himself. Although the word punishment needs to be interpreted in relative terms. In this scenario, the soul, which is aware of its multidimensional identity, in the long-term sees new possibilities to come to forgiveness and thereby let go and make new choices. But first it is important to experience the downside of the lust for power 'from on high', from the other side. This is how people describe it to me in my practice, while from the depths of their being, totally vulnerable, they go through intense and emotional re-experiences.

Sometimes it seems that souls reluctantly incarnate when they 'have to' start a life.

Nevertheless, the soul-in-essence cannot wait. It seeks to become whole and therefore knows that entering this kind of life trajectory gives it the opportunity to do so. For the soul, an incarnation to a difficult life is comparable to a visit to the dentist when you have a severe toothache. However, we suffer more from ignorance of karma than karma itself. In fact, so much has already been worked out karmically and virtually ripe to be forgiven, that during sessions you don't even have to work unduly hard to let matters yield to surrender. Ripe apple sessions, I sometimes call them.

How a general, who died at the line of communication, is buried... and how the proletarians slaughtered at the front are dragged away.

OPPOSITE ROLES IN THE SAME WAR

CHAPTER 19

Stringing war lives

"War is nothing more than a continuation of political interaction by other means."
– Carl von Clausewits

The stories in this chapter provide insight into how multiple lives of the same soul are thematically connected to each other. Some clients are quite driven to rid themselves of old ballast through reincarnation therapy. The starting point for them, is a deep awareness that multiple lives are lived and can affect the current one. The advantage is that the inner critic does not always feel the need to keep control over the information provided from the subconscious. In that way this area is more easily accessible, and on a broader scale. It also makes it possible to work quite purposefully so that the exploration of past lives, where necessary, runs smoothly. It would even seem that more is achieved with less effort from both client and therapist. A therapeutic question put to a client in a trance during a session, such as: "Can you now see in which situation in your previous life, the exact same convictions arose as in this situation in your current childhood?" is then answered quite clearly. Being able to grasp this insightful dialogue would usually be much too remote if too much thought was given to it.

Obviously, the success of a therapeutic trajectory depends on many factors, but sometimes the time is just ripe for people to knock down the house of cards that was built a long time ago, in which they have been imprisoned for quite some time. How special and powerful is it when the cause of deep-rooted patterns suddenly comes into the picture in a logical way, in a very broad, transpersonal spectrum? The various lives with so many differences between them now turn out to be very clearly the chapters of the same book, in which the protagonists flow together internally even though they were different characters at the time. It also becomes clear which life experiences people need, in order to negate tenaciously stuck patterns, so that they can open themselves up again to new life adventures and associated life visions. Stringing lives!

It makes sense to process the childhood pain that someone suffered due to the psychological and physical aggression of his father. It makes more sense to learn to see that dad's behavior stemmed from the early loss of his father, or his grandfather. And it is even more meaningful to learn that that grandfather, overcome by fear and mistrust arising from the war, died because he had to work his fingers to the bone to pay off a bank loan to keep his head above water. And when it also becomes clear that systems are deliberately devised that entrap millions of people in similar ways, even in the course of many lifetimes, then – finally – an even bigger picture becomes visible. But consider the story below. Isn't it incredibly encouraging to see how determined a soul naturally is to want to end up with its feet on the ground again after so many detours?

CASE HISTORY – FRANCOIS FROM LIEGE

When Francois from Liège was 21 years old, he was called up to take part in the First World War in 1914. He departs with a feeling of excitement. A raw recruit, part of a much larger battalion of raw recruits. Francois promises Germaine, his lover, to come back in one piece. They have a child together and the second one is on the way. Francois offers her and their children a bright future. He does not consciously experience that he is being opportunistic, although a gut feeling gives off other signals. It is the young male bravado as is so often present in wartime.

The senses are incapable of processing the reality on the battlefield. To some extent, a built-in protection mechanism shields the overwhelming amount of hopelessness, horror, and neglect of human values. Francois' soldier's eyes see an incredible number of dead bodies of young men wearing the same uniform as him. With torn limbs and the most abhorrent mutilations. As if uniformly scattered over a muddy landscape with craters and shattered trees, he sees carcasses of horses, human bodies, and the wounded everywhere. The living are in the throes of madness. They move automatically. Groaning to themselves or one other and moaning under their breath, dragging their bodies forward, because walking is no longer possible. He more or less gets used to the continuous flow with which he filters his observations to manageable proportions. He wakes up to these images, if he even managed to sleep at all.

In his experience, the German opponent turns out to be a vast powerful military god. Francois is not one of those soldiers with polished helmets who received training that made them invincible. Proud soldiers in a well-organized army with much better weapons than his simple rifle and bayonet. Soldiers with superiors who knew strategically what they were talking about and always had an organized and well-thought-out battle plan. Soldiers who could stay strong because they were well fed, so that they could always be one step ahead of the enemy.

With numb hands, Francois opens his pocket diary one last time in which Germaine longingly looks at him from a sepia photo degraded by moisture. The more he weakens, the more she comes to life. With a look that has been in his dreams the past few weeks. His cold, hungry body has no strength left. The infection from the huge leg wound caused by an artillery shell explosion has exhausted his body. And now that his end is approaching, he tries to persevere, not to give in to a desperate attempt to be saved by men with stretchers, whom he sees walking back and forth in the distance. Francois fights against the desperate realization that he will not be able to keep the promise he made to his sweetheart. He muses about what it would have been like to win the war, come home glorious and feel proud. A basis for a long and happy life. To no avail. He doesn't even consciously experience his last breath. Francois is already too dissociated from his battered and half-frozen body, which has almost fused with the mud and snow in the trench. Energetically entwined with the miserable reality of his last moments of existence, he must have thought; so long as my leg is throbbing and hurting, the cold is there and I am surrounded by hopeless sadness, I am still alive. Until the candle goes out.

His intense desire for connection, sharing love and experiencing fatherhood, sends Francois into a new incarnation. His memories of the misery of the war left two very defining thoughts in him. "Anyone born in the Netherlands does not have to go to war." He knew that from the Dutch branch of his beloved wife's family. After all, the Netherlands was neutral in World War I. And the second thought: "if you're taking part in a war, make sure you join the most well-organized army with the best and most weapons. Then you still have a chance to come home in one piece and live a good life with your wife and children."

Mainly regarding the first consideration and in the hope of finding traces of the family of his (former) beloved who probably fled to the Netherlands, Francois is reborn in the Netherlands. Somewhere in Limburg, near the Belgian border, so that he could get a sidelong whiff of the once familiar energy of Belgium, while for his new body a life path has been rolled out in another country. Willem is his name now. By the time Willem is twenty, a new threat is already looming over Europe. The echoes of the First World War form the breeding ground for a new bloody conflict. When the Netherlands, together with Belgium and Luxembourg, is taken by Germany in 1940, Willem is faced with a terrible choice: which army am I going to join? The German Army recruitment program wins out. Willem joins the Waffen SS, a paramilitary organization with which you can become a full member of the German army. He takes for granted both the horrors and the humiliations suffered by the German officers who gave him his military training in Munich. They did not outweigh the prospect of a successful outcome to the war. Willem turns his back on his Dutch family, and thus his birthplace. He cannot do otherwise. He makes his decision from deep inside, based on the ultimate conviction of coming out of the war alive this time. "One day my family will understand why", Willem thinks. Against his better judgment, he hopes for their approval once the outcome of the war is clear in the future.

The war years are once again horrific. William is sent to the Eastern Front and during the endless journey, he kills and violates Russian women. He gets carried away with what has become commonplace within the group of frustrated soldiers consisting mainly of Dutch SS men. Wherever possible, the German SS men who feel superior remain aloof to their inferior fake colleagues. It results in a mutually tense atmosphere in a freezing cold climate during a hopeless mission, in which the Germans keep the warmer clothes and the best food for themselves. It gradually becomes clear to Willem that he would never be able to live up to the ideal image of the invincible soldier he dreamed about. He is shunned not only by his own family, but now also by those he hoped would be his new family. And again, he finds himself in a no man's land. Everything is cold and hopeless again and yet again he longs, in vain, for someone who is unreachable. Where it was once Germaine, now it is his mother, whom he is convinced is disappointed in him. That she condemns him as a gutless quitter. His dream is already in ruins even before he will die again. He now realizes that there is no future in joining the ranks of this side in the war either. Whether as an ordinary Belgian soldier or a Dutch SS soldier, it doesn't make any difference. Willem had such a completely different idea of what it would be like.

To make matters worse, when the war is decided differently than he initially believed, he is executed as a war criminal before a firing squad, together with many colleagues. He never comes home and neither does his body. No one will ever know what happened to me, Willem thinks. Multiple bullets strike him in and around his heart. Several last thoughts are deeply etched inside him: "I am bad, I do not deserve to live, love does not belong to me, I am unworthy of a woman, my death is justified, and I am worth nothing."

Once dead, in a dimension after physical death, Willem's soul experiences being under a grey veil. He has no idea where he is and is hardly aware of his disembodied state. There is an indefinable but compelling need to want to make amends. In 1955 Willem is born again, once more in the Netherlands, as the third child of a family that suffered enormously from the consequences of the war. His name is Dirk.

Dirk's eldest sister is called Jenny, then comes his brother Jan, then Dirk and after him three other children. Dirk and Jan are very close. Together they are able to stand up to their mother who favors Jenny enormously and heavy-handedly lets her sons know how worthless they are, that they are nobodys and only cause her trouble. Jenny is her 'everything'. Mother herself lost her father and brother in a bombing raid during the war. As a result, she was very much left to her own resources and had to do a lot on her own. Emotionally, she is a wreck. As a child she was the apple of her father's eye, and she experienced his death as a personal rejection. She cannot put the loss into perspective by seeing it from the point of view of war. Mother projects the pain of her father onto her husband and sons. She dominates her husband and makes him do the dirty work. Against his will, she urges him to punish their sons regularly, not shying away from severe physical violence. Dirk grows up under the influence of a mother who finds him worthless, confirming to the utmost his ingrained belief that he is unworthy of a woman. Dirk is 18 when, after the umpteenth beating by his father, he no longer wants to live. It's 1973. While doing his job, he deliberately works his way into the rotating parts of an agricultural machine and dies a horrible death. He sticks his arms in, knowing there is no way back. Driven by the beliefs 'I'm worthless ', 'I can't make up for it' and 'I don't deserve to live'.

Once the family hears the news, it's Jan who is most devastated. Although Dirk's tragic death is presented to the outside world as a fatal accident, his mother has been touched to the deepest core of her perception of the world. For the first time in many years. It marks a turning-point in her trapped feelings, awakening the memories of her father and brother from many layers and years of denial and isolation. Mother makes an inward journey back to her younger years, before she lost her beloved father and her lovely brother. Tears come, old tears that now mix with those of the loss of her son. She painfully realizes how brutally they raised him, wondering wordlessly whether her evil influence was part of Dirk's 'accident'. At the same time, she realizes how she has influenced her husband who has battered their children so often.

Once dead, Dirk has not realized the full extent of his emotional legacy. It overwhelms him. What keeps him bound to them is not only the realization of the enormous grief his death triggers in his brother Jan, but also he can now experience all his mother's sincere but painful considerations from a place of deeper feeling. At the same time, he experiences that his self-convictions and feelings of guilt still bother him. What is more, as a soul entity, he clings especially to his brother Jan who is inconsolable. They cannot let go of each other internally. Jan was on the verge of leaving the parental home, but now does so with a heavy heart. Apart from all the blows he himself received and his mother's painful rejection, he has now also lost his favorite brother. He starts his life as a violated man. His mother's rejection cause all sorts of problematic relationships with women. What follows are three marriages, three divorces and seven children.

Mirjam is born in Jan's second short-lived marriage. Father Jan and his partner have already become separated during the pregnancy. Mirjam, however, is determined to make her appearance. She is the new incarnation of Dirk, this time as a girl. "Because girls are not rejected and do not have to go to a war if it breaks out."

Mirjam has a huge desire to be with her father Jan, who was previously her brother. She wants, in the name of her earlier personality Dirk, to make up for everything because he has abandoned him so abruptly. "I want to see my father happy again, I want to be meaningful to him," she says. Before Mirjam was born, her mother had been pregnant with Jan. Under the circumstances at the time, Jan pressures her to have an abortion. Mirjam says that it had been her. "The doctor who performed the abortion pulverizes me in the womb with his equipment when I'm almost three months old." The word she uses brings the memory to the surface of Dirk's being pulverized to death in the agricultural machine. "They don't want me. You see, I'm worthless," are the delirious thoughts of the fetus. But they don't stop her from getting a second chance. Another incarnation follows in the same womb. Now that the birth is imminent, Mirjam still feels a great deal of reluctance. She is pervaded by the thought of really having to become visible this time. The contractions cause her to feel threatened, making Mirjam resist. Then the forceps appear. "I am pulled into life," Mirjam tensely says. The resemblance to Dirk's accident, in which he was also pulled, is immediately envisaged. "The agricultural machine pulled me to my death, the forceps pulled me into life. How is that possible?"

As an adult now, she says: "I go berserk as soon as anyone starts pulling at me."

There is a moment of panic during the delivery when the little body is being pushed through the birth canal. After all, Mirjam has been resisting and therefore gets stuck at a certain point. Her breathing stops. Again, that reliving of Dirk's moment of death. "I can't go back." Yet now, thanks to the forceps, she is emerging. Shuddering, but also deeply touched and in a kind of surrender, she experiences her first breaths. "I am living... again", Mirjam now emotionally observes, still breathing in fits and starts.

Mirjam is now 29 years old and my client. She suffers from temper tantrums and immediately becomes defensive as soon as there is a hint of anyone expressing an opinion. Especially when there are expectations or when people or situations appeal to her. Frustrations that, as it turns out during the therapeutic process, have their origin in the inability to 'make things right with her father Jan'. She never really got to know her father after her parents divorced. He was always somewhere else, purportedly not interested. Because Mirjam already sensed a divorce while she was still in the womb, she has identified herself as the cause for his departure. "He's mad at me, he doesn't want me," she concludes. Now she "sees" her father in every man who crosses her path. She anxiously wants to bind herself to men through sex, each time repeatedly experiencing extreme anger. It is an energy-consuming game of excessively attracting and repelling men. With her current partner she now has two children, a boy and a girl. He has been offered a job in Germany so that the family will soon be moving to Hamburg. The turmoil Mirjam feels is enormous. "I'm so ashamed," she says now, referring to Willem's part in the war. "I never wanted to have anything to do with him again." She associates Germany with him in a very general way. She is now able to put it into perspective, given the awareness of the previous history as Francois. "He was also just a poor soul looking for happiness who didn't know what he was doing."

And so, we see Mirjam's previous personalities correlating in a very transpersonal context. Francois from Liège in the First World War, followed by Willem, Dirk, an abortion and finally Mirjam. Before that there was probably already a line of personalities in past lives, but for Mirjam it was not yet necessary to do any more research. She had reached a point of contentment with herself after this whole process.

This makes it clear that the soul continuously searches for situations or possibilities in which to incarnate and uses them to enable healing and completion of old unfinished events. The new players, family members in new family constellations, all have an important role to play in this. They have a reflective effect on the soul, which reconnects it with those emotional charges it left behind, but that still require attention. Of course, Mirjam also has a mirroring role for her fellow players here. Seen in this way, everything is interactive, and the soul strives for reunification and harmonization of old, damaged scenes.

Mirjam makes little effort to remember the content of all the sessions. If necessary, the broad outlines can be called up. But she is doing well now, there is no more agitation, the turmoil has decreased, and she is doing fun things, with her children as well. There are also no more spasms in her body after having once relived being mangled in an agricultural machine. “It is special that we live close to the Johan Willem Friso Armory,” says Mirjam. “That way I am still reminded of that military stuff. And maybe that explains why I always wanted to be a boy as a child.”

Emperor William II by the grace of God.

Keizer Wilhelm II, bij de gratie Gods.

“War is an element of the world order determined by God.” (Count Molte)

„De oorlog is een element, van de door God bepaalde wereldorde”. (Graaf Moltke.)

OPPOSITE ROLES IN THE SAME WAR

CHAPTER 20

The Black Hand

"Don't criticize your fellow man until you've walked in his moccasins for a day."
– Lakota piece of wisdom

The many stories I heard about the lives of ancestors are insanely compelling. Frequently characterized by intense heartache and incredibly mordant fates. I am regularly amazed by what ancestors went through in a single lifetime. It is sometimes beyond comprehension how it is possible for someone to cope with so much adversity. At any rate that they could survive in one existence.

The life story below is about Susan's family. It serves as an example of someone who has been through so unimaginably much in a single lifetime. Remember that the offspring, in this case Susan, walks the earth in the now. You see people everywhere, but you don't see their history, their ancestry. How fascinating is it to see how everything turns out to be connected? The common thread of this story concerns the life of Susan's grandmother, Johanna. Follow her, and imagine how it must have been to walk in her 'moccasins'.

Susan is 31 years old when she pays a visit to my practice. She is married and has two children, a four-year-old son and two-year-old daughter. "I have a lot of trouble with my children," she says. "I keep them at a distance all the time and find it very difficult to get attached to them. I'm ashamed of it, but I regularly fly into a fit of temper and am just able to suppress my feeling of wanting to beat them. They take up my space. There's no place for me, it's just like I'm not allowed to be here." She makes no bones about it and is immediately in tears. Close to despair, that's how Susan feels.

When Susan turned 16, her mother, Meta, told her that she is actually one of twins. The other child died during pregnancy after five or six months. "It was just thrown away, like garbage."

Susan's parents are 51 and 53 and they are still together. Father Gijs has been out of contact with his own family since he was 14 or 15 years old. He never talked about it. He always works hard, is introverted, never speaks about himself and always keeps his feelings inside. "He was there but not really," says Susan. Mother Meta is very caring, to the point of being overprotective. She is an expert in effacing herself for the benefit of others. "I don't know how she manages it, but my mother always has someone around her who is more important than herself," Susan stresses. As a child in the parental home Meta was already the caring daughter alongside her own mother. She was always used for all kinds of housework and taking care of her younger brothers and sisters.

Father Gijs has an older half-brother and a half-sister. When his mother Johanna's first husband, dies, twins are born from a new man she is forced to have sex with followed by Gijs, also born from a rape.

Grandma Johanna, Gijs' mother, and Susan's grandmother is originally from Indonesia. In the early forties, when she is only six, the family is brutally removed from their home. A 'black hand', as she once said, pushed her into a closet and then locked it. She still hears her mother screaming among the foulmouthed, menacing voices of soldiers. She intuitively realizes that she shouldn't react to that. After a while, the locked closet becomes so oppressive that in desperation Johanna kicks open the door. There she is, a child all by herself in the abandoned parental home. Dazed, she shuffles into the garden where she is taken care of a little later by the old neighbor who, as it turns out, was the black hand. He wanted to save her from the horrors of the camps because 'children certainly don't survive there'. Johanna is taken by the neighbor to a shelter. There is a nice woman who takes care of her. Finally, after a few years, Johanna, now nine years old, becomes reunited with her parents. The reunion is incredibly emotional. Separated from each other, Johanna's father and mother survived the camp horrors, consumed with anxiety about whether their daughter would still be alive. Like so many fellow sufferers, they decide to go to the Netherlands to find happiness and a future. There, somewhere in Amsterdam, however, they encounter a reality that is not their own.

However much he tries, father is totally unable to feel at home here. He has been deeply wounded by the horrors of the camp. As time passes, the trauma takes its toll. Nightmares and fears plague his existence. Psychologically, he is so dislocated that he can no longer have normal social contact. He alienates himself from life and from his environment. He dies when Johanna is only 12 years old. Johanna is now alone in Amsterdam with her mother. Together they try to build a life. When Johanna is 17 she meets a Dutch man with whom she falls in love and marries shortly afterwards.

They have two children, a son and daughter. Her husband has a hidden, dark past. During the war he became entangled in a dangerous network where he had to do odd jobs for the Germans. Although the war has been over for years, he is recognized, arrested, and summarily executed by firing squad. A post-war act of revenge. Johanna totally panics. Her husband's death brings the trapped grief of her own father's death to the surface. All of Amsterdam reminds her of her husband. She wants to leave. With her mother and two children she flees to the east of the country.

She diligently goes in search of a new partner to protect her and her children. In desperation, she clings to the first man to give her attention. An easy prey, as if she has sensed it. Paul had originally been something of a backward child. Regularly made out to be crazy, no one really took him seriously. She seduces him by offering herself and two children as a family. That's an incredible thing for him. No one ever imagined that he would find himself in such a privileged situation. They even get married. Their deep-seated hidden agendas and emotions make it impossible for them to grow accustomed to each other in a healthy way, moreover Paul still bears a deep trauma from the war. The seeds of estrangement have already been planted from day one of their marriage. In the meantime, Johanna's thoughts are always with her first husband.

Paul was arrested as a teenager during the war and taken to Dachau in Germany where he was put to work. He was abused there and the reality he encountered was so overwhelming that he cannot integrate it. Everyone thinks he's dead. He stays away for a long time. Completely unexpectedly, Paul returns one day, totally screwed up and distraught by all the horrors he has experienced in the camp. He becomes a quiet, introverted, emotionally damaged man. On the surface he looks calm, at most not very sociable. Joanna does not know Paul's war history. But as the years go by, his camp experiences take their toll. Already condemned by his own family who never took him seriously, he can't really get used to the fact that he now has a wife and two children by his side that are not his. He does not know what position to take, and communication stagnates on all sides. Paul drinks too much, causing his silent demeanor to become severely interrupted by tantrums. His behavior becomes unpredictable and increasingly unstable. "I don't recognize him anymore, he's completely insane" says Johanna. She rejects him, as his family already has, and that makes Paul's blood boil. He rapes her, staking his claim to Johanna's promise that she wanted to offer him a family with perhaps another child of their own. The rape results in Johanna giving birth to twins, a boy and a girl. She totally rejects the children and cannot deal with them. Another child, a boy named Gijs, results from yet another rape. Paul distances himself from Johanna and the children. Johanna is seduced by a neighbor and completely ignores Paul. Her children grow up with this new man and Paul dies of cardiac arrest a few years later.

The twins and Gijs are ordered to do whatever their mother and stepfather want. Their demands are excessive. They leave the parental home and grow up in various shelter homes. When Gijs is 14 matters escalate between his stepfather and him; he breaks off contact with his mother, stepfather, half-brother, and half-sister. A total break. When Johanna dies of colon cancer in 1997, none of her children are at the funeral.

After her death, Grandma Johanna, remains stubbornly attached to her granddaughter Susan, as a confused spirit. She directs Susan's every move. Susan is the only one who still connects her to her family. Internally, she is consumed by anger, aggression, and despair. Something that Susan constantly feels from the energy generated in her by her grandmother. Grandma considers Susan's children to be hers and wants to compensate for her own violated motherhood by throwing herself at Susan's children. Susan now understands why a wedge has been driven between her and her children.

Grandma Johanna's harrowing life story is given space. She allows herself to hear about all the low points and all emotions are let go. Susan and I help discharge everything. Now the realization is starting to sink in with Grandma Johanna that she has an undermining impact on Susan and her children. She can then finally let go and let her granddaughter Susan live her own life. Susan's life takes a turn after this. Peace comes to the family. And more importantly: she can now really start bonding with her children and her own life. "It's unbelievable what my Grandmother Johanna went through in a lifetime", Susan sighs with understanding.

CHAPTER 21

Perpetrator lives

"The New Testament is the only detective novel that clearly points to the reader as the perpetrator."
– Jan Hein Donner

Anyone who takes reincarnation seriously and discovers its most basic principles cannot avoid the realization that you have also lived lives as a perpetrator. That you carry experiences in you where you have wronged others in the most diverse ways. Whoever excludes reincarnation outright also excludes that idea, and perhaps that is also the purpose of exclusion. But in doing so, many former perpetrators, the internally convicted, are deprived of their right to be. That's a different approach than non-believers who claim that people who adhere to reincarnation do so because they cannot accept mortality. Creation does not know the phenomenon of exclusion, so if perpetrators are in a zone of exclusion, something will always have to be done to reintegrate the outcast back into the fold. The person who has to take the basic responsibility for this must again be made aware of the presence of these aspects in order to make the process of working through something, and forgiveness, possible. In the first instance, new personalities, people who have reincarnated again, are confronted with these things through mirrors held up by their immediate environment, in the form of family members and relationships and circumstances that arouse all sorts of turbulent emotions. The interactions with these people leave behind charges that accumulate in the body and manifest themselves sooner or later. It is a laudable goal to want to let go of the past, but that can only be done if the essences of these old experiences are allowed into our consciousness. Otherwise, you have undergone those experiences for nothing. In concrete terms, this means that it is important to be able to show compassion and understanding for someone who has hurt you enormously. That person was in fact a mirror of yourself from past lives that allowed you to experience what you once caused yourself. Because the outcast usually manifests itself through complaints, such as illness, problems, and blockages, that is not really appreciated. We don't recognize those demands for attention as such because we grew up in a culture of exclusion. That is why we have become specialized in symptom control.

Anyone who, under the auspices of his own much-needed titles, also concludes that we are 'our brain', has gone too far. A more advanced form of excluding past lives does not exist. In that case there is a pressing need 'not to remember'. The identification with rational thought then has such a grip on you that you are no longer aware of the pitfall in which you yourself are trapped by the limitations of that same rationality. You tell yourself, through extensive research, that you have come to these conclusions without acknowledging the limitations of your research methods. But those conclusions were actually already drawn in advance because you don't want to remember things for which you did not want to take responsibility. The sole purpose of your findings, which are in fact predictable, is confirming your own conclusions. Preferably in the hope of gathering many supporters to make the field of influence you wish to believe in, as large as possible.

No one is to blame, for we drink from the Lethe, the river of oblivion, before we incarnate. We remember what we can handle, which in turn depends on your development of consciousness, and on the degree of judgments within the society in which you now exist. Do you feel safe enough?

The case history below concerns the courageous personal report of Saskia, a client from my practice. It is the story of someone who wishes to remember, even if that is a real struggle. But the results speak for themselves. These experiences are by no means a rarity in my practice and that of many colleagues, and worth highlighting in every respect. That illness and health are closely connected to facing yourself has been proven as far as I am concerned. I would like to encourage everyone to dare to investigate themselves like Saskia. It delivers more than you could have ever imagined because all is Love, but you have to discover that for yourself.

SASKIA'S STORY

The reason for my session with Maarten was physical: I had back pain, knots in my upper back and eczema on my eyes, on my face and in my cavities. For this story it is important to know that in my current life I am a musician, a cellist. My connection with the cello is intense and has existed since I was six years old. Music helps me express what I am not able to put into words. Even when I receive messages, this often goes through the 'ray of music'. Through a previous session with Maarten, I already know that I have had something to do with being a perpetrator in a war. At that time, the theme was only acknowledged and not dealt with in detail.

Maarten says that the physical complaints I have now may have to do with a life during the war. The perpetrator in me has completely closed himself off and made himself small. I feel it near my heart area. He is nervous because of the fear that when he comes out, he will fall back into the indignation of the past.

Maarten led me back to the Second World War. The perpetrator in me was a man, whom I will call Verlin. Verlin was working in a concentration camp at the time. He held a high position and took his work very seriously. His position of power meant everything to him. His task was to sort the deportees who entered the camps: who had to go to work and who had to be sent straight into the gas chambers? He sorted by man/woman, young/old, vital/weak, Jewish/non-Jewish/Aryan appearance.

Sometimes he gave people the benefit of the doubt so that they were put to work first. He was quite harsh and ambitious. People never lasted long. He smelled death and destruction day in and day out. He thought it was disgusting. But Verlin stayed put from an idealistic belief in Hitler's ideas.

The intensity of camp life only served to make his faith stronger, precisely because it was the only thing he could hold onto. Cut off from his emotional life and from his body, he relegated himself to living only in his mind with this faith. Where did Verlin get this? As a boy from a large family, he was raised with a heavy hand. His father, who survived the First World War, but came out of it badly damaged emotionally, was always in charge and excessively strict. His mother was not taken seriously by his father, she was even scorned. Father looked down on mother and found her totally unimportant; all he cared about was playing one big happy family to the outside world. The boy Verlin also learned that from his father. What's more, mother was approached with distrust. She was not that big, she often wore white clothes, had brown and long and curly hair and dark brown eyes: her appearance indicated Jewish ancestors.

Father, who gradually began to adopt Hitler's ideas, started to suspect and detest her. This terrified his mother who thought that she would be caught one day and arrested. And her fear came true. In a swift raid, in which a few men in uniform invaded the house, mother was arrested and taken away never to return. At that moment, the now young teenager Verlin died inside. He froze with grief and, above all, was terrified that he would be the next to be arrested and handed over. However, this did not happen. His father took the boy with him for a career in the SS. The boy followed in his father's footsteps. The boy's compulsion to prove himself was fueled even more by the fear of getting caught for having Jewish blood. He went on to overcompensate for himself, for his alleged Jewish origin, in the figure of an SS man.

During life in the camp, when sorting out prisoners, Verlin's attention was mainly focused on the children. This appears to have caused him the greatest pain. When he pointed to the right with his arm, he sent them to the gas chambers. When he pointed to the left, he sent them to work. He sent far too many children to their deaths with his right hand. Hungover for the umpteenth time from the previous night, when he had to go back to work sorting the children all over again, just seeing them made Verlin wish he would be the one who would die. He realized that it was he who ought to die because of his Jewish blood. In fact, time after time he sent himself to death whenever he raised his right hand.

How did Verlin survive? And what did he do on the days no trains arrived? He then had two distractions. Women and booze: he drank and fucked like crazy. He selected his women himself during his sorting jobs. They had to be full-bodied and look anxious. "Resistance is more fun than some feeble submission." This pastime was a perfect way to strengthen his position of power vis-à-vis his colleagues and that is why Verlin sometimes allowed them to share 'his' women. To him, gaining a position of power was essential. "I must set a good example here. Otherwise, we won't get anywhere with this screwed up bunch."

What method did Verlin use to select people? Which sense did he use the most? That of sight. His eyes played a crucial role in this process. The eyes were so connected to the suffering they saw, they energetically took the blame. The eyes have seen so much suffering, so much pain and many disgusting things. A person's fate depended on his eyes. That was the cause of the eye rash in the current incarnation. During the session this point had to be clearly stressed by saying to the eyes that they were innocent. And that they had purely and simply received a task. Realizing this: how does Verlin look back on the judging, the good and the evil, the feeling of superiority, the selecting? He realizes that it is an illusion, a disgusting illusion. Deep down he knew that from the beginning, but he did not dare admit his feelings. That would mean he would fall from his position of power and, moreover, it would throw him back to being the little boy with Jewish blood. The turning point came one late night, after a day's work. Verlin was walking across the campgrounds, to the spot behind the gas chamber where the corpses were piled up. He was only a few meters from the first pile. Only then did he fully realize just how many corpses there were. A horrible number, piles as far as the eye could see, way too many...

He smelled death and destruction. This was the moment when something snapped in him. He felt so guilty. Every fiber of his being was filled with the realization that he had sent all these people to their deaths. "What did I do?" It was an intensely emotional moment. At one point, his eye falls on a child's arm. He can't tell if it's a boy or a girl, as it is buried under other corpses. In the session I say 'he' to the corpse, so afterwards it turns out to be a boy. Verlin grabbed the cold boy's hand and realized, "This should have been me."

The next thing he knew, his fear and shame almost kept him from doing what he did, kissing the boy's hand. He felt that he loved the boy, and that he was so sorry for what he had done. He promised himself right there and then never ever to kill anyone again. With the kiss on the hand, he identified himself with death. Verlin then broke down and fell to his knees with the corpses behind him.

"ECZEMA IS A REMINDER OF HOW DEPLORABLE MY ACTIONS ARE"

In my current life, my eczema is in the cavities of the knees and elbows. In the moment of falling to his knees, the scar of death stuck to Verlin from behind. On a deep level he chose this because he identified himself with death. The connection with the session was that I wanted to get rid of my eczema. Do I still want this, now that I know what it stands for? "No, because I'm not entitled to that. I feel terrible as a perpetrator. It's a reminder of how deplorable my actions are." Maarten said: "I get that. Maybe the secret is that you don't need eczema anymore now that you're completely aware of what happened. You don't need a reminder anymore because you remember everything now."

Finally, Verlin was caught out by colleagues, and branded a weakling defector. Crying and weakness, of course, were not accepted. Everything collapsed for him after that, and he lost his powerful position. Verlin was swiftly seized by his upper arms and dragged away. He tried to defend himself with lame excuses. They didn't fall for them and took Verlin to be hanged. It went through his mind, "Oh, all that remains now is making a big show out of it." During his hanging he tried desperately to cling to the last vestiges of his imagined position of power. At that moment, mortal fear, firmly attached itself to his neck and upper back. In my current life, these are exactly the painful knots in my muscles that always bother me. With Maarten's help I experienced Verlin's choking to death as physically as possible, with all the resistance he put up. Then Verlin lay down and it was quiet.

After a while, he realized that he felt groggy. Being dead did not bring him the relief he had hoped for. "This groggy feeling is yet another way of escape, of not having to feel." Maarten helped him to realize that this piece of 'not having to feel' meant he had now incarnated yet again.

Looking back on all those corpses, Verlin realized that he has never felt so small. He wished himself dead and felt he was not entitled to anything else. At the same time, there was the suffering he had inflicted on so many. "I'm so sorry, I'm so sorry. I don't think I have the right to say anything to all these victims. But I would like to wish everyone to come through this terrible drama of karma and continue on the way to the Light. I realize that we are all one and that there is no judgment. Judgment is an illusion of separateness. Maarten, would you like to say that to them?" Maarten replies: "Yes, but I think these people would much rather hear it from you. Without me in between." "I'm so sorry, I was the perpetrator... and all those children... I wish everyone a path of light, and hope that one day I can be forgiven. I realize that we are all one." Maarten then heard a voice resound. "Maybe you would like to play for us sometime?" I was moved on the spot and immediately agreed. "Yes, of course, I'd love to..." The voice turned out to come from the boy whose hand Verlin had kissed. The little boy was standing next to me... "I was musical too," he said. The souls of the boy and me turned out to be connected to each other, because an entanglement of karma has been played out. This time I was the perpetrator, and he was the victim. In another life, I was the victim, and he was the perpetrator. Because no experience is complete without having played the role of the opposite. We wanted to do this for each other. It also helps to put Verlin's childhood that underlies these dramatic events firmly into perspective. It doesn't make up for it but makes it somewhat understandable. Trauma begets trauma for as long as it is not brought out into the open and not allowed to be expressed.

PLAYING CELLO FOR THE VICTIMS

The day after the session I played the cello at home for all the victims from the camp. I invited everyone and decorated my living room with beautiful crystals and candles and a lovely wooden gate.

I had a palpable sensation of the space filling. It made me nervous, but most of all it fulfilled in me the urge to want to play for everyone. It was so necessary. I improvised in three phases. First based on my own story, my guilt and sadness. It made me feel small again, being among people. Instead of powerful, and being above them, like I was at the time. Then I played for the deceased, letting them go with respect.

I enjoyed improvising from this feeling of vulnerability. Thoughts and music went hand in hand. In the end, I dared to wish everyone a path of light, in which the drama of this karma comes to an end. And other beautiful light wishes, which I brought out with music. I also played something about the unity consciousness, and on 'Together through the Gate on 21-12-12.' My kindred spirit, the musical boy, clearly manifested himself. He wished me to kiss life. The candles burned for quite some after the playing ended. Profound stillness filled the room. I promised myself and everyone that whenever I play the cello, I will also play a little for these souls.

The following afternoon, during a meeting, I spontaneously received a big hug from a seven-year-old boy. It was truly incredible. I had tears in my eyes. "I love you, boy," I said. He gave me a card with angels on it. I was totally overcome with relief, even when I tell others about this. Finally. I feel it in my body and hear it in my voice. It's so wonderful and important finally to be able to pass this on. Moreover, my physical complaints have practically disappeared already even as they continue to impact me. Immediately after the session I felt relief in my upper back: it was no longer blocked so that I could breathe normally again. Unbelievable after a lifetime of tension in that spot. My eyelids are no longer red, and my eczema is also greatly reduced. When I get itchy sometimes, those are the moments when I prefer to withdraw and do not dare to choose life. I see the connection. I am very grateful for this experience, the lessons and all the help.

CHAPTER 22

Traces on the skin

"Is my disease very dangerous doctor? – Let me put it this way. If I can heal you I'll become world famous."
– Wiet van Broeckhoven

We conclude this third part of the book with two case histories. The story of the German Eva, who in her current life still has the traces of burns from various lives on her skin. And the story of Lenna, who died in 1943 but is far from forgotten. In her story you can see the influence of the Second World War in a dreadful combination with interference from the church that has incited some people to insane acts.

CASE HISTORY OF EVA FROM MUNICH

'Psoriasis reminds me of dying from a mustard gas attack...'
In September 2015 I met Maarten, at a conference of the German network 'Schamanisches Netzwerk Europa' at Ludwigstein Castle. I ended up at his workshop by chance because I was lost while looking for another workshop. Maarten said that his work consists of pulling up a chair for our ancestors, so that they can tell their story. This statement fascinated me and touched me immediately. His story, and especially the case histories, made a deep impression on me.

Suddenly there is a logical connection between complaints and a deep conviction from a past life. Because of the respect and empathy with which Maarten does his work, I decided to attend one of his seminars. I underwent an experience from a past life in which I was burned as a witch, based on unfounded accusations. It explained for me my irrational fear of showing myself in my current life with all my knowledge about healing and curing. And my fear of making mistakes. I have also been suffering from psoriasis since I was 14 years old. According to Maarten, this skin condition already refers to an old core theme about that burning.

I've tried a lot, from salty baths to taking cortisone, which helped for a short time, but you don't want to take this medicine permanently. Radiation treatments are expensive, and I question the effect. At first, I had the rash mainly on my head and elbows, but in the last two years the symptoms had worsened, and it had spread over large parts of my upper abdomen, lower back, and forearms. In addition to the itching, the idea of wearing a bikini during the upcoming beach holiday in April caused me serious concern. I was too ashamed. So, after another masterclass in 2016, I went with a friend to Maarten's practice in the Netherlands in January 2017. During the session we talked about the influence of alcohol on my disease, especially the hard stuff. Consuming liquor can trigger psoriasis within a day in places that take months to clear up. So, I haven't been drinking much alcohol for many years. But in the last two years, that didn't help either. The psoriasis came back even more widespread, now also with small fiery red dots on my face.

GAS ATTACK

During the session Maarten brought me back into a body during the First World War. I immediately found myself in a trench. Totally drunk, I was unable to walk away when a bomb exploded nearby. Without knowing it, I knew it was a mustard gas attack that burned my entire body, while many other soldiers were still able to get away. Because of all the liquor I had in me from a stolen bottle, I had lost all feeling, had no control over my body and had to experience not being able to escape the disaster. I cursed myself: "If you hadn't guzzled it down, you would have gotten away in time!" The blistering clouds of gas penetrated deep through my uniform causing my body to be burnt deeply in several places and the gases to eventually suffocate me. But my body didn't understand that it couldn't survive this. A deep conviction took hold in the consciousness of my numb body.: 'As long as my body is burning, I am still alive.' In addition, a profound desire to be able to come home kept me fixated in that dramatic moment, so that I never fully realized I was actually dead. Three attempts were needed under Maarten's guidance to relive the moment of death, until the last breath was taken, and it was clear it was truly over. The last things that went through my mind at seeing the body with all the burns were: "If only I hadn't guzzled so much, I would have gotten away in time", "I never want to be wracked with so much pain and misery ever again" and "I don't want to lose; not this war, not this life, I never want to be on the losing side."

I shed a great deal of tears mourning the death of this young man. In my mind I bandaged the burns, took care of the body, and laid it on a beautiful field, in a clearing on the earth. That brought peace and quiet. On being asked, I was able to tell Maarten that it was a young man who had fought on the side of the French during the First World War.

Over the next two weeks, my skin began to recover without me doing anything about it. Within two months, large parts of the scaly and bleeding parts were (almost) completely healed. During the holidays in April, I could go to the beach in a bikini without long sleeves, without hiding. What a huge relief.

This experience has done a lot for me physically, but it has also given me insight into how illness can be related to your own (incarnation) history. I was also able to look at relationships in my family history from a new angle. The current way disease is looked at, especially symptom-oriented and focused on the individual, is quite short-sighted.

This approach to disease and death goes beyond the limits of treatments with chemical medication and modern medicine techniques. It gives me a freer and more decisive feeling in how I deal with illness.

SS-ER IN WORLD WAR II

A month after the session, in February 2017, I visited one of Maarten's masterclasses. I was looking for advice regarding the care of my parents. My mother was demented, and my father was barely able to take care of her and himself. When asked what was important to me, the answer came: "To be a good daughter to my parents, especially to my father." When we looked deeper, I ended up in a life after the existence of the soldier who died from the mustard gas bomb. I was now born In 1923 as the daughter L. of a German soldier from the First World War, but I died of pneumonia after only fifteen months. It was an incarnation in which I went through a deeper transformation to reconnect with being a woman after a life as a man. But it was still too early, too fragile, and not viable. The choking carried deeper elements of suffocation, both being burned as a witch earlier and later by the mustard gas attack, according to Maarten. The rejection that I experienced as a witch by the one who had me burned at the stake was rekindled by the fact that my father did not want any daughters either. After that I was born into the same family, in 1926 as son M. Four years later, in 1930, a second son arrived, and in 1936 the father died suddenly at work at the district office, where he was allowed to get a job as a war veteran from the First World War. Father left his wife behind with two sons, aged 10 and 6. In 1943 the eldest son, me that is, as a sixteen-year-old joined or had to join the armed LSSAH – '*12, SS Panzerdivision Leibstandarte Adolf Hitler*'.

I am brought back to a situation where a group of drunken soldiers and officers are standing around me laughing and screaming, forcing me to rape a girl lying on the ground in front of their eyes. Someone pulls my pants down and starts penetrating me from behind. I feel so helpless, humiliated, and so full of shame that I strangle the girl under me by the throat. I kill her to end the situation. I feel totally guilty and deeply ashamed.

A dramatically short life follows in which, as a professional killer, I go far beyond the limits of what is humanely permissible. The core feeling that I have harks back to the trench warfare after which I resolved to be the one to decide on matters of life and death from now on. It is short-lived. Even before the official end of the war, I commit suicide by shooting myself in the head. The shame and guilt were no longer acceptable. M. dies in the military hospital in Lower Austria, on May 4, 1945. This was a few days before the takeover by the *Rote Armee Fraktion*, three days before the war ended on May 7, 1945, four days before M.'s 18th birthday. His last thoughts were: "Don't trust anyone in positions of authority, always put attitude and integrity to the test," "It's better to be a girl, then you don't have to go to war," "Don't touch alcohol," "I have a deep aversion to drunk, fat middle-aged men," "I will take good care of girls and women" and "I want to be close to my mother and my brother."

I came back in a subsequent life as the daughter of my then younger brother L. During my grandmother's funeral in 1982 the tears came thick and fast, without me being able to explain why. She was old and sick, and I had a good relationship with her, but I wasn't all that close to her either. In this farewell I realize that I must have felt M.'s pain, who lost his mother at that moment.

Research brought me to information on Wikipedia: "The LSSAH is responsible for numerous war crimes on the Eastern and Western fronts. (...) among other things, the murder of thirty-four French civilians in Tavaux and Plomion (also involving soldiers from the twelfth SS Hitler Youth armored division)." Did I hail from these regions as a French soldier? Who's to say? At its deepest levels the story of this session is the root cause of a massive feeling of self-condemnation. I no longer feel that, and I'm allowed to live again. My skin does not have to put people off any longer because I am dangerous and unpredictable. It's a huge relief.

LENNA'S CASE HISTORY AND DOWN'S SYNDROME

Dagmar, who was born in 1973, has felt a very strong lifelong responsibility for the well-being of her mother Ingeborg. "As if I always want to please her, make her happy." On the one hand that is a powerful connection, on the other it deprives Dagmar of a sense of freedom. She finds it hard to really live for herself. Dagmar is her mother's only child. In addition, she has two half-brothers from a previous marriage of her father.

Dagmar says that her mother Ingeborg had an older sister. Her name was Lenna and she had Down's syndrome. Lenna died in 1943, when she was 5 or 6 years old, from a 'vague condition'. Dagmar experiences a strong sense of connection with this deceased girl, although she can't explain why. She has a picture of her. The story of what happened to her slowly starts to unfold.

Dagmar's grandmother and grandfather have a total of six children of whom Lenna and Ingeborg are the fourth and fifth. The eldest is the only son. He became a priest, driven by the expectations of his parents. The family lives according to very strict and stringent church principles. Grandma is clearly the one who wears the pants, grandpa has nothing to say. Grandma feels that she is better than 'common people'. This has been instilled in her by her upper-class family upbringing. Her husband, granddad, comes from a simple working-class family. This situation makes her conflicted with the entire situation. It feels to her that she has disappointed her parents. On top of that, granddad is unable to actively serve in the German army due to physical disabilities. He is at home, but to compensate for his passive role regarding the war, he becomes a fervent verbal supporter of Hitler's ideology.

Lenna was born in 1938 and Ingeborg a few years later, in 1941. Grandma is totally incapable of dealing with Lenna having Down syndrome. Grandma completely distances herself emotionally from her deviant daughter. She views it as a scandal in the eyes of the church and the parish. It is a disgrace, because a mongoloid bears a mark from God, or in fact, is a punishment from God. Moreover, a mongoloid in Hitler's ideology means a profound disruption of family systems and a sign of impurity. Lenna's arrival completely shakes the family to its foundations. 'Aktion T4', a program started by Hitler in 1939 to preserve genetic purity of the Germanic people through the systematic murder of mentally handicapped and deformed people was already in full swing. The idea behind this program that these patients, just like Lenna, would have a meaningless existence, became the cover that was supposed to appease her conscience.

A SHOT TO 'SET HER FREE' FROM THE DOCTOR

Grandma takes refuge in practical matters. When Ingeborg is born a few years later, she is put on public display to as many people as possible. She must become the epitome of the ideal daughter, to camouflage Lenna's disgrace. The family, meanwhile, withdraws and isolates itself more and more from society. A father who, for vague medical reasons, does not take an active part in the war and a mongoloid. What will people think?

Ingeborg and Lenna are now very close. Ingeborg loves her special sister, and she takes on a protective role towards her, which goes against what her mother expects of her. She puts increasing pressure on Ingeborg by constantly making sure she fulfills her important responsibilities. Lenna, for whom the connection with her sister Ingeborg still gives some joy, starts missing her sister more and more because of her mother's increased discouragement. After a while Lenna gets sick, she has a bad case of the flu. Grandma, Lenna, and Ingeborg's mother, instructs her husband to go to the doctor with Lenna. "Go, take her with you, and make sure she never comes back," she says resolutely.

Under pressure from his wife, father convinces the doctor that their daughter is in very bad shape. He encourages the doctor to give her a shot to "set her free". The doctor is persuaded and injects Lenna in her upper arm, causing her to die a horrible death.

From now on, Grandma must live with the realization that she had her child killed. She can only do that by leading a frenetic and practically oriented life. It puts a burden on the children. After the war has ended and the circumstances of Hitler's theater of war become clearer, grandma can be found frequently in church. She constantly prays, wanting to clear her conscience. Her 5-year-old granddaughter Dagmar reminds her intensely of Lenna. That's why she anxiously tries to keep her at a distance as well as her daughter Ingeborg. In the end, grandma dies in 1978 fraught with inner resistance. Because she is convinced that she is going to go to hell, there can be no detachment from her earthly condition.

Once deceased, grandma attaches herself to her two descendants Ingeborg and Dagmar. For fear of going to hell, she cannot surrender to death. As a confused soul, she becomes frenetically entangled with her daughter and granddaughter, because in her relation to them lies the whole unforgivable trauma with which she cannot identify. That brings things together, a layer of her soul ultimately longing for the potential that can free her from her self-condemnation.

In trance, Dagmar relives Lenna's death, with the emotions, bewilderment and confusion that go with it. Dagmar realizes that she is the reincarnation of Lenna, with whom she wanted to reconnect to life as the daughter of her former sister Ingeborg, who made her feel safe and noticed. Grandma is also present as a soul during the session. After the necessary explanations and reflection on the most profound events of her life, she too relives her own death. This time in a way that frees her from so much clinging and denial. When she expresses her incredibly deep regret, it is heart-rending. The madness of the zeitgeist that held her captive and even enabled her to perform such an act was so great that she was unable to open herself to it during her lifetime. At an emotional level, Dagmar experiences reconciliation on Lenna's behalf. Lenna can forgive her mother. Grandma can now let go of her daughter Ingeborg and her granddaughter Dagmar. After this session, Dagmar succeeds in allowing a great sense of freedom to enter her life. Now she can start living for herself.

PART IV

INFLUENCE OF THE CATHOLIC CHURCH

CHAPTER 23

Church legacy from past lives

"A theists express their anger against God even though, in their opinion, He does not exist."
– C.S. Lewis

We have now discussed in detail the impact that the Second World War had on those living at the time, and succeeding generations of people, at all conceivable levels. Another area of work that requires attention in my practice to an equally large extent concerns the influence of the Roman Catholic Church. Compared to the various wars that have a beginning and an end, this influence spans centuries. Therefore, this part of the book also has more chapters than the previous one. It is about the Roman Catholic Church and its branches. By branches I mean all denominations that have emerged from the Catholic Church over the centuries. The Protestant church, the Reformed church, the Mennonite, Remonstrant and Reformed church, the Apostolic society, the liberal church communities. And from the Ledeboer Reformists to the many monastic orders, to the Pentecostal churches. Clearly this religious institution has determined the course of human history to an enormous extent. Could that have ever been its founding principle? Those open to the idea of having lived several lives quickly realize that a church, or another dogmatic religious institution, in those several lives, must have been the influential focal point of the society you were once a part of.

I would now like to take you on a journey through the probing adventures of clients who, in current and past lives, were marked and mangled by the church. Regardless of rank or position. They are about lives that were determined at all levels by the position you held and your attitude towards the church. Ranging from total devotion to intense disgust, from hypocrites immersed in lies, to the torture that staying true to yourself could cause. Lives that gave rise to all sorts of issues that also caused people to remain trapped their entire life.

I saw a clear underlying pattern unfolding in all my sessions. As a changing landscape in which people lived through various images of time, with a church at the center of the communities. In this picture it became increasingly clear the extent to which the church exercised its sphere of influence coloring in its own picture of society. Take, for instance, the example of the Martinikerk in the northern Dutch city of Groningen that only installed a lightning rod in 1837, after numerous strikes had claimed several victims. The main objection from the church community, besides of course the financial one, was that a lightning rod would disable an important instrument of God's punishment, namely, lightning, causing the wrath of God to be invoked even more upon the people. It just goes to show that God and punishment went hand in hand for many, while punishment and guilt are, to this day, the most necessary and effective ingredients to manipulate a people.

My work clarifies what really moves people, especially when it comes to layers of meaning and spirituality. And, how in these regions it is possible to create such effective confusion about our spiritual origins that a wholly distorted experience arises about the laws of the unseen world that can hold us captive for life. An interpreted illustration that says that the real forces of love springing from the source of creation, from which we come, and to which we return, may only be experienced by adhering to all sorts of strict conditions. Talk about a lightning rod. Even the organ, which people automatically associate with ecclesiastical trappings, was once called 'Satan's whistling cabinet' by Calvin (1509-1564), which would overly distract people from the word of God because of its pleasant sounds. That too would have been enough to call God's wrath down upon anyone who believed it. Reformer Luther, on the other hand, thought that the organ reinforced God's message. How confusing it must have been to get a clear focus on what God wanted and meant. Just as diverse as people are, were the explanations put forward by influential people dressed in robes, chasubles, and cloaks, who pretended to the many God-fearing citizens, that they knew what had to be done because of their personal friendship with God. One thing remained intact everywhere: it is not so much what brought down the wrath of God through the ages that really matters, but what could be called down by something that you could put a name to.

How cause and effect connections really work is constantly shown in practice. Clients ultimately propose the irrational solutions to their own conflicts, which were previously veiled in the subconscious. And so, I always have a front row seat to gain insight into the genesis of human dramas.

In terms of the influence of the church, clients repeatedly talked about the deeper shadowy dimensions behind this spiritual organ. Especially in terms of power and control. The loom with which the religious system was woven seems to be in obscure hands. Most clients already had such a sneaking suspicion of this, but when stories become concrete, those gut feelings really come to life.

These conclusions are, as it were, the landscape of this journey. I ventilate them freely through the concrete reports of sessions. I must admit that this was accompanied by some hesitation. Because I know many people believe that they, or else their parents or ancestors, draw strength from their faith in some way, and it seems as if I am infringing on that with all these reports. In the end, this hesitation was not the decisive factor. I trust that everyone retains the truly good in their perceptions of any religious experience, and at the same time is willing to be critical, and especially to look at my findings with a brushed-up point of view.

What the real intentions are behind the worldwide image of God remains a big question to which I would be hard pressed to give an immediate answer. However, many clients feel extremely close to their own truth in certain trance alignments. A powerful therapeutic interplay of question and answer enables them to rapidly find their way into deeper layers of inner knowledge. And so quite a few visions of faith, however ingrained they may sometimes be, were rigorously fine-tuned during therapy. Not primarily as a therapeutic goal, but more resulting from processing. It makes you wonder.

Many also feel overwhelmed by fear and uncertainty in these intermediate dimensions as they come to realize that the way their lives were determined is now crumbling. At the same time, these processes always go hand in hand with deep sensations of experiencing freedom. The idea that "my grandmother drew a lot of strength and support from her faith", then changes into a different approach. "Because my grandmother lost a child and considered it a punishment from God, she gave herself completely to God out of fear of hell. Therefore, she forgot to really live and everything in her existence revolved around prayer and inner doubts and self-punishment. Ouch, I never looked at it that way," follows the progressive insight, "but it does explain why my mother could never even be spontaneous and cheerful."

ACTS OF LOVE LEAVE NO BALLAST BEHIND

From my practical experience, I reason that where acts of love, respect and compassion took place, no emotional ballast was left behind. On the contrary. Call it favorable karma. After all, countless people lived lives, framed by religion and religiosity, while no (significant) adverse karmic burden was accumulated. When old traumas are processed during sessions, an interaction between the so-called perpetrator and the victim plays the stereotypical leading role. It is simply not possible to have an experience of being a victim if a perpetrator did not exist. Even when someone jumps off a cliff out of sheer loneliness, his act of despair stems from the influence of others who have prompted him to make this decision. The perpetrator-victim situation is less prominent here, but nevertheless present. In practice, attention is generally and primarily paid to old experiences of being a victim. But the traumatic aspects of being a perpetrator are often also discussed. In fact, to be able to dispel certain themes properly, it is even necessary to see that one was not always a victim, but also once embodied the other party.

Without wanting to show any approval, at a certain moment it is possible to have sympathy for a perpetrator who harmed his victim. Especially as soon as the motives for the perpetrators' actions come into the picture. They engender a deeper insight into the cause of an event, which is quite healing. The insight that perpetration stems from victimization and vice versa is an intense one and therefore powerfully transformative. Like the father of a client who died at the age of 51 who was prosecuted for pedophilia during his life. He also abused my client's brother when he was a child. During the contact with the father in a session, he hesitantly told me that his parents sent him to boy scout summer camps when he was a kid. He was regarded as a nuisance at home, and they were better off without him. At the time they were living in the U.S. The counselors at those camps sexually abused quite a few young boys. The father learned there from the age of 8 that it is what makes you a 'man'. In fact, in his twisted need to be a man, he later sought out young boys with whom he committed the same acts. Thereby connecting himself as a perpetrator to his own inner child. My client was later able to verify this information. They found her father's old scouting certificates. Research on internet confirmed for her that quite a few cases of abuse took place there. This fostered a sense of understanding for her father, which allowed her to reconnect with him. In short, these insights play a vital role in the process of clients who were once victims of one or more perpetrator(s) working through what happened.

But the bewilderment and indignation are many times greater when a globally organized institution ('Catholic' comes from the Greek 'katholikos' and means 'universal') propagates the word of God for the well-being of humanity. Also when it turns out afterwards that there is a dark, manipulative agenda behind it. The engine behind a huge layer of perpetrator-victim entanglements over centuries appears to be hidden at a much deeper level. The entire orientation process of understanding the development of trauma then shifts to another plan. Seeing through the magnitude of such a field of work, with the immense consequences that go with it, is not something you can learn by taking a quick course. To be able to realize your own freedom, it is necessary to learn to see through the façade. Digesting and processing something are therefore carried out in stages over a longer period than a single human life. Practical experience with reincarnation therapy shows that souls remain thematically linked to series of lives with religious influences.

CHAPTER 24

From shadowy cardinals to child abuse

"No one is more hated than he who speaks the truth."
– Plato

In past lives grafted onto the church, you will find the stereotypical characters that we know, ranging from shadowy cardinals or other illustrious, ecclesiastically consecrated dignitaries to child victims of (ritual) sexual abuse in secret underground church vaults. Miraculously, powerful, and transformative therapeutic interventions are also possible at these levels. The client's soul is always decisive in the end and always retains its autonomy. The soul determines when real change may take place, and whether stories from these heavy categories may be tapped into.

Consequently, the therapist does not have to have any illusions about his influence on the client and can take a modest position. However, a position that can of course be taken forcefully. And also one that screens a soul as a form of energy: what potential reveals itself in the interaction between this unique combination of client and therapist? And which layer can be touched during a session? The one who dares to ask the deepest questions, and in so doing is essentially taking the soul seriously, can count on a close friendship with that soul and on all the necessary cooperation to conduct a successful session. Regardless of the nature of the story, regardless of the level of perpetration. A soul makes no distinction whatsoever.

For example, what I often do as a therapist with the category of dark characters is to work on dispelling the absolute secrecy that was sworn at the time. That secrecy is still in effect over time. High-ranking positions were gradually acquired, resulting in more and more conflicts of interest. The unscrupulousness they learned that was empowered by the occult is the hardest nut to crack. This was learned deliberately so that not a shred of conscience was allowed to penetrate. The enormous burdens of guilt, shame and disgrace that can always be found in the repressed areas of feeling are reactivated during a session. They are felt again. A beautiful and important step for the therapeutic process. Although a psychopath is not very likely to go to a reincarnation therapist, these examples are about lives in which this person would then be diagnosed as such.

When it comes to child victims, it's all about their enormous vulnerability. Fundamental fear of life, physical wounds, and injuries with the corresponding dissociation and symbolic or ritual incantations. In children's lives where the life energy was seized with the help of lugubrious rituals, often through the blood, it must be released from captivity by dispelling the incantations made at the time. Of course, there are plenty of reasons not to talk about these horrible traumas, but I do anyway. These stories have also come to the fore, and it was possible to work well with them. I sometimes make the comparison to a good dentist, who does not differentiate the degree to which a tooth is rotten. These lives just need to be given appropriate attention. "It's just part of the game, period."

Those rituals could only be successful because the children were terrified at the time. When a person shines new light on the ritual with his current consciousness, it is possible to start a transformation moving. Seen from this perspective, it is worth realizing that if people need the blood of children to feel alive, they will also remain dependent on these children on a soul level. That will cause a turning point in the long term. The soul simply wishes to get rid of these dependency patterns. That is why entanglements between perpetrators and victims remain in force so long as there is no change of theme. Life situations will then be arranged with the need for a child, or several children, to die in the presence of the one who had become dependent on it. Perhaps this time as someone with a deep kinship, such as a parent or relative. One will be plunged into an enormously deep sorrow which ultimately results in the disconnection of the earlier energetic entanglement of dependence. Drinking children's blood literally means that the life force of these children in one's system will take on a life of its own. One does not realize it at that moment of course, as there is no real spiritual awareness about this yet. That way, you might be able to imagine that the ingested, non-own-child energy can begin to translate into serious physical ailments in a new life. One's own death caused by it will result in the release of the child's soul energy. Call it a sacrifice. "This time I give my life for the freedom of the child, because I once took this child's life." In this way, the child teaches you that you should not make yourself dependent on someone else's life force for a human existence. Life should take place out of love and being connected to yourself, and in the end, you always come back to that principle, if you ever abandoned it.

CASE HISTORY – SACRIFICIAL KNIFE

Laurens, a young man in his early twenties, has a tattoo of a sacrificial knife on the inside of his lower right arm. An imaginary shake of his head is all it would take for the knife to fall into his hand. He can tell you a lot about knives; he has always been attracted to them, and the sinister stories that go with them. Laurens has a serious blood disease, and the prognosis is not good. During a session, he discovers that he has been a high priest in a certain culture in a past life. As a member of a high-ranking society of several high priests, his particular role was to wield the sacrificial knife. During extremely lofty and sacred rituals, children were sacrificed for "a higher purpose." It was precision work, and for this reason he held a prominent position in these secret circles that were unattainable for the common people. Laurens now realizes that his blood has become impure because it was mixed with that of children, without him having any real awareness about it at the time. He belonged to a group of "wise men" whose task was to instruct the people, and thanks to the children's blood, these high priests remained supernaturally lucid and sharp and divinely informed. Laurens says that he now sees this fulfilled a need for unseen evil creatures posing as gods. They feasted on the energy of the children released through this society, and in return gave information and direction to these high priests, who had to keep the people in check with threats and insider information. Laurens died a few years later. Shortly before he passed, I received a letter from him in which he writes that the session was an incredibly valuable experience, because he can now surrender to a deeper order of the soul enabling him to give the children their freedom back with his death.

DISOBEDIANT CITIZENS, RENEGADES AND SINNERS

In the area that lies between these extreme roles of perpetrator and victim, we meet many priests, sometimes missionaries and further, nuns, monks, disobedient citizens, and sinners. The large number of inquisition victims is remarkable. For instance, denounced and cursed, they once ended up on pyres having to swear off their natural talents to be able to heal or be self-sufficient. The latter caused great displeasure to the soul. In situations with such enormous disruptions, it immediately comes into play again, preparing for future steps to bring repressed divine talents and abilities back into balance. Massive numbers of inquisition victims seem to have incarnated in the current era. Making use of the powerful transformative potential of altered consciousness on earth, they want to resurrect their once lost natural talents. Clients with such inquisition-like backgrounds are recognizable in their current lives by enormous frustration, where they somehow feel they are unable to live their own individuality. They have often adapted to prevailing norms and expectations, but actually want to do something alternative, usually quite literally. There is still a defining, underlying fear that terrible things can happen when they publicly express their own opinion or trait. At the same time, there is a force, at a deeper level, that apparently wants to take precedence again. The original potential that has fallen into decline wants to be set free after many hundreds of years in captivity. A moment always arrives when this is re-released, and it seeks its original form of expression again. It really is the nature of our spiritual beast. What you then see is that clients, after reclaiming their assets from old lives, open a practice as a magnetizer or for giving other energetic treatments. Or you see that they go to study and practice certain forms of alternative medicine, finally write their book, start transformative coaching based on a holistic view. Or they move on into a new era, with accompanying possibilities, where once they had been silenced.

Therapeutically, I notice that it is very effective to confront clients with their own findings, outrage, and conclusions about their personal actions from past lives with the deeds that went with them. So long as objectivity and non-judgment are guaranteed in sessions, these rusty stories feel invited to be adequately pulled out of the muddy catacombs of a human consciousness. They have lain there far too long. The journey of the reincarnating soul contains so many themes, encounters, excesses, learning processes, adventures, remote corners, mountains, and valleys. They are all chapters which together form its book of the soul, an account of a journey.

CHAPTER 25

Religion, pain, and wounds

"Of all tyrannies that affect mankind, the tyranny of religion is the worst."
– Thomas Paine

Every era has open or covert discussions, about whether the Catholic Church and world religions, in a general sense, produce anything good for a society at all. In some previous life experiences, it was literally life-threatening to question an image imposed by the church. Whoever did so openly was no longer sure of his life and those of his loved ones or followers. History repeating itself is not just something in the past. A grim and ominous climate surrounding faith and religion still pervades our reality today. In many countries, the decision whether to worship a faith still has far-reaching consequences. The punishments meted out in antiquity to those who held deviant views is notorious. To endure abuse and all the pain inflicted, one had to forcefully disconnect from oneself. The mind dissociated from the body to keep things bearable, until death usually ensued.

Such extreme attacks cannot be experienced to the full extent. What is not always consciously considered is that the effect of inflicted injuries reached much further than just the physical, emotional, or psychic body of the victims. These wounds lodge in the immortal etheric body of the affected person. They manifest themselves again in a successive new body with its corresponding living conditions. And so, it is reexperienced, because if it is not integrated its bearer basically remains connected to an old, unfinished story. Depending on the degree of processing that has already taken place, old wounds will begin to demand attention in a new setting, i.e., the present life. So-called stigmata that bodies can exhibit are physical manifestations of previously sustained injuries. In a current body, which has not gone through that experience, an old pain becomes visible. For instance, in the form of a birthmark or birth defect, which can be a manifestation of a burn or severe skin condition. Or something serious, such as someone who is born with a hole in his heart resulting from an execution in which a bullet pierced the heart. These are the least understood, abnormal physical changes that can manifest themselves even in spontaneously bleeding wounds without logical explanation. Prof. Dr. Ian Stevenson reports extensively on this phenomenon in his groundbreaking work *Where Reincarnation and Biology Intersect* (1997). It is true that the book focusses mainly on making physically demonstrable connections with past lives, but it makes it very clear how concretely we are still connected to old trauma. This also includes states of mind, such as fear of life, depression, fundamental insecurity, and timidity. It should be noted here that physical imprints from previous lives do not always have to be distressful, think of a scar from a wound that has healed.

DISCONNECTING FROM OLD WOUNDS

The impact of inflicted injuries and punishments on various layers of souls extends far beyond the pyre, dungeon, public demonization, or the scaffold. For those who see this far-reaching effect, this is of course unfavorable to the credibility of an imagined almighty loving church god, surrounded by massive numbers of images, with his only representative, the crucified son.

Every religion that is forcibly imposed and practiced is steeped in interests that serve not so much our experience of spirituality, as certain human positions instead. Sooner or later, it throttles the soul-bearing human being. If a doctrine of faith is going to be substantively interpreted and constructed by delusions, such as the existence of a hell and an all-seeing condemning god, it will lead a life of its own. That is disastrous for gullible people, who under these threats gradually sink deeper and deeper into an abyss. And especially because of the sneaky way in which it works. One only starts asking the real critical questions when the way back can hardly be found. It is never too late, of course, but then meant in the sense of multiple lives.

A natural, friendly, all-encompassing and above all unconditional image of God, as it should originally be felt and experienced from love, is also very effectively kept out of reach. How many people nowadays prefer to believe quite convincingly in 'nothing' so that it cannot have nasty consequences or cause pain? If we are spiritual beings, it is very unnatural to exclude that aspect of yourself, which normally wants to experience a cosmic connection. It's like a cow that doesn't like grass, and who over time also thinks he has a darn good reason for it. Fortunately, the time span is shrinking between the imposed threat and the legitimate critical questions about whether it all adds up due to the changing consciousness in our '2012 time'. That is why new religions are being shoved down the throats of society more and in ever cruder and more transparent ways.

FEELINGS OF GUILT HAVE A NEGATIVE IMPACT ON DYING

Devising systems based on debt and then persistently camouflaging the hidden agendas behind them is proving to be very effective. It is a blatant lie that a punitive god awaits after death. I have been able to conclude that with my own eyes and ears countless times as a travel guide of the deceased. The instilled fear of it does exist. But when the transition is made and one looks back, this doomsday version of God and his afterlife was actually nowhere to be found. When you have been duped with misleading ideas about your right to be, it inexorably complicates the whole process of passing on. Depending on the extent to which these beliefs were rooted throughout life, they will cause a disruptive effect in any natural transformation process, such as death. Feelings of guilt can have a huge negative impact on dying.

For example, a grandmother who dies from Corona can suffer unnecessarily during her transition, because the doctor, who was instructed by his superiors to diagnose terminal patients as corona patients, had told her that she suffered from it. While that was not the root cause of her disease at all. As she was dying, she wonders in an excruciating inner dialogue whether she may have also infected her (grand) children, when she went to a family birthday party six weeks earlier and everyone gave one another big cuddles. Or a grandfather, who after he dies bequeaths considerable debts to his children and is deeply ashamed and unable to let go of this feeling. What is remarkable, to say the least, is that, apart from the church, the financial world also relies on the principle of debt systems. There are many parallels, on which I do not want to dwell too much because it is not my field. Sinners, as is true today, arose out of nowhere. The similarity is that the church depends on sinners for its salvation since they can be punished so that other people submit for fear of the same fate. Under duress they accept the ideas imposed by the church. Banks depend on money made from thin air, in the form of interest. People are enslaved for a lifetime with repayment obligations. In the past this also created, and still does, a strong need by and for systems of power to introduce all kinds of absurd regulations. Public penance is extremely effective in sowing a mood of fear and anxiety among the people, so that the unsuspecting spectator ultimately does not even think of still being critical. It is the mainstream media of yesteryear that, like today, thoroughly played on the sentiments of the population by producing waves of fear. By means of papal indulgences, which were actually the preliminary stage of paper money, you could buy off your guilt (feeling) and thereby come clean with God. Or, to put it more bluntly: without indulgences you will end up in hell. So, pay. Your neck was temporarily saved again, with the emphasis on temporary. Meanwhile, without them knowing it, one became dependent on the person who had profiled himself between God and man as being his representative. Thus, "God's word" grew into an immortally dogmatic paradigm that was aggressively shoved down people's throats wherever it did not resonate with its intended purpose.

Clearcut responses are given when I ask clients why they had let themselves be led by a church system in a past life. Or what effect, for example, baptism, communion, or another religious ritual has had on them. Meanwhile, somewhat resigned comments are made of a large-scale deception to which they fell prey. Quite concretely: "It's a made-up story", "People are trapped there", "We've been fooled", "There's no hell." But also extremely loaded responses: "They have to come up with a system for their pedophile sexual needs", or "It's the work of the devil." Not so much dominated by an atmosphere of reproach, but more self-critical. "I didn't listen to my heart", "I didn't know any better", "I felt trapped", "I was blinded or deceived" or "I didn't see it for what it really was", are the responses most often expressed. As far as the effect of church rituals is concerned, you will hear: "It sucked me deeper into it", "Now the cross has been seared into my soul", "My mother thinks I am protected now" or "Now there is absolutely no way back."

STRUCTURAL INDUCTION OF PAIN

The results in my practice show that on average people start to feel much freer after a Church knot has been disentangled, an old contract has been cancelled or a ritual or initiation dispelled. They are no longer hindered by an imagined idea of a judgmental "big brother entity" that watches admonishingly and punitively from on high. Someone may even experience this without the church playing a role, but that this 'looking down on you' can be translated through a father, a grandfather, a boss, or a partner, with whom he always had a feeling they were looking over his shoulder. Or there will be a guilt-free attitude to life, a need to develop spiritual talents or less hesitation in expressing an opinion. Where someone makes himself more easily visible, feels calmer and connected through love with deceased family members. Especially with those who were previously unfathomable and unreachable. Where there is a much more vivid sense of experiencing being part of larger whole.

Can't this whole long history of influence be better explained in the context of a trauma that has been consciously produced, and even transferred? I know, it's quite a claim. The broad field of vision required to see through that, gradually revealed itself to me. That the introduction of an invented image of God could take place on such a massive scale among fellow humans, does not go down well with quite a few people. Unfortunately, it is a falsely reassuring idea. We are often tempted to scale back our feelings to manageable proportions to keep life livable for ourselves. How many do not wish to believe in the innocence and goodness of men, and if necessary, regard the painful events as incidents that got out of hand? It often happens that clients have a romanticized image of their grandparents who grew up in a time when the church was center stage. They prefer not to approach the life experiences of the time too deeply for fear of discovering the pain that was hidden behind it. "It wasn't too bad", or "My grandmother lived to a ripe old age with it because she drew strength from it." But when the sharper questions get through to the real answers, a completely different picture appears to unfold. A picture that shows the shady side of their existence and on which all kinds of details become visible that marked their lives in the unseen. That is why I regularly question the romanticized images which often arise to maintain a certain image in the family.

Just how refreshing is it to get to reveal the whole elephant, and to be able to distinguish the noise on the line from the true story? After all, it concerns our well-being and that of our ancestors and children. As far as I am concerned, there is no reason to question 'the good' in man, but our history clearly demonstrates that we are capable of excessive behavior. And how can we really bring healing into the equation when we only naively keep looking at the surface? Here it is good to note that people suffer more because they keep a lid on things instead of taking it off.

ATTRACTION AND REPULSION

Structural pain induction takes place, on a mental, emotional, physical, and spiritual level. Across many lives. In such a way that each new generation is constantly burdened with restrictions that ensure people are blocked from developing to their full potential and thus remain easily manipulated. Supported by a cleverly conceived worldview that is snuck under people's noses thorough propaganda channels and immense pressure. A worldview that is focused on chronically distracting people from who they really are, and how in reality, earthly life works. It is an incisive conclusion, I realized countless times while writing this book.

The definition of power is the ability to determine the behavior of others. One must produce a reason to create fear, a reason to control and do so in an atmosphere of apparent transparency. Of course, a prerequisite for that is for people not to realize it. A field of tension must arise that gradually tears apart the harmonious foundation of polar society on our earth. Society consists of men and women, irreverent pluses and minuses, or yins and yang's, who are on the same playing field. All born from a spiritual source of unity through the sexual energy that our parents experienced during conception. Even if new life comes about through rape, there must have been sufficient power of love at a deeper core level. Sexual energy has the capacity to connect extremes and bring them into contact with each other. That might be easier to imagine when you can see that a rapist is actually desperately seeking the connection with his mother, who he himself has missed terribly. Or if you can see that "hate" is in fact a corruption of love. Either way, in human society men and women together generate a fluid magnetic field of attraction and repulsion. That's the field we live in. The more this field is disturbed by pumping up traumatic circumstances, the more people end up in dependency. It is no longer a matter of attraction and repulsion; severe trauma causes a new phenomenon to present itself that is alien to the soul: splitting. People unwittingly subject themselves and develop an almost childlike need to use their life force and talents to give direction to their lives. Like a child tends to want to please his parents, who radiate displeasure and set conditions. People become slavish to the one who ostensibly protects them from the threats of the world. At the same time, they do not see that they expend their life force for the plans of the very people who create their misery. In this way they learn to hand over their commitment and the proceeds of their labor to the higher-ups and so surrender their freedom. It automatically becomes a tax levied on life, which you pay as a price for living. Literally and figuratively, which I refer to in the subtitle of the book. The split between these two poles, as desired by the authorities is now a fact, and it only needs to be maintained. A split as a condition to continue this dark game.

Life on earth is borne by a fundamental frequency that, according to indigenous peoples, stems from the heartbeat of mother earth. As soon as those frequencies are disturbed, the residents also become disturbed and stray from their path. That split makes life force leak, and that life force is then used by the splitter to give them the feeling of being alive. As if you want to form a partition between the minus and plus poles in a light bulb, but at the same time enjoy the warmth of their appeal. This way, one simply strives for a restructuring of existing creation into a new, artificial order.

This exposition is also a reflection of how someone can ultimately also function as a person. The traumas a person once suffered create corresponding disruptions causing him to put his own life frequencies under pressure. This is how people also carry inner authorities, such as sub-personalities, within themselves, who call the shots for the rest of the person but, are actually anxiously dwelling in a survival mode based on old experiences.

LEARNING TO SEE THROUGH THE GAME

What do we need to let the scales drop from our eyes so that we learn to see through the game? Several lives, perhaps, that release us from this captivity. Life experiences that lead us out of the maze we once unsuspectingly stepped into, an experience richer, to redraw our own life plan.

What is typical of that contrived, misleading concept of how earthly life works for people, with its smuggled in view of our spirituality, is that it is so warped and complicated no one can really understand, let alone experience it. It simply does not reflect how we really do experience spirituality since all sorts of pretexts and conditions have been contrived in and around it. The creation stories now taught in schools and universities simply crank it up a notch. Big Bang theories and Darwin's theory of evolution lead many to believe that this is the normal evolutionary process of humanity. In the meantime, that includes a self-inflicted climate problem. And an idea about God that has been reduced to pitiful proportions. As if, with the help of a president's vote, he would bless the U.S. or other countries and peoples, at the expense of their enemies. How on earth can this narrow vision of God take into account what our spiritual well-being, our health issues really need?

A religion that crept in as a now more or less accepted part of human existence. With extreme consequences, ranging from all sorts of beliefs that restrict freedom, resulting in dull, narrow-minded lives, to total (religious) madness and ungraspable dictatorship. And what do the painful aspects of people's self-reincarnation experiences teach us? That these wounds are so deep that after physical death, in energetic form, they remain connected to the journey of the soul of the persons concerned and seek healing. What does a soul do if the virgins it has come to believe would be there after blowing itself up, turn out not to be there? And what does the child left behind do, whose father does not return home for that reason because he has performed a fatal 'heroic act'? How clouded does your outlook then get? A new episode is simply added to a bloody trajectory, which still has to extricate itself from the entanglements that have arisen.

Trauma-related behavior, such as sexual, physical, or psychological (power) abuse, domination, delusions of grandeur or all kinds of (self)chastisement, are therefore outside the realm of the finiteness of material life cycles. They move with the soul to new lives where a new layer may be peeled off, like a magic ball. Just until the core is reached again, and one starts to feel and experience oneself again from one's own unvarnished truth.

Mental imprints from past lives are largely responsible for the formation of our new DNA, of both a loving and twisted kind. It is a challenge, but if it turns out that we can regain autonomy for its formation, not through technological interventions, but by living through it, then a great deal could change quite rapidly.

CHAPTER 26
Waning power?

"The church: a businessman in bulky durable consumer products."
– Arthur Adamov

Ironically, disbelief is a common reaction when people are confronted with another truth about the faith that already resided within them. Especially when they hear that there could be powers with invested interests behind it in pursuit of control. Powers that manipulate on a large-scale and play on human opinion in all kinds of ways. The extent of such an idea is so incomprehensible it simply cannot be digested (all at once). In addition, one does not realize that the prevailing concept of faith and religion crept in quite some time ago. It formed under all kinds of forgotten, painful or invasive circumstances (and rituals) from childhood. However, confusion and disbelief are a necessary and inevitable preliminary stage for being able to admit new ways of thinking. If people are confused after a session, that is therefore a very good sign. A dedicated priest can only come to realize, as part of a process, that there were fundamental gaps in the institution to which he once pledged his soul and salvation. Sometimes multiple lives are required, each of those life events leading step by step to that realization. Once that insight has been gained from confrontation with one's own actions, the realization penetrates deeper and deeper. Discovering and accepting one's own part in a dark history is the most intense process and at the same time necessary for transformation. But many tend not to want to read beyond this point. The power of reincarnation therapy is that people can find themselves as well as their so-called shadowy sides. It is 'part of the game', to discover that we are not random victims of domination, but rather of a deviously conceived concept in which we were tempted to play a role.

As I have previously pointed out, there are countless people who have acted with warm-hearted and well-meaning intentions in the name of the church or any other kind of religious philosophy. If a nun "in the name of God" responds to someone in a loving and helpful way, then it says more about the person behind the appearance of the nun than about the religious setting in which this takes place. That is what makes it sometimes so misleading, especially since the church will claim all the credit to strengthen its position.

After my father died suddenly in 1965, Pastor Lansbergen, an emissary of the local church parish, regularly visited my mother, my brother and me to give spiritual support. A fantastic man who taught us magic tricks and always left behind good vibes. I remember that he could magically move the Catholic cross pinned on his jacket from one side of his lapel to the other. I still have no idea how he did that. But what does that have to do with the church as such? He was simply a man who wanted to help his fellow man.

WHEN IS SUFFERING EVER ENOUGH?

A basic principle of the church is that we as human beings are sinful from birth. You are burdened from childhood with original sin, which causes a separation between God and man. That separation necessitates redemption. In the best-case scenario, you pray, confess, repent, and behave in a sufficiently pious way in your life so that this supposed distance from God is slightly reduced. And you must do this in time, before dying. Completely bridging this gap and reaching the state of enlightenment is a utopian dream. That is reserved for the most holy.

Because people have tormented themselves day and night over the centuries with the question of when suffering would ever be enough, life as such becomes a serious, melancholy, circumscribed, and on a spiritual level, hopeless event. At deeper levels, the daily way of life that arose is then experienced as very unnatural and inhibiting. Priorities, decisions, upbringing and behavior, everything is colored by suffering. Heaven was promised for those who were cleansed, purified disciples. That's what people believed, deep into the grave. The key question is what the implications of this are for the dying. If the question of whether one was sufficiently converted also lingers in the perception of a soul after death, what does a deceased person do with that uncertainty? More concretely, what happens to what someone has repressed or prayed away for fear of judgment? And what was all that doing penance and confessing good for? And then consider the fact that in earthly life not a day went by without there being a gnawing doubt about it.

Many people sense beforehand that repression will no longer be so easy when death is on the horizon. How much is known about this perception of the world and the influence of the deceased? The question on many people's minds is whether the deceased can even experience their environment. The dominant influence of church and science leaves little room for self-examination, especially in the previous generations that, after all, were the breeding ground for the people now living. Many, therefore, grossly refrain from asking essential questions about the process and dying and afterwards.

POSTMORTEM ASSISTED DYING

Many people die from a disease. Illness was seen by deep believers as a command to suffer like Christ on the cross. But could a disease also stem from that idea? Or from the lack of freedom experienced by the endless list of rules that people thought they had to follow their entire lives? In what way did the desperation grow rampant under the skin about the harsh living conditions and accompanying 'incidents', such as the frequent sexual excesses? How much life energy went into all the frantic attempts to come to terms with it?

During sessions with my clients, I had frequent contact with deceased people who had succumbed to a physical condition. To diseases that, upon further questioning, could simply be traced back to uteruses or fallopian tubes that had been abused when they were young, or throats and thyroids which had suffered oral abuse. Or in the lungs because the fear of life from the church protocols had become so suffocating that one simply could not breathe anymore. Or otherwise, because a stillborn child was seen as punishment from God, or because a mentally or physically disabled child came into the world, like Lenna from chapter 24. Mother or father could make themselves sick so that suffering could already start, before they would end up in hell after dying. I have heard all these variants countless times. If only I had made it up! How many diseases in the stomach and intestines resulted from indigestible, unspoken events and secrets that finally took their toll? How many mothers could not share the secret of who the real father of their child was? How many elderly people in psychological distress feared the reprisals of God because they masturbated or had cheated, usually out of desperation? Or had to get married, which caused an entire marriage with children to end up in a shadowy world, with severely broken family ties, or at least damaged for life?

The inner world of a dying person in the run-up to his last breath, where there are so many considerations, uncertainties, assumptions, and hypotheses, would thrive on having a timely dialogue. People at this stage wonder about the most basic things about themselves and the life they have lived. From my work experience – I sometimes call it postmortem assisted dying – I notice how much it still relieves and liberates people to be able to express all kinds of pent-up inner emotions. They did not take the opportunity before, because they did not want to burden others, or from fear of condemnation, rejection or disapproving self-judgement.

HUGE INDIGNATION AND BEWILDERMENT

Would all confessional moments, all abstentions, compensatory forms of behavior, Hail Mary's and self-punishments have been enough to pass over with peace of mind? It may seem that way sometimes, because after the last breath and the anointing, it is quickly said that he or she fell asleep peacefully. However, the truth is often different.

Once I was in contact with a deceased father of a client who had died of a heart attack. He said that he had not succeeded in acquiring another heart during his lifetime, which caused his own to break down. That idea was based on the assumption that people come here with a heart that by definition is impure. In other words, as sinful beings who set themselves a lifelong goal of acquiring a pure heart. This man had taken it quite literally.

Of course, it is not the case that everyone remains attached to the earth after dying. I wouldn't dare put a percentage on that. I do dare to say that the numbers are enormous – beyond our comprehension. To get a good picture of this perhaps it would be clearer and reassuring to limit yourself to your own family. Or to a partner, friend, or relationship. Or possibly a client or patient if you have one.

In the big picture, there are countless deceased who are still confined to the terrestrial in energetic form, for fear of hell and purgatory. Trapped souls in a web of conditions, composed of threads of menacing precepts and judgments. Sometimes for centuries.

Let's delve a little further into the purpose behind this controlling need. Soul energy, which in this way remains trapped by fear, feeds the spider, the 'devil in disguise', that has spun the web. Clients, looking back from a past life or on behalf of a deceased parent or ancestor, literally speak of an upside-down world. The realization that, "it is not so much God as his opposite, that is the driving force behind this religious world," leads to huge indignation and bewilderment. Often it is only after sessions that one realizes what the constructed image of God is, and what this name really stands for, and that it actually forms a kind of wolf in sheep's clothing. The realization dawns that man has allowed himself to fit too easily into the dark dream of the institution of power as dictatorship. Modified by intrusive prayers, menacing theories, and false prospects. It is a painfully acquired but crucial realization for a new incarnation, which allows one to freely determine how a divine principle can be experienced during a human life. As CEO of a carefully concealed mega multinational, with the Catholic Church as a cover, this wolf mines life force fuel and sells it to those who have become dependent on him. God gives what you need, the devil what you want. A shadowy game whose engine runs on premium fear. The parallel with oil for the internal combustion dependency of our visible world is also not that difficult to see: "The greater the need, the higher the price."

This manipulation must result in dependency through fear. That's the ultimate goal. Securing your business with foresight, with a plan for the future. Preferably in a way where this conditionality seems voluntary. Conditionality is the last key word of a powerful triptych that maps out the policy plan: sin, guilt, conditionality. "Sin" stands for a violation of a divine law or rule. Whoever makes the rules defines what is sinful as well as formulating the repercussions and can reap guilt. After all, for those who experience enough guilt, their right to be is at stake and that brings fear, lots of fear.

IS THE POWER OF THE CHURCH ON THE WANE?

According to official figures, there are currently about a billion Vatican supporters. It is important to emphasize that the influence of the church is of course not limited to this group. My brother-in-law from Argentina confirmed that the Mormons, Jesuits, Seventh Day Adventists, and Jehovah's are triumphantly operating at full tilt there and getting a hearing everywhere. So, all over the world, groups are still active in propagating and practicing all kinds of religious experiences.

When I see a range of dignitaries, such as Willem-Alexander and Máxima, standing next to Pope Francis, I also suspect that their meetings serve greater interests than devoted believers can imagine. The romanticized sight of the characteristic church towers in the center of nostalgic villages has become so completely familiar to us that we would miss them terribly were they no longer there. Originally, they were all dependencies of the Vatican, built with tragic mortar, mixed with loads of spiritual, emotional, and psychological injuries. Down the centuries many millions of the reincarnated have been deeply damaged and brainwashed. Keep in mind that this usually happened out of everyone's sight. Abuse did not take place in the church, but in its shadow zone. What did happen in the church was intended to give the impression that it was all about divine devotion. The truly dark spectacles I encounter in my practice took place behind the scenes. In the visible part, everyone showed themselves to be pious and loyal. It is comparable to the image presented by the present-day media to the public about what is going on in society, while the shadow world remains meticulously hidden.

Pope Francis makes remarkable statements. He speaks out about the need for a corona vaccine, and he condemns the rumor mill in which other news is circulating concerning this. According to him, we can consider that as fake news and conspiracy stories. A spiritual banishment of impure language. We hope that his entourage will not still attach eternal consequences to this. He recently stated in an interview with an Italian newspaper that a new dimension has been added to the explanation of 'hell'. Suddenly hell no longer exists. Souls who did not live in accordance with the guidelines simply disappear, according to Francis. In that case, a hell would at least offer some form of existence, but with its disappearance the right of a soul to exist is completely erased. In other words, those who do not comply with the guidelines and conditions no longer exist. Fear already reigned, but Francis changes gear. Where are all those supposed souls who are in hell if it wasn't there? Are they all in a state of emergency?

Is the power of the church really waning? It looks more like the effectiveness of its influence, in addition to millions of practicing believers, has moved to deeper regions. In that sense, you could say, power still reaches very far, without this being recognized as such.

CHAPTER 27

Herman as a child of the devil

"The devil can cite scripture for his purpose."
– William Shakespeare

CASE HISTORY

Herman is a middle-aged man. He has a remarkably impeccable appearance. Hair parted in a neat, almost old-fashioned way. Ironed shirt and trousers, shiny, polished shoes, Harry Potter glasses and a fancy sixties briefcase.

Herman shares his concerns about the social isolation he has gradually ended up in over the years. His inability to connect with his surroundings causes him to have hardly any contact with his wife and son. He rarely experiences them anymore and tends to run away when any kind of appeal is made to him. He can't enjoy good food and doesn't really know any expressions of happiness or merriment. Everything is experienced entirely within narrow structures and margins. Herman says himself that he has narcissistic traits. "Just like my father. I closed myself off at a very young age to the world around me. I'm there but never say anything. If there is a quarrel or conflict, I completely clam up." Herman also reports that he's terrible at handling any form of criticism. He totally shuts down if the slightest hint of it comes in his direction. His wife plays a crucial role in this. Her dominating presence constantly gives him the latent feeling that whatever he does is not good.

Herman says that he was an altar boy at a very young age. Because of his serious demeanor, he was favorite as cross bearer at the head of the funeral processions. Once he was also allowed to be an altar boy at a wedding, but it soon became clear that this boy was incapable of looking happy which immediately "put him back" to "funerals". Herman says: "I was always surrounded by sadness, but it didn't touch me, I just don't feel anything. Nothing touches me actually."

When I requested his biography, I learn that he lost his father Kees in 1987 to stomach cancer. Father is 56 years old at the time and Herman 18. We immerse ourselves in Kees' life. During the Hunger Winter of 1944 Kees is 13 years old. A time when people ate stickleback soup, and sugar beets had to sweeten the taste of flower bulbs. A time when green soap was collected because it was a precious item to exchange. Kees is followed by three more sisters and two brothers. His mother wields the scepter in an authoritarian way in the heavily Roman Catholic family. Father hardly plays a role and is only present in the background. Every day, as the eldest son, Kees is reminded of his great responsibility towards his brothers and sisters. A task that gives him the opportunity to be seen by God in a positive light, who, according to his mother, is constantly watching. Kees is encouraged to share his own minimum ration with the younger children. What he doesn't know about his mother is that she trades her body now and again for food. A shameful and desperate way for her to scrounge a meal. She compulsively and constantly ignores the consequences the church attaches to extramarital sexuality. She has to.

Under great pressure, Kees must become a responsible, self-sacrificing savior. Every day his mother reminds him of the watchful gaze of God. It's also his task to go out looking for food and gather wood. One day, due to an unexpected twist of fate, he finds a bread roll. Feeling overwhelmed and confused in equal measure by this gift from heaven, Kees decides to keep this treasure for himself. When he gets home, he hides his loot, but mother catches him in the act. The repercussions are enormous. Mother is seething and crushed. At a single stroke the ideal image of her son falls to bits causing her own suppressed truth to start to emerge. In her inability to express herself, under the influence of the misery of war and indoctrination of the church, she lets Kees know that he is "a child of the devil, because they too steal from the poor." In doing so, she also projects her own confession of guilt onto him.

Kees deeply internalizes this condemnation. Without a word, without expression. It takes on a life of its own inside him. For punishment, his ration is cut in half, so that Kees experiences a gnawing feeling of hunger in his stomach over a longer period. The overriding thought in his narrow perception is, so long as I feel this hunger, God cannot punish me anymore. In other words: so long as my stomach hurts from hunger, I have been good. A yawning gap grows between mother and son. Somehow or other he avoids her while at the same time she stands for the one who determines his own right to be. After all, this condemnation came from the lips of the one in whose womb he had spent nine months. The one who had welcomed and fed him at the beginning of his life.

DEEP GROOVES ON AN EMOTIONAL AND PSYCHOLOGICAL LEVEL

Everyone eventually survives the war, at least physically. On an emotional and psychological level, it leaves deep grooves in everyone, especially Kees. Mother loses herself even more than before in prayer and devotion to the church, and the bond with her family and life in general disintegrates further. Father disappears even more into the background. He never learned how to make his presence known. His wife took care of that. At the same time, Kees' father was the safe haven. He did not judge him and made no statements about God. So long as father was still around, Kees somehow still felt the connection with someone who it felt good to be with. Where he was allowed to 'be'.

Once Kees becomes a father himself, he knows no joy, no form of joy about life. He is skinny and incapable of enjoying a morsel of food. Because he is so desperately withdrawn and believes deep down that he is indeed a child of the devil, he develops patterns that isolate him socially. A 13-year-old child is locked up deep inside him, a child who believes he has no right to be. Herman calls his father a narcissist, a father with whom no one can make contact.

Some years after Kees' father, Herman's grandfather, died in 1984, Kees developed stomach cancer and dies a few years later. Kees' father meant more to him than just a father. The presence of his father provided him with a right to be, as a counterpoint to his mother's extreme pronouncements. Father is life, mother is death. In his inner world, now that his father is no longer on earth, he experiences that he has also lost the person with whom he still felt safe enough to be. By developing a disease, he basically follows him, so that he can be with him in a 'different world'. Another world where his 'no right to live' cannot be determined by mother any longer. Three years after Kees' death in 1990, his mother passed away. We make contact with her, Herman's grandmother, through Herman.

In the contact with grandma, we discover how eaten away she has become inside. The condemnations she made, based on all kinds of insane views, especially about her necessary extramarital sexual behavior, are disastrous. She has completely handed over her natural authority as a mother to an ecclesiastical institution, which has presented her with a devilish image of God. The image of an authoritarian, all-powerful, God who sets strict conditions. A super-powerful supreme being who condemns human souls and can put them in hell forever. With no way of escape. For grandma it has become an unfiltered assumption. She, in turn, became indoctrinated by her parents and environment during her childhood. Her position in that family, along with her receptivity to the influence of both her father and mother and various events that took place there, framed by ecclesiastical contexts, were already breeding grounds for subsequent misery.

Because of this, grandma is damaged to the fiber of her being. Even though she has physically died, she cannot let go of the earthly realm. She is still consumed by feelings of guilt towards her son Kees. She has been harnessed by the tenacious energetic layers that prevent her from acting out of her original role of being a mother.

We release the ingrained pains and condemnations through a dialogue with grandma's soul. This is accompanied by intense emotional discharges that express themselves through Herman. At the same time, deep insights arise into how thoroughly the Catholic belief system has worked its way into this family. We connect grandma and her son Kees. Admittedly this takes place at the level of the soul, but Herman experiences it as completely real and true. Although they had both died, there has never been conscious contact between them. For that, even in that dimension, they were still too far apart, just as it had been on earth. Kees and his mother experience the beginning of an exchange. For the first time Herman experiences a profound discharge, but especially a feeling of relief, both in his emotional world and his intestines. These sensations are difficult to describe. A spectator can see it clearly through an alternation of all kinds of facial expressions, emotional discharges, tremors, sighs, and tears.

In the period that follows, Herman undergoes a substantial transformation. He feels more understanding and recognition for himself and experiences a heartfelt connection with his father. He releases himself from his own restrictive behavior and feels freer. The questions he is now going to ask, about himself and his life, bring him into different territory.

THE DECISION NEVER TO CRY AGAIN

In a subsequent session, we discover the existence of a Jewish boy around ten years old in one of Herman's past lives. This life takes place at the time of the Second World War and the persecution of the Jews. When the boy is brutally separated from his mother in a concentration camp, he cries his eyes out. A guard's piercing and menacing look lets him know he should never have cried, and that now it's his own fault he was taken away from his mother. In a paralysis of fear from deep within, the boy decides never to cry again. He somehow hopes to get noticed and be reunited with his mother as a reward. He blindly follows the commands and orders of the guards and capos and emerges as a good and obedient boy prisoner. He is allowed to work with the dead bodies in the camp, an honorary job.

Removing clothing, searching trouser pockets, collecting rings, earrings, and other valuables. The dead are familiar to him, there he can show what he is worth in the silent hope of seeing his mother again. In the meantime, living conditions are appalling. Hunger is a greater enemy than the guards. At some point, he can't resist the temptation to steal food. Convinced that no one sees it, he puts a piece of bread in his pants pocket. But then that guard is standing there who gets a huge kick out of catching the boy. A disgusting, sadistic grin appears on his face. The kid is completely beaten up with particularly vicious blows to the stomach. Cowering and numb with pain, he remains true to his promise not to express any feeling. Much to the displeasure of the guard. Strangulation follows with the guard's hands clamped around the boy's neck. The death struggle that he no longer consciously experiences, deeply engraves the need not to show any expression. Because now its crunch time. After all, dying without ever being able to see his mother is out of the question.

The emotional discharges that follow are impressive. Step by step, more awareness begins creeping in about his (then) death. Herman laughs when he really wants to cry. He has unlearned how to do the latter. Still, it was a close call, and ironically, there is nothing to laugh about either. When I underline that, then it actually becomes laughable again, which makes for more laughter and therefore the need to cry. In any case, his frozen emotional world is finally thawing. Herman is overwhelmed by it. He spontaneously remembers making a powerful decision as a 10-year-old boy in his current life. His mother, who was outrageously normative and demanding, threatened to leave. If things didn't go 'as they should', mother went out of her mind. And Herman automatically felt responsible for that. Then Herman decided never to cry again, to close off his emotional world once and for all. "Bizarre – that was at about the same age as that little Jewish boy during the war," he says.

Naturally, we also make a connection between the same themes that his father had in this life and Herman in a previous one. Namely, that stealing food leads to death. The extreme intention to close off one's own emotional world and to switch to a blind conformation to one's surroundings. In both cases that was essentially embodied by a demanding mother who set strict conditions. In the previous life it was a guard who made the separation with mother a fact which caused a separation between mind and feeling. How fascinating it is to consider that such circumstances appear to be able to facilitate such disorders, that we, usually in one or more subsequent lives, call narcissistic or psychopathic.

In any case, Herman's face is open, as well as the rusted door to his emotional world. Time can now heal the wounds because everything can start to flow again.

CHAPTER 28

Systems of power behind the church

"The truth will set you free, but first it will piss you off."
– Gloria Steinem

Clients, as I have said, make mention of a kind of illustrious power organization behind the church décor so often, that it seems to have every semblance of being there. Although naturally the personal therapeutic process always has and gets priority, it raises questions when so much trauma seems to be consciously controlled from behind some dark desk. Even though I had been thoroughly immersed in this matter for decades, I received the strongest confirmation for the existence of such a conspiracy from my clients. Maybe I should turn it around: because I received so many signs in my practice, I started to delve into it. It was certainly not wishful thinking. The effect of a session gains a much broader perspective when these areas also come into the picture, as it turned out many times. And that can only become clear as soon as it is also reported regardless of whether it is stimulated by questions. Independently of each other, clients talked about it themselves, some in more detail than others, while most of them had never explored this matter. It is of the utmost importance here to ask the right questions. Things frequently do not turn out to be as they seem.

For example, after a grandmother told me that she was raped under nasty circumstances, I ask her sincerely and very neutrally if she may have experienced any feelings other than the miserable ones she described. But the cat comes out of the bag here. Because it turns out that she has distorted her experience in such a way, emphatically calling it rape, out of the fear of being judged by her environment, which is permeated by imposed norms and values. She did this so powerfully that she started to believe in it herself. In the end, she admits in all vulnerability that she enjoyed the physical togetherness because she felt love for the first time. Obviously, this is certainly not always the case. You can simply check it with the right question at the right time. And once it opens doors to a deeper dimension of truth, the insight increases on a greater scale.

Indeed, there seems to be a lot going on. On a huge scale. When people's traumas are essentially the result of a consciously filled-in agenda, who dares to really see said agenda? Isn't the scale of this so daunting that it is tempting to regard all kinds of tragedies in history as a more or less logical consequence of human evolution? If all these painful human events from past and present lives form the pixels of a bigger picture, what does that bigger picture show? An elephant in the room that is so large that we do not perceive it because we are always distracted by all kinds of unimportant details and messages.

Precepts and announcements imposed on us and constantly demanding our attention, with a weekly highpoint during the high mass, in which everything is neatly rearranged back into place, have an important purpose. As a significant part of the power game, we need to be functionally distracted so that we don't get to see the big picture. Once upon a time, we were consciously part of that total picture, like "the wise Indian" who knows himself to be part of one great divine creation. Until for many it crumbled, in stages, across many lives. There seems to be a program behind it, a sphere of influence, a brain. And now the soul wishes to awaken that memory, so that the whole can be lived again. The first rays will shine for everyone once more, re-illuminating the entire image, causing the mists of deception to lift.

Did this ever happen to you before? At school, sometimes at the fair or if you were lucky at a children's party. Whenever there was a puppet show, and everyone was breathlessly following the action, some annoying wise guy would always get up at the most exciting bit, pull the curtains aside, look inside, pointing, and then laughing sarcastically. He wanted to reveal to everyone that there were people hidden behind that puppet theater. Sometimes he was so clumsy he knocked over its outer panels. A little conspiracy theorist no one needs. At least, not if the show is really engaging and childishly innocent. It's a beautiful metaphor for a TV, just about the most penetrating propaganda tool of our time. A child is not yet interested in the real motives that breathe life into Punch and Judy's adventures, but if they were to profoundly influence and disrupt this child's world, then it is time to discover whose hands are pulling the strings and making them move. Preferably before everyone is so familiar with these figures that they are no longer able to accept that the characters are being manipulated. Literally by invisible hands. The ease with which the shouting children want to warn Punch about the bad guy hiding behind the curtain matches the ease with which adults assume that the bad guy, the terrorist, the virus, the alarmist, is a self-contained danger operating all on its own. If there were no such bad guy, no one would look at the puppet show anymore. Meanwhile, it keeps us constantly occupied: the puppet show, on TV.

SPIRITUAL GARBAGE COLLECTOR

I sometimes jokingly call myself a spiritual garbage collector in this work. Just like a good cook who wants to know where his ingredients come from before working with them, a garbage man also wonders what he is working with too. Doing no more than transporting garbage bags only adds to the fact no real insight is gained into the history of the waste. And so, the working method remains unchanged and does not evolve. Meanwhile, old systems can continue, without them evolving with the times. My Mohawk grandmother Sara once told me I ought to use "vulture medicine" in my work. She authenticated that statement with the help of a feather from a griffon vulture that she took out of a drawer and gave to me. She emphasized the uniqueness of the vulture as part of creation because of the enormous potential it has for allowing transformation to take place. A vulture has a very specific quality, namely, the ability to transform the most contaminated remains on earth. Its digestive system can handle this. In this way it contributes to a profound cleaning up operation in our circle of life. I think it's a very respectful comparison. Waste, in this context the indigestible layers arising from unprocessed feelings and emotions, however, becomes increasingly difficult to digest and dispose of, if all kinds of tricks have been pulled with it. It requires a great deal of creativity from the vulture, and the garbage man.

Anyone wanting to understand how power exercises control must be able to travel some distance down the rabbit hole to discover what is really being concocted there. And who better to tell that than those who were dragged into it? So, my clients. Incidentally, and at the risk of repeating myself, clients were not only sucked in as victims. Many also experienced being part of power organizations that manipulated and abused people. Even though those lives took place in a bygone era, they essentially employed the same methodologies as they do today. The massive spreading of disinformation and fear appear. In obvious synergy with the corresponding zeitgeist.

COMPLICATIONS IN THE DYING PROCESS

What my clients taught me to see is that the human process of dying contains an inordinately unnatural number of complications due to people having been fed anxiety throughout their lives. Beliefs about hell, punishment, damnation, or the non-existence of a spiritual essence, as science claims, have a catastrophic and stagnating effect on the course of dying. All this complicates the extremely delicate and vulnerable process. Deep-seated misconceptions about life and death, poisoned beliefs about one's own parents, partners, or children, or about oneself, also cause stagnation. Ideas and programs that assume that life mainly has to do with social success, competition, being pious and restrained and not making mistakes. That war is necessary to get peace, that we need leaders and authorities above all else, and that excessive medical treatments are needed to guide someone to a final stage in a desired way. You name it. During the process of dying, the soul prefers to shake off as much as possible that does not tie into its own inner truth. As well as what the person himself had wrongly assumed was the truth but does not appear to belong in this category. The consequences of his actions are shown to him introspectively. In essence, all those assumptions, deceptions, and beliefs are showered with love.

The soul is unable to carry all the foreign energies with it through the eye of the needle, as a symbolic representation for the process of dying. The residual processing, the excess ballast, everything that cannot be taken to the spiritual world, lingers like smoke in a café after a busy evening. It clusters around the stragglers. Therefore, incomplete dying is a burden not only for the person who is dying, but also for those who survive them. To be clear, I don't want to make a value judgment about it, and I believe that in a sense we are always dealing with burdens that have been passed down that lead to new growth opportunities for our successors. What matters more to me is to expand on that and closely examine the things that are deliberately manipulated and created. To understand the specific working methods of a world of power, it is important to realize that stagnation is the desired condition for those in power. The most important starting point for their policy. This feeding of fear and disinformation brings about a strong lockdown in the transmission of life force and life experience, of ancestral information between generations.

FRAGMENTATION OF FAMILY TREE TRANSFERS

So, is it precisely a question of disrupting these family tree transfers beforehand in such a way that separation and fragmentation arise? Quite a few of those who have undergone past life regression say they are – those who are so sensitive to trance that they can draw answers from dimensions that go beyond their own perceptions. There's no denying that. What can we learn from this? What can we do?

The flow of the original vitality, also called life energy, prana, Qi or 'the breath of the great mind', decreases through these interventions. Connections between the various family members are weakened and the confusion that this brings creates clouded exchanges that do not resonate on our sounding board. We feel like our lines are crossed and we can no longer understand the essence of our ancestors. It could be, for example, that an ancestor is held captive in the conviction held by his own family tree relatives for far too long, so that those certain acts he once committed remain buried in a condemnation, as in a status quo. The question "Why did he behave that way?" is not asked and therefore not answered. Due to the leakage of energy, the curiosity that someone should normally have about the actual circumstances also weakens. Hence my advice, revive your curiosity about your ancestors as much as you can and encourage your loved ones to do the same.

I remember an example of a Jewish woman who married a man with a non-Jewish surname during World War II. This kept her safe and she was not discovered. Her father, mother, brothers, and sisters were taken to an extermination camp where hardly anyone survived. The woman was ashamed to the core that she had survived and been saved, and that she could go on living. Talk about the right to be. To survive, she developed a behavioral structure that made her very hurtful and distant towards her immediate environment, including her children. A strategy that ensured that no one got too close, which meant people found her nasty and cold. To some extent, of course, that is quite understandable. However, there has never been any substantial understanding and openness for the pain at the root of her actions, in the generations after her. This woman went down in the family history after her death (she was only 56) as a gloomy mother and grandmother. I consider this condemnation to be the cause of a torpid state of being in the family.

No one knows how to break through this and the person who asks challenging questions is quickly considered difficult and dismissed. No one wants to be reminded of grandma. Grandma, in turn, is unable to let go of her family. For that to happen, her own deeper truth must first awaken for her progeny. A truth that does not match the misinterpretations and ignorance of her descendants. That is why she remains attached to a granddaughter. She can still compulsively manipulate her from her own spirit, jealously clinging to the old survival patterns she had developed in her lifetime. The truth behind all her pain comes out during a session in a poignant dialogue with grandma, with this granddaughter as the medium. Acceptance and recognition finally emerge through the understanding of her having genuinely suffered as a victim of war. Recognition from one of her own descendants, because that is what really counts - not if an outsider understands it for her. Only now can the life energy, blocking her and her family tree, flow on again and find its way through the lives of her (grand) children. And the latter is tangibly quite noticeable for those involved. Even for family members who were not present at the session.

HURT FAMILY TREES ARE EASIER TO MANIPULATE

What can we conclude from this? Hurt family trees are easier to manipulate. The business plan for a controlling mechanism of this order, entails exploiting maximum energy leaks in family trees. They provide space to infiltrate. The result is that all participants or generations must hesitantly reinvent the wheel again and again, and for that they draw increasingly less from original sources and more from artificially devised systems. You cannot plant seed in the fertile soil of your ancestry in this way. This brings to my mind the following metaphor to make the comparison.

The biotechnology company Monsanto uses the same principle. By means of genetic modification, seeds are processed in such a way that the crops yielded are themselves incapable of producing fertile seed. This is a radical artificial intervention in the cycle of the original biological growth processes of Mother Nature. Since I don't do therapy with plants, I cannot substantiate that plant consciousness is also traumatized at these levels. What shamans, medicine people and seers have to say about this is unequivocal. Every gross, violent and artificial intervention in total disregard of divine life, yields fissures with accompanying trauma, regardless of the life domain in which it takes place. I don't find it hard at all to see it that way. Manipulation and tinkering take place at molecular level, to conjure a property in a plant that is alien to nature and can be instantly patented. For what purpose? To make the farmer dependent on the seed supplier every year and to sell pesticides which make the plant artificially resistant. So, this also causes stagnation in the growth and evolution of family energy flows. To put it into human terms – maybe that way we are eating autistic, epileptic and stress-infused foods. Power organizations that dictate with the obligatory propaganda how they think everything should be, are given a reason to exist. It is important to emphasize that they are completely dependent on our ignorance about this.

Trauma also partly determines the arrangement of DNA structures, which manifests itself in damaged coding. As nicely shown by the studies of Dr. Masuru Emoto with his water molecules. There, in the spaces created because of the damage caused, infiltration proves very effective. The unadulterated foundation on which our ancestor's experiences are based is becoming increasingly difficult to reach. Through the holes that have emerged in it, a surrogate breeding ground is laid for unwanted parasitic visitors. When ancestors were formed by strict religious upbringing, or rather deformed, this very often led to transgressive behavior and distorted situations. Practically always arising from the initially frantic attempts to meet the standards and requirements that were imposed. Actions sprang from an excess of prohibitions and conditions, which always had a counterproductive effect, that could not bear the light of day. This created a shrouded, murky hell of a world of abuse and misery. One that was never talked about again, that was swept under the rug. This is how it went with many great-grandmothers and fathers or grandparents. 'Bad' deeds snuck up on them and guilt complexes arose, the preliminary stages of the secrets taken later to the grave. Such secrets are the events and life stages that were undergone in which too much unresolved misery was trapped. The life energy continued to keep the one trapped in captivity. Events that ended up in isolation and whose doors are kept closed deep into the grave out of shame, disgrace, guilt, and fear of reprisals.

THE GOD STANDARD AS UTOPIA

The idealized image of someone fully compliant with the standard of God is not only utopian, but also something quite unnatural to pursue. People need it in their various incarnations to experiment and experience. The extremer the conditions, the more excessive the consequences. In this way they gain the life experiences associated with their karmic journey and grow towards a natural and self-realized 'soul personality'. A soul manifested in matter, as a human expression of the ultimate aspect of the divine in an earthly world. In fact, we become 'only' ourselves. There are no appropriate words that can describe what that means. If there were as many words to be found as the countless tones between the musical notes that are familiar to us, but to which our hearing is not attuned, then things would probably be better. The more artificial boundaries that are placed on human living conditions, the worse, more violent, and bumpy those various lives will be. Every quest has a reason. The most important is to find where we lost ourselves, regardless of the circumstances under which that happened. Even though your head was sometimes handed to you.

Obviously, it's not all doom and gloom. Lest we forget. Previous generations left us a lot of beautiful things that we could build on. Where ancestors got stuck, new growth opportunities open for the offspring. Many parents see it as their natural responsibility to provide their children with as much good as possible. And for that they don't always have to set a good example. In this way we invest in our own future. Especially if we are going to travel this world again.

Still, when it comes to the downside as described in the many examples, ancestral influence is literally unprecedented, and especially invasive. The influence of old, painful, mostly church-related stories remains very strong in family systems, so long as they remain couched in such spellbinding expletives as hell and damnation. The many dead, who are held in captivity behind the scenes of our power of vision, give the dimension between earth and heaven a fixed structure. They cannot be released and so the frequencies in this intermediate field remain of a low order. There can no longer be a beneficial exchange with them, even though that need is there. The day must come when appropriate attention has to be paid to intergenerational dilemmas, as is ultimately determined by universal laws. You can't escape that; everything eventually wants to start flowing again. But in the meantime, in our conditioned world, everything is done to prevent the stories from coming to the surface to keep putting that off for as long as possible. Over time the water accumulated behind the dam and has built up an ever-increasing desire to be allowed to flow again, which will cause the dam to burst, no matter how thick the concrete is.

Based on a similar principle, many an ancestor comes off a pedestal during sessions, tired of having to uphold their image or keep secrets intact. While yet others become visible again and get their voices (back). All parties ultimately experience this as very liberating.

Contrary to what was (and is) held out to us by the church, through romanticized representations of things, weighty promises, pretexts and hypnotizing togetherness, the well-being of many parents and ancestors appears to be painfully and transpersonally affected. By transpersonal, I mean previous personalities that we carry within us of those we once were, in previous lives. We were regularly one of our own ancestors. In that case we are in incarnated again in the same families, a (number of) generation(s) later.

In summary, the most destructive aspect of the image of God, injected on such a massive scale, is that it exists outside of ourselves, that we are looked down upon by a conditional and punitive majesty, whereby those who do not adhere to "His" precepts are sinners who end up in hell for all eternity after dying.

GIGANTIC COMMUNICATION GAPS BECAUSE OF A LANGUAGE BEING BANNED

My intensive contacts with indigenous peoples helped open my eyes further. The suppression, subjugation, and decimation of entire populations 'in the name of God' has left deep wounds. It is still transparently observable today how this trail of devastation extends to the current generation of these peoples. Under violent duress, they were no longer allowed to live according to their own original values, which in fact bear a much deeper essence when it comes to the experience of spirituality. We all know it, but when you are among them on a regular basis it really hits you.

Natural peoples have all had their turn worldwide, that cannot be denied. One of the Canadian first nation tribes, the Iroquois, were systematically forbidden by the church and government to speak their own language. Right up to the end of the last century. The punishments were inhumane. In practical terms, the English language imposed on them never covers the energetic overtones of what really wants to be expressed. This leads to gigantic communication gaps. A stunned silence that prevents the stories of the grandfathers and grandmothers from being heard and which are no longer a living part of the treasures of the family tree. In countless forms. The traumatization that this results in literally translates to an entire generation. There is currently an epidemic of thyroid disease among women in the reserves where I work, which they have often had ever since they were teenagers. We discovered the connections during the workshops in which I do so-called 'demo sessions' in learning settings, surrounded by dozens of interested parties and stakeholders. Diseases that basically turn out to be physical manifestations of millions of unexpressed, pent-up sounds and words from previous generations/lives. Or put more clearly, the silenced cry for help, understanding and recognition, or the pain that has not been screamed out, translates into matter in the form of dysfunctional thyroid glands. The medical world prides itself on having developed ever better treatments and medication. But how much awareness does it take to see that the real healing is genuinely a matter of unblocking things that have literally been rammed down people's throats? And that it does not take place by chemical management that focuses solely on the physical effects of all this internalized chaos that makes it seemingly more bearable. This is but a single example of the many other consequences of damage inflicted throughout the course of history. It shows that a great deal of the influence of the church has spread like an oil slick wreaking disease through countless eras and populations.

Historically speaking, I don't imagine being able to add anything spectacular to what has already been written, although the authenticity of our case histories is peppered with "Native American stories." But I can add something about how this burdened history is passed on to new generations – and that this seems to be a consciously organized route.

CHAPTER 29

Authentic spiritual dedication

"Devil made religion and stirred it in a pot. And true believers bent to the east others prayed to a cross."
– 'Devil made religion' – Cuby & the Blizzards (famous Dutch blues band)

There are certain moments during a session when it feels like the voice of a client's soul is particularly resonant. This is distinguished by a subtle but noticeable change in intonation. It is a truly special encounter. My natural reaction, as a guide, is a slight tendency to make a reverent bow, without feeling submissive. A deeper, place of wisdom residing in my client then comes more to the fore and holds forth. I assume that this wisdom has always been there in the background with everyone. Somewhat veiled.

A kind of silence ensues, a moment of peace, and one's spiritual essence shines through, wishing to clarify a few things. It is a voice that comes through like the sun on a cloudy sky. Remarkably this voice often emerges in the space that arises after certain emotions have been expressed that have been pent up for so long. The content of what is then said is so pure, so striking and so gently poignant, that it vibrates from soul to soul. The voice comes as a kind of gift, where the client realizes that the heavy lifting had to be done first because explaining alone does not bring any real change.

Children can have that too. Such an 'out of the blue' intervention. Suddenly they say something at the right time, with a certain timbre, with a certain look in their eyes or with specific sign language that makes the missing explanation clear. Unfiltered, their message comes across to the person they are speaking to, usually a parent, in a way that is truly moving. The usual control melts away for a moment, and bang, a tear or valuable insight appears, or both. I sometimes ask where this voice comes from. The answers are always along the lines of someone's 'inner self', 'a deeper awareness', or 'spiritual essence'. Originating from a tirelessly loving character, eternally connected to a source of love from the power of creation. A source from which the soul is born and allows itself to be propelled as though in the current of a river. It knows no other goal than the pursuit of self-realization, of perfection. Crucial intuitions, as you can sometimes get at the most unexpected and unguarded moments, seem to emanate from the same source.

THE ENVIRONMENT VIBRATES ALONG WITH IT

What is remarkable and surprising during sessions is that the environment reacts and participates in the vibrations that are raised stemming from the activated stirrings of the soul. It is not only the changing atmosphere that is emotionally noticeable at important moments, but also things literally move. Suddenly, a bumblebee comes flying out of nowhere into the practice room just as a grandfather makes an important revelation. In the view outside my practice window, a buzzard unexpectedly spectacularly swoops down through the garden, just when someone finally feels connected with his long-suppressed anger. One time I even witnessed a hawk ripping into one of our unsuspecting chickens just as a client was telling the story of how he was being attacked from behind in a war situation. Indeed, that's when you think things couldn't get much crazier.

A squirrel with a walnut in its mouth euphorically passes the practice room from a short distance while someone is undergoing an experience from the Hunger Winter in which a secret storage space with stolen food is discovered by the wrong people with fatal consequences. At some crucial moments during a session, dark gray clouds suddenly gather from a clear sky when a client opens up to all the overwhelming sadness running through his mother's family since practically everyone was transported to camps during the war. Thunder, lightning, downpours and rays of sun suddenly bursting through the clouds – apparently everything joins in. It undoubtedly helps that my practice is in the beautiful northern Dutch province of Drenthe, somewhat remote and surrounded by natural beauty.

Hares, passing deer, woodpeckers, even dogs that have broken loose from the leashes of local hikers appear at the most appropriate times to reinforce a certain sensation. Yes, even annoying blowflies join in, who have chosen the nose of one of my clients in a state of trance, as a favorite landing spot. It doesn't take much imagination to place them in the context of the story that is coming to the surface. I remember a session with a nine-year-old boy with a deep-seated fear of planes flying over. And yes, to his and his mother's great astonishment, one promptly flew over, the moment I asked him about that fear. As if I had a secret remote control to make that happen. And to be clear, aircraft hardly ever fly over our place.

When a person opens deeply to inner emotions, the environment seems to respond to them. This is something that probably happens all the time, but during sessions where, by definition, processes of transformation are activated, it is quite pronounced. We rarely consciously perceive it, but everyone knows these kinds of magical moments. This comes as no surprise to many indigenous peoples. After all, everything is interwoven. We are constantly creating movement in our environment. In other words, we create our own reality. They call the creation of everything that exists in conjunction, in relation to each other, the Great Mystery.

THE SOUL KNOWS NO PREFERENCE

The point I want to make with the above is about the interface of this voice of the soul with what we usually call the divine. These special dialogues of the soul in no way give the impression that there is any need to express our divine nature according to specific customs, conditions, systems of debt systems or invasive symbols. If there were to be any kind of preference, it would be something based on unconditionality. And that can safely be celebrated and assented to. If so desired with symbols and all kinds of expression. So long as love is the intention behind it. For the soul, it does not matter whether this is done through a stone, a tree, a star, the sun, a color, an animal, or song.

This unadulterated spiritual devotion has quite often given way to systems that interpret, set conditions, and restrict freedom. Now they are so ingrained and passed down for so many generations that few want to openly question them. Some, for example, prefer to stifle the physical reactions to the nauseating incense swished their way during church rituals, rather than daring to say they don't really like it. Is it human nature that we first must become so sick to our stomach before we take other paths? Perhaps. However, the need to see the forest for the trees again also seems to be innate. No hype is blessed with eternal life.

When I watch and listen to a group of dedicated, dark, corpulent men and women gospel singers, joy tingles down my spine. They go crazy, swinging and swaying in a church practically bringing the house down with their beautiful à cappella singing. Thereby expressing their deepest devotion to their version of God, represented by a symbol of a cross that hangs behind them on the wall. The colorful clothing and radiant white teeth in the full, dark faces completes the spectacle. It feels so sincere, powerful, and beautiful that it has a very life-enhancing effect. At the same time, I find it incredibly easy to imagine the same group of people who would stand singing and dancing with equal devotion in a circle of stones around a chosen tree with colored strings fluttering through the wind, while wearing a symbol of the four wind directions around their necks. What does that matter to them? The form is of secondary importance, but the passionate expression of gratitude remains the same. The extremely sad facial expression of the suffering and bleeding Jesus, who is always the main character behind many of these settings, unfortunately remains unaffected despite this passionate cheerfulness. As if He is in the throes of eternal depression that, no matter what we do, he must constantly remind us of the eternity of our guilt. Authentic devotion to our spiritual nature, regardless of how we experience it, is separate from imposed norms and conditions.

CHAPTER 30

Attachments with the deceased

"Sometimes you have to fall into traps so that you learn how to get out of them."
– Vaker Vrolijk (Dutch lifestyle blog)

It may sound strange, but a deceased person needs to realize that he is dead. This is not always the case for all kinds of reasons and new generations can be adversely affected by this.

In the chapter that follows I have worked out a detailed account of a session from my practice. It is the profound story in which Aafkje, my client, very clearly bears the consequences of an anxiously hidden tragedy that previously took place in the same family. In the runup to this, I pay extra attention in this chapter to the phenomenon of 'entity attachments'. This is an attachment of one or more deceased person(s) to a living person and vice versa. Dramatic events that once took place are crucial breeding grounds for this and are a prerequisite to give these connections the right to exist.

The most typical features of this family drama are very similar to many other church-related sessions with ancestors. You see how literally we remain connected to old events in new generations. Not just psychological but certainly also serious physical complaints, which often occur in my practice, clearly express what "was never allowed to be talked about in the past." When serious physical ailments reveal themselves in someone, this is accompanied by entanglements with entities that feed them. No major complaint is isolated. The basis of the complaint can be found in the original event that once took place and in which the now deceased person, usually a family member, played a role. There is a lot of uncertainty about these entity attachments, while the phenomenon is constantly manifested in my practice.

THE ABSOLUTE REFUSAL TO ACCEPT DEATH

A person in a process of dying while fearing hell is like a cat backed into a corner. He, more than any other person who is dying, is incapable of passing away well. Distraught, afraid of the misleading stories with which he was burdened an entire lifetime, often from early childhood. He now projects the doomsday scenarios he came to believe onto a self-spun web seeking the opening of a passage that he knows he must go through. But he prefers to keep himself locked up. Anything better than the horrible reality he expects afterwards in which his right to be will no longer be the starting point. He wants to postpone dying and slams on the brakes with all his might. Meanwhile, the weary, dying body descends deeper into inevitable death. These opposing forces characterize the well-known death throes. Ultimately, sucked into a state of violent disorientation, he is hardly or even completely unaware of the fact that he physically died.

To consciousness it is one huge mess in which the connection with physical reality, the actual dying, has become disconnected from the eternal soul. Underlying this is the absolute refusal to truly accept death. He still perceives surrender to mean that he is doomed to go to hell. That manipulated imagined authenticity is completely alien to the soul. For the soul no such thing as a final destination exists, a place where you would not have a right to be or where the basis is formed by all sorts of punishment. This reality can only be created temporarily, so long as the soul still lingers in a vibrational level close to the terrestrial. Because the idea of no longer existing after death is something that does not take root in the consciousness of the soul. People continue to resist dying because hell has been presented as something that is eternal. Then you have no other choice but to cling to the material.

Incidentally, not only in situations where one is afraid of hell does one cling to earthly familiarity. A scientifically minded rationalist, who during his life categorically ruled out any form of continued existence after death, is also incapable of dealing with a reality of sensations and awareness after his death. The perception he built up over a lifetime does not allow him to do so. Although he still 'is', he continues to deny this by clinging to old patterns and connections, such as his children. This soul does not experience that time passes here on earth, and that he is still clinging to circumstances that have passed. Someone who died twenty years ago and still holds on to his son, who was five at the time, does not realize that his child is now 25 years old. He can only perceive and influence him from the phase of his death, without him having consciously experienced his dying. Confusing?

AS A SOUL CLINGING TO FAMILY TREE RELATIVES

Although these deceased may very vaguely notice that something has changed, they remain in a state of confusion. A deceased person simply needs to realize that he is dead. Compare it with the following idea: anyone cycling on a country road where the road is a metaphor for the path of someone's life – with a pasture full of cows on one side and an empty pasture on the other – and who has only focused his attention on the empty one because he was told from an early age that that was what was real, may eventually be convinced that there are no such things as cows. Once he has died, he experiences that everything has remained the same: the empty pasture is still his only reality. He can't see anything else. He has also based his identity, his views and his actions on that image that has become familiar to him. The transformation of death has not yet manifested itself on all levels of his being. His focus remains unchanged. It is the same areas of focus as when he was still alive. The difference is that he notices that some of his relatives are less easily, or even no longer, accessible to his influence and presence. They don't respond like they used to. Others, conversely, appear to be very open and still receptive to his influence. As a result, he focuses on them with all the power in his soul. Often even to the point of obsession. And so, as a soul, he continues to cling to these family tree relatives. To a certain extent he is still able to experience the earth-bound state to which he was accustomed. For example, an entity can even smoke, bleed, and have a drink with someone and experience sexual energy. He can even experience the energy of a match in a football stadium when his (grand) son goes there. And to do that, he must influence them. There must be an energetic exchange, an interaction that continues to connect them. For him, life goes on, as it were, albeit in a disembodied way about which he has no awareness. We speak here of 'entity attachments'. In other words, of deceased ancestors who settle in the energetic field of a descendant who is still on earth.

The degree of disturbance depends, of course, on many factors. Only if there have been substantial conflictual and unresolved situations do these types of attachments continue to have an obstructive effect. Sometimes very long-term. A major portion of these associations dissolves naturally. This happens through dreams and all kinds of spontaneous exchanges, or because someone else points them out, touches upon them. It can also happen because people make important decisions about their lives, or that new loves or circumstances appear. The inner processes that are released again imperceptibly lead to letting go, processing and healing without a therapeutic intervention necessarily having to take place. Often it goes unnoticed, or at least not always in a directly conscious way. For example, because the death of a mother-in-law brings up the previous death of her own mother. The mother who has been attached to her up to that point can now break loose because the previously unexpressed emotions are now suddenly given free rein. It is always good and appropriate to rely on that. It concerns 'biodegradable spiritual waste'. The process is naturally fueled in the everyday human stream of life. The powers of the seasons also do their work here. Time does indeed heal wounds, and this has a natural course, on condition that life offers that space. However, so many influences thoroughly distract people from these natural possibilities. So much so that we have become alienated from the existence of such cross-links with the deceased.

RECEPTIVITY HAS A BASIS IN MAJOR LIFE EXPERIENCES

The phenomenon of entity attachments usually takes place from subconscious regions. It doesn't happen randomly at all. The so-called hosts must be sufficiently receptive to the presence of the spirit of a deceased person. It is about emotional connections, such as parents or grandparents with their (grand) children, or siblings or partners, or close friends, who have passed away.

This receptivity has a basis in major life experiences in which both have played a role.

If a child suddenly loses a parent, it is not possible for both the deceased parent and the child to let go of each other immediately. That requires a grieving process, longer or shorter, depending on the complications that were there and the space that that process gets. If the child's life leaves no room for going through this, for example because the immediate environment does not attach any importance whatsoever to processing, then those connections will last for a very long time. Over time, under the skin. The energetic presence of such a deceased person can even feel like it is your own in the long run. I remember a client who, as a 3-year-old girl, was saved from drowning by her father. He fished her out of the water just in time. Her father then told her many times, "If I hadn't been there, you wouldn't be alive anymore." After this lady later lost her father, she became seriously ill. Her utter conviction that "I can't live without my father," still troubled her. She thought she should always have him around. Her father, as a soul, could not let go of her because this contract was still active on his part. In a way, he always felt he could control her by constantly emphasizing this. After we were able to dispel these things, and she could then let go of her father, she got better. She had a tough time getting used to being able to lead her life under her own steam.

"IF I HURT, YOU HURT"

The consequences of entity attachments are played out on multiple levels: mental, emotional, and physical. They have a disruptive and in the long run even literally sickening effect. Someone losing a parent who suffocated to death, after which that parent keeps holding on, can also develop respiratory complaints. Or intestinal complaints if the cause of death can be found there. A descendant of an injured family member may begin to experience the physical pains caused by the accident, such as a blow to the head or shoulder against the street. Or a tightness on the chest because the body was crushed against the steering wheel.

In practice, the more severe cases of entity attachments usually come to light. Although the severity is also relative, because by far, most attachments take place out of ignorance. The bad consequence of holding on do not really get through to people. It is relatively easy to work with. As soon as there is more awareness about the state of being of the deceased, a liberating process of letting go is the automatic consequence.

However, there are also attachments that have a clearly hidden agenda. In addition, on an energetic level, fear is consciously fed to the male or female host. It sometimes happens that the deceased person is actively trying to force an illness, accident, suicide, or other doomsday scenario. At its core, this is done out of a compulsive need to be reunited with that person. Or a hateful program is running that is based on fear; 'If I hurt, you hurt.'

There is no reason to be unduly afraid, none of that just happens, but I still want to draw your attention to it. You often see such situations if a twin brother or sister has died in the womb. They cling to the living and still wish to be reunited. A kind of jealousy for the one who survived is then manifested, while the severe influence the dead twin still exerts, proves exhausting to the twin still living.

As mentioned, the energetic field or aura of the bearer must be accessible to these manifestations. And such fields are accessible in those places where major events once took place and damage occurred. The protective nature of the aura weakens as a result and becomes, as it were, available for unwanted influences. For example, people who from childhood have repeatedly been subjected to the menacingly raised voices of those drumming a religious belief into them, develop a weakened auric field around their head. In the long run, the head with the associated chakras is not sufficiently protected against people with loud voices. If they later have dealings with someone who speaks too loudly or intrusively then they dissociate. Or, for example, young people who had had all kinds of orders barked at them in military settings. They have become receptive to the instilled militaristic ideas that they are no longer able to filter out. These ideas make their disruptive appearance without being part of the original, authentic way of thinking. That can take extreme forms and even lead to hearing voices that inject compulsive messages into them.

KNEALING ON A BED OF VIOLINS

If a grandfather has sexually abused his (grand) daughter, this not only damages the physical part of the body around the sexual organ (or near the mouth, throat, or anus), but also the energy in and around it. The associated chakras no longer function optimally and start to exhibit disturbances. If this grandfather dies, it is very likely that he especially views that vulnerable place as one in which he can entrench himself – and therefore remains jealously earthbound. The management of the vital energy of the host has been chronically reduced. On top of that, old power relations can still play a role. At the level of a child, the person who is now an adult may still feel that "grandpa is the boss here." Or that, "it would have nasty consequences if I publicized what grandpa did." Grandpa's threats at the time still play an active role: "If you tattletale on me, I'll do something to your mother or your brother," "Then I'll drown your dog" or "Then you'll go to hell." Time has stood still here. Fifty, sixty or seventy years after an abusive past, a person may still believe that it will have serious consequences to talk about this. I have often heard this from clients who, through manipulative discouragements of confused, attached spirits, made the appointment for a session but kept putting it off or rescheduling it. They did this under the influence of the attached intruder. Even getting lost during the drive to my practice, resulting in being late, is common. In that case, I already know what to do. Somehow understandably so.

From grandpa's point of view, he must continue to exercise power over his (grand) daughter so that he does not have to face himself. In his experience, the latter also means that he would have to pay penance in hell for all eternity. A view that he also learned and came to believe in his childhood and resulting in his natural maternal bond being damaged early on. To compensate, he later abused his (grand) daughter. And so, it continues to fester, through generations. And yet these kinds of intensive cross-links want to be untangled. There is always a desire for letting go and healing.

Film can offer us more insight into the zeitgeist in which such stories originated. Think of the movie version of the novel by the Dutchman Jan Siebelink entitled *Kneeling on a Bed of Violins*, or the films *The Magdalene Sisters* and *Deliver Us from Evil*. Based on true accounts they sketch in an extremely realistic way the period in which our ancestors were still young and in which people became religiously caged with all the consequences that entails. When I look at the facial expressions on the old sepia family photos that clients sometimes bring with them, I see remarkable expressions. Sometimes you see exactly where the pain is and how the power relations must have once been.

They involve stories whose contents are disconcerting and usually horrific, which explains why many prefer to turn away from them. "Just the thought of it." As a therapist, I am used to that, but I understand that this can also be the case for the reader. The most prominent side effect of traumatization is precisely that no one wants to be involved in any way. And that's why those things keep festering for so long. Meanwhile, I have endless reasons to continue to share my experience because the outcome always brings improvement.

Let's get ready for Aafkje's story!

CHAPTER 31

Sex with God

"There is hardly anything that causes as much harm as the good: the deliberate good, the know-it-all good, the conceited good, the good that for the fool must be imposed on your fellow human being."
– Johannes Anker Larsen

The influence of the church plays a key role in the experiences of my client Aafkje. This story shows to which insane acts people can be incited if the claim to their right to exist was shrewdly manipulated with hell and damnation. Sometimes persistent silence out of sheer fear of life is the only option imaginable to get through life after extreme dramas have taken place.

CASE HISTORY AAFKE

Aafkje (1965) has had migraines ever since she was a teenager, which became more severe when her mother Jelly became seriously ill. She has since passed away. Aafkje does not believe that she will ever be cured of this again. "I've been on medication for years that slightly relieves the pain, but the side effects are at least as bad." With a stretched-out thumb and forefinger, she marks an imaginary line across her forehead, from temple to temple, and indicates the main area of pain with a contorted look on her face. Aafkje also talks about the extremely bad relationship with her mother with whom she has never had the experience of being able to make any connection. Throughout her life, she was plagued by frustration, as her younger brother was always held in high esteem, which was in stark contrast to the way her mother treated her. "I have developed an inferior self-image because of it," she observes self-consciously. "Since my mother's death, I have been inflicted with an indefinable sense of inner turmoil. Sometimes it's like I feel her around me. She still makes me feel like I can't do anything right. It drives me crazy. It controls me."

The biographical information about her mother's family leads to Gran, the mother of Aafkje's mother, who lived from 1912 to 2004. Gran and Jelly come from a good home. Well-to-do with prestige and a distinct voice in the parish. Everything in their lives was indisputably founded on the word of God. All fingers pointed to the Bible. At the same time, the family led a separate existence excluded from the village community. Having a high social status creates distance with ordinary citizens. They even had permanent places to sit in the church, at the front of the choir. Granny's remains have been lying for years under an imposing funerary monument in the cemetery of an idyllic Frisian (terp) village. It is sometimes said that a tombstone bears a characteristic reflection of the person lying beneath it. But what she took with her to the grave turns out to be very much alive. “Gran was an unpleasant, unfathomable woman,” says Aafkje. “Surly, aloof, very judgmental and even threatening. Authoritarian, right up to her last days. No one liked to come near her, and no one ever dared to answer her back, let alone get involved in a discussion. Gramps, who died much earlier because his lungs ran out of oxygen, suffered under her influence. He was a submissive, docile gray mouse who didn’t say much and smoked cigars.”

Gran’s dominant manners exhibit deeply etched trauma. Trauma that has influenced not only her own behavior, but also that of her husband, children, and grandchildren. We are going to investigate, via Aafkje. After she has closed her eyes at my request, I ask Aafkje to focus her attention inward. With a few simple trance-inducing instructions, she makes an inner connection with Gran. So much so that, through Aafkje, I can start a direct dialogue with Gran, as if she were a medium for her own ancestor. It happens in the blink of an eye. I see her face contort with pain and even take on a surly expression and we come into deeper and deeper contact with the energy, that is, Gran’s soul. In this phase of the therapeutic process, I am always determined to make this contact. Because there is often resistance and reluctance from the deceased in the beginning, as if they were being put on the spot, this brings some sort of compliance. As soon as it becomes clear that I am not out to caste any judgment whatsoever, there follows a kind of ‘okay then’, enabling the connection to remain for as long as necessary.

Nevertheless, the exchange with Grans gets off to a difficult start. I didn’t expect anything else. First of all, Gran was always used to pulling the strings herself, and at an even deeper level she did this with her domineering and threatening behavior in order to keep a big secret from the outside world under lock and key. Traits that still characterize her. Even though she is deceased. Coldness, relentlessness, and condemnation still permeate her charisma. Punishing her environment for what she in fact, blames herself for, as it will turn out later. As a therapist, I know that there are always huge hidden secrets behind such behavior. I have a lot of faith in that and that is precisely where the key lies. That is why I need to adopt as neutral and safe an attitude as possible.

RAPED IN THE NAME OF GOD

It soon becomes clear that Gran’s main doormat is her daughter Jelly, Aafkje’s mother. Jelly was the last of her four children. “The two of you are doing the devil’s work,” I hear Gran pedantically say to Aafkje and me, through Aafkje’s voice. “You have to leave me alone, it doesn’t concern you,” she continues. I hear despair in the tone of her voice. In any case, it testifies to the fact that we now have good contact. We can continue in this vein. Through some inviting, not too elaborate questions, we come to a different alignment.

These kinds of questions offer the possibility of giving short answers, without having to tell whole stories. That is not desirable in this setting. "What's the first thought that comes to mind when I remind you of your father?" "How did you experience his presence as a child?" "What makes the deepest impression on you when you think of him?" "Which of God's words reach the deepest part of you?" "Which ones do you fear the most?" The short answers I hope to get are sometimes faltering. In the meantime, a better picture emerges about the deeper experiences that have always remained hidden.

It turns out that after her first three children, Gran got pregnant by an illustrious church father from the community. Her own upbringing as a child was already a very God-fearing one. She was also terrified of her own father, or Aafkje's great-grandfather. With his ominous thunderous voice, this man reigned as if he were God himself. Gran says that she sometimes saw him slaughter animals on the farm. "It was as if the devil awoke in him." And then the for the first time Gran distraughtly reveals in an upwelling of emotions, that her father, in the name of God, sexually abused her. Several times. He had a stranglehold on his daughter by threatening her with hell and the devil. Summarized bluntly: if Gran, as a child, swallowed his seed and allowed herself to be penetrated without making a sound and without resisting, she would not go to hell.

In her childlike experience of the world, Gran figured out that when she did what he wanted, his temper remained within limits, allowing her to somewhat regulate his unpredictable and domineering character for the whole family. How twisted can it be? Gran, who as a child comes to believe that by allowing perverse sexual acts with her father, she will look good in the eyes of God the Almighty. A God who was magnified to monstrous proportions in the child's experience of the world. To make matters worse, as Gran gets older, she learns, how sinful sexuality is, explained in the Bible, which in no way rhymes with her experiences as a child. A schizophrenic personality structure forms as a result. On the one hand there is a child, loyal to her father and therefore to (her conception of) God, and on the other an adult woman who has compulsively conformed to all conceivable forms of chastity and self-punishment. And over the course of her lifetime, she gradually projects this self-flagellating attitude onto her environment that she punishes.

ALL SHE DID WAS SEEK APPROVAL FOR HER OWN EXISTENCE

The later secret intimacy with the church father, who in the name of God was also in for a bit of distraction, gave her a veiled sense of security in line with her father's actions. In other words, he became her father in a new capacity and she merely sought approval for her own existence. An unsatisfactory, childlike need for approval, sought in sexual matters, something that her own husband could not provide for her. As if Gran could stave off a diabolical wrath with this by meeting the not exactly chaste expectations of an authority with a hypocritical cross around his neck. This is how programmable children are under the right form of duress.

Gran has always kept the feeling that her father, who apparently died young, was looking down on her with his penetrating gaze from heaven, she says, still via Aafkje. When I ask her how she managed to keep from getting pregnant by this ecclesiastical invader, she is frightened. A tricky question, of course. And so, the atmosphere changes immediately, as if she hadn't seen it coming. From my work experience in similar situations, I know how to enter a deeper level within this low field of vibration. It is fine to notice that I always have a kind of 'gratitude from the soul' experience, from Gran's soul, which helps me to access the crux of the matter through multiple layers of resistance.

Beppe turns out to be pregnant, but not from her husband. The highly charged sense of tension is palpable. The first harbinger of the great secret presents itself. I cautiously continue my inquiries with the subtlest questions I can think of. Gran herself is unable to connect with what is growing in her belly. She knows the consequences that have been instilled in her: extramarital intimacy and certainly one which results in pregnancy is diabolical. So, she has spawned a devil's child. Followed by several attempts to get rid of the child by tumbling down the stairs on her backside, pouring liquid soap in her vagina and punching herself in the abdomen, all to no avail. Thwarted but adamant, she pretends her fourth pregnancy is her husband's child. His suspicions are no match for her coercive instructions not to ask difficult questions. She completely ignores the childish compulsion that underlies her behavior. It's everyone's fault even though she can't name anyone. Not even the real father of this child, because he is, after all, a church father.

When a child is born some eight months later, assisted by a midwife under Gran's influence, it turns out to be physically disabled. "The curse of God," Beppe's voice cracks, as she sneaks a peep at the fruit of her womb for a second, weary from the contractions and childbirth. Gran's fear is as terrible as it is merciless. She orders the midwife to get a spade with which she single-handedly splits the skull of the child through the forehead while the afterbirth is still in her womb. "This little devil must not be allowed to see the light of day," she mercilessly swears. Gramps is ordered, without any explanation, to bury the tiny corpse. Far away and without letting anyone see him doing it. No one is allowed to talk about this. Gran's regime is taking on unprecedented forms. The starting point of a black period of life that lasts for years. As this story comes out in this therapeutic setting, Aafkje experiences the pain of the dying child intensely. "My head is exploding," again drawing that imaginary line of pain with her fingers over her forehead covered in beads of sweat. It is this horrific moment that visibly moves her the most.

ENERGETIC ECHO FROM A PAINFULLY HIDDEN PAST

A few years later Jelly is born, Gran's fourth... er, fifth child. Jelly is raised in an imaginary straitjacket. She must meet a huge list of criteria that has to camouflage the fact that something stupendous had once happened. Jelly becomes Gran's ultimate project. She must behave in full accordance with church guidelines, not cause problems, be entirely subservient to the interwoven family system spun by the church. She cannot act from self-interest; Jelly does not learn to say 'no' and her life consists of accommodating and adjusting. Femininity should be covered up, sex is reprehensible and sinful, having your period is filthy and takes place in a zone where, if necessary, dressings sometimes must be changed.

When Jelly leaves home, she remains energetically under the guardianship of her mother. With every decision she makes, she asks herself through an inner dialogue, over which she herself does not seem to have any say, how her mother would feel about it. And when she becomes pregnant with her first child, Aafkje, even before birth she experiences that the child is actually under her mother's control, who, in an almost familiar way, interferes with everything from a distance. From the very beginning of Aafkje's life, she is followed and surrounded by an energetic echo from a painfully hidden past.

Gran's incredibly powerful hidden pain, her self-condemnation, her fear, and bewilderment at what she was once capable of, persists after she physically dies in 2004 after a period of dementia in old age. The feeling of her impending death was so threatening and fearful that the possibility of 'forgetting' on a certain level is a welcome intruder. The dying itself was very difficult. She now fell prey to her own intransigence and ruthlessness like a tough old woman who absolutely could not surrender. Such stubborn mechanisms appear to be able to persist even through her physical death when the heart stops beating. As a result, the awareness of dying does not really get through, while the event has already taken place. The soul settles in the energy field of its descendants.

Deep in her being, even after her death, Gran suffers from the equally current and awe-inspiring reluctance to end up in hell. She is still completely connected to her last personality, even though she is already dead. That is why she cannot let go of the earthly existence. She anxiously seeks an opportunity to cling. This is almost magnetic, as a matter of course, with those who are most receptive to her influence: daughter Jelly and granddaughter Aafkje. Gran literally says, "I have always seen my dead child in her, in Aafkje." She finds this extremely threatening because in that way Aafkje triggers her bizarre act. She therefore deployed a controlling mechanism through Jelly, that had to ensure things did not get too close. But now everything suddenly seems to be breaking open. As if Gran can no longer hold it back now that attention is being paid to her frozen drama. Gran's tears run down Aafkje's cheeks. They look like water from melting ice. My practice space fills with an atmosphere of gentleness and surrender. The words "Please forgive me, I didn't know what I was doing," can be heard. And a helix of healing soothingly spirals through the deep wound of this family artery. As if driven by an invisible force, pieces fall into place. I can lean back; the hard work has been done.

I ask Gran to orientate herself on the surroundings that become visible around her. It is light, gentle, and beautiful. It seems to take her hardly any effort to behold these spiritual regions. To her surprise, she sees figures there who approach and beckon to her with a loving radiance. I don't have to offer her any suggestion or interpretation, it's an involuntary movement that she apparently makes, driven by an indefinable force. "Is there anything holding you back?" I ask. "No, it's done," she says softly. I remind her of her fear of hell and purgatory. With some newly shed tears of compliance, she says, "It's something evil-minded people made up, it's nonsense, meant to drive us crazy, to enslave humanity. I was totally in a daze, practically my entire life. There is no hell as represented by the church." These pure insights, that need no discussion, emerged naturally. On deep levels, everything now seems to achieve clarity. Gran's former personality flows apart, as it were, and her inner self, or soul, sees through everything as she merges with the new reality to which she is intensely drawn. "Is there anything else you want to say to Aafkje before you let go completely?" I am barely able to ask my question before she says. "Live your own life, dear, I love you."

There is a lot to be said about the aftereffects of this session. Unblocking a harmful, ancestral cross-linking has a lasting liberating effect on those directly involved in this family system. People experience a new sympathetic connection with their predecessors, in this case especially that of Aafkje with her mother, but also with her Gran. As if a heavy impalpable burden has given way to acceptance. What remains, after the actual letting go, is a loving, natural feeling, and unconditional soul connection.

And 'on the other side' a reunion also starts. Gran's former partner Gramps and the other children they had are now automatically accessible and embrace Gran here with surrender and love. Depending on possible old disturbances that may still be current with certain people involved, deceased children, brothers, sisters, great-grandfathers, and mothers often also appear here. Even Gran's father can show himself, usually in a cloak of shame and guilt, but at least accessible. Brought together by spiritual management. I have often witnessed this. They are emotional reunions that the client in question consciously experiences, even if he or she is in trance. As a supervisor, I can't look much further than these layers. But that fundamental things change in the energetic composition of this 'maternal line' is obvious.

The most remarkable thing is that Aafkje's migraine has completely disappeared. Like snow melting in the sunlight. It seems like a miracle but of course that is not what it is. It only seems that way when you don't understand the story behind her pain. Her own translation is that she has returned to the same family system, has reincarnated, after having lived a life of a few minutes as a physically disabled child that ended dramatically. Murdered by her mother who bashed her forehead in with a shovel, thereby frozen in the curse “I am God’s punishment, a devil’s child,” with the fixated pain that went with it. The soul, on the other hand, comes back, a generation later, to the suppressed daughter of her then mother, now Gran. This fixation must be broken. In this way, the original purpose of the former incarnation, the disabled baby, can finally be experienced. That goal was to break through totally institutionalized ecclesiastical dogmatism in a particular family. That breakthrough could be realized coming from an impossible conception by a church father, by being born and becoming visible in an impossible situation, as an illegitimate child. Think of it as a step-by-step plan. The soul has plenty of time and does not get put off by a single lifetime. In any case, the goal in this family system now seems to have been reached. And it may very well be that Aafkje has successfully dealt with the consequences of having lived and especially suffered from a past life for such a long time in which she herself was a dark priest. Someone wanting to make herself invisible forever. A life in which the karmic damages you incurred as well as those of others could only be healed again through various journeys. A life in which her current Gran was perhaps her chosen victim at the time.

CHAPTER 32

The Pope and the inquisitor

"Ask a hundred people if they know a single memorable statement made by the current pope. You can't stop laughing."
– Fons Jansen

LE PAPE ET L'INQUISITOR BY JEAN PAUL LAURENS (1882)

For this story I was inspired by a painting on the wall of the torture museum in Carcassonne. Although it is a fictional story, the history of the inquisition time is drenched with hugely influential situations and events.

I see a lot of people in my work. Of course, I also look into their eyes, the windows of the soul. Not all the eyes in which I stare reflect me. The eyes staring at me here are, however, very challenging. They make me search quite deeply.

During a summer holiday in France, I am with my nine-year-old son at the Torture Museum of Carcassonne, a beautiful, imposing, medieval, fortified town in the heart of the mystical Cathar country, in the French department of Aude. The last word on the bloody history of that area has still not been spoken and written. Somewhere amid the great stream of blood that was shed, the chief representatives of ecclesiastical institutions cloaked themselves in holiness. Once inside, despite the holiday mood, it still chokes me up. Even though I have some idea of what to expect, I also look a little through the innocent eyes of my son. I am unpleasantly wracked with doubts about whether, despite his repeated insistence, I may not have been a bit too overconfident to pilot him here. After all, this is the place where the blackest pages of our history are on colorful display.

The layout of the museum takes us from bad to worse and starts with the old scaffold. I jokingly toss imaginary pulpy tomatoes and rotten eggs at Justin, who has worked his neck and wrists deftly between the two planks. What follows is an impressive collection of torture devices, that is equally as shocking, ranging from a rusty chastity belt to filthy and horribly conceived tools and devices, which are intended to torture the human body in bizarre ways. That the effectiveness of these devices did not leave much to be desired is evident from the illustrations and the explanations that accompany them.

Justin of course immediately wants to know more about the medieval contraceptive for which a separate display case has been made. "What are those two holes for?" he innocently asks. An elongated oval and a round hole, in front of the vagina and the anus, both with vicious serrated edges and then at the top a keyhole where things locked and ensure that it cannot be taken off. First, I have to explain to him the device's low hip level position around a woman's body. "That round thing makes rosettes out of turds", I nervously joke to downplay the seriousness of the exhibit. Then I explain what it's really intended to do that he gets without really understanding it. I gather from the loud, cracking noises he produces with the wet palms of his hands on his mouth, that my initial explanation clearly appeals more to his imagination, and which makes other museum visitors turn around to look with annoyance.

UNSCRUPULOUS MALE RULERS

In a specially decorated corner of the museum, you can see how a gruesome scene from antiquity has been staged with the help of mannequins. A handsome, half-naked young woman in rags, is tied to a stake around a prepared pyre, awaiting her fate. All around her are church fathers in priestly robes, whose austere facial expressions betray not a trace of emotion and seem to rigidly consent to the execution of the umpteenth sentence. It does not leave me unmoved; I must confess. The epitome of pure beauty and innocence, in the form of this beautiful but battered young woman, versus the cold unscrupulous male rulers who have declared themselves superior to all that lives in the name of God. On impulse I would have liked to save her, but because her head is bent over, I can't look her in the eye to see if she would still want to be saved. God knows what had already been taken from her and meted out before the fire was actually lit, as the one display is harmlessly electric.

Several impressive paintings are displayed on the walls in addition to the many disgusting torture attributes, of which the ancient thumbscrew appears the least harmless. One of them, *Le pape et l'inquisitor* from 1882, by a certain Jean Paul Laurens, makes a deep impression on me.

It is a beautiful depiction of the Pope and the Inquisitor together in a whispering conclave during the heyday of the Inquisition in the second part of the 15th century. The period when the power of the church was unprecedented and heresy had been declared a contagious disease. Justifying mass killings of countless "witches, whores, heretics and rioters" was among their many responsibilities. In the painting you can see how these two sinister gentlemen discuss matters in a private conversation and are forging nefarious plans, the content of which can be guessed. It has been painted in such a fascinating, detailed, and lifelike manner that I take a moment to let it sink in. My son, who seems to take it all in quite soberly, surprises me by asking me what I see in it. Halfway through my attempt to answer him, I realize that it is almost impossible to explain in language a child can understand, and he deflects my explanation by asking what we are going to have for dinner that evening.

Encouraged by something illusive, I try to empathize with the world of these two extremely macabre figures, as if something involuntarily compels me to show a genuine interest in what must have driven these people to do what they once felt needed to be done. I am extremely curious about what I can hardly comprehend.

A POLITICAL AGENDA HIDDEN FROM THE PUBLIC

I fall into a slight trance as I scrutinize the pale mugs of these cunning, impenetrable dignitaries laced with viciousness. Searching for possibly concealed messages that could have been hidden in the painting, I get the spontaneous impression that the conversation could well be about women. The perspective Jean Paul Laurens' brush renders in relation to the Pope on the canvas gives us no opportunity to look into his eyes. Who could have done that at the time? The inquisitor has shrouded his viewers in shadows.

The pope's holy slippers camp on a dark red velvet cushion. The men's gazes focus on a phrase designated by the inquisitor in a document whose content no one knows. The index finger of his left hand makes a resolute gesture. The way I see it, it appears to be a decision that must be made. A difficult choice perhaps, for which the inquisitor needs special permission from the Pope, the human embodiment of God who has the last word on everything. It is clear a decision is being taken here based on a political agenda hidden from the public. A dark sub-bible.

Although the imagined scenario of the convicted woman at the stake and the painting in the museum seem to have nothing to do with each other at first glance, I suddenly get a new insight. I think it could well be that her name can be read on a death list under the inquisitor's fingernail on the paper edged with black borders.

Then, in my mind's ear in a soft gray, crackling tone, I hear a ruthless voice whispering sentences, shrouded in a foul breath. The inquisitor says that this woman is the daughter of a prominent and charismatic merchant from the city. A man whose influence is given too wide a scope, and who clearly conveys a different message than the church deems desirable. To put a stop to this state of affairs, the inquisitor proposes declaring the young lady extremely unchaste and accusing her of fornication. A clear case of heretical disease in an advanced stage.

The consequences are then coolly considered and discussed. Cunning as foxes, they now devise anticipatory measures to convince the citizens of the evil with which this woman is possessed. The logical consequence of this is that the attention will automatically focus on her family members and therefore her father. Only now am I struck by a detail in the painting showing the slightest hint of a curl around the corners of the mouth that betrays satisfaction. Before this item on the agenda is checked off, the Pope instructs the Inquisitor to arrange for this woman to visit him that evening for questioning in the specially equipped room. With a dry cough he makes a note of it. It's not the first time.

"Dad, come and have a look!" shouts Justin, who is already in the next room. I wake up from my sinister digressions in a daze and realize just how much I have empathized with, and especially given free rein to my imagination to what might lie behind the tableau depicted in the painting. " This is what they used to cut people in half," he continues enthusiastically. Brought back down to earth, I break free from Le pape et l'inquisitor and join my son who is hoping for a reaction.

AN INNER PERPERTATOR EMERGES

After a wonderful holiday I go back to my work recharged and inspired. There are a quite a few appointments in the practice diary, and I am always curious about new clients. One of them is a young woman. There is a gloomy look on her good-looking face. She doesn't want tea or coffee. It is not easy to look into her melancholy eyes because her head is always hunched over so that her straight, black hair partly covers her face. She tells me that she comes from a very strict Catholic family. Everything that happened there, including several nasty intimate experiences she had when she was too young, keep her from experiencing any happiness. She even regularly has suicidal tendencies. She has never had relationships. Sex is dirty and frightens her. The contour of her shapely body underneath tight-fitting clothing is unimportant, she says. "Dominant, authoritarian, physically violent and unpredictable," is how she describes her father. He has long held a prominent position in the local church council. "Everywhere I go, he seems like an all-seeing eye watching over my shoulder, so I don't feel safe anywhere," she says. She anxiously flicks her head up, seeking eye contact to make sure I heard this.

When we start a regression, where I give her an instruction to go back in time to the kernel of the judgment about femininity, she immediately turns pale. Her body stiffens and she suddenly sees herself sitting on a large wooden chair with a very refined ecclesiastical motif embroidered on her slippers. Slippers resting on a dark red pillow made of velvet. "It's in a musty room, as if I'm waiting for a meeting with another high-ranking person," she says. An inner perpetrator emerges. Initially to my surprise, because it's usually victims who emerge first in these kinds of heavy cases. After several intensive sessions, some light is finally shed on my client's darkness.

And me? When I look myself in the eye in the evening while brushing my teeth, I suddenly recognize something deep that I had lost for a long time: my innocence.

When I arrive at my office the next morning, there is a drawing my son, who has now gone back to school, made while we were on vacation. He has drawn a huge cake with brown rosettes on it. *Chokolate rosettes*, it says when I follow the pointing arrows. In the sky above the cake, he draws a child's version of the chastity belt that we saw in Carcassonne. He has clearly not lost his innocence. When he comes home in the afternoon, we laugh so hard it makes us cry.

CHAPTER 33

The Filthy Stinking Rich

"Religion is embraced by the people as truth, by the wise as false, and by rulers as useful."
– Seneca

Those who were rich could afford a place after their death under the vaults of a church, close to the altar, where Jesus was expected on the day of the resurrection. So, the most expensive places were those around the altar, after which the rates, depending on the distance, became lower. Even the most expensive coffins did not always close hermetically, so the stench wafted through the church. The rich stink. The non-rich too, of course, but they were out of olfactory range. 'The filthy stinking poor' has therefore not become an expression.

Why did they do everything in their power to obtain a place for their corpus as close as possible to an altar? And could that also have consequences for the soul? All in all, it simply has to do with the belief that the Messiah, Jesus, died for the sins of mankind, our sins. Just as Jesus was nailed to a cross, so too have many jealously become painstakingly hung up on his existence. Jesus as a bearer, as a database, of our sins. Thus, we can never learn from the consequences of our own actions and free ourselves from them. We relinquish control over this. That makes us inextricably dependent on Jesus. Simply put: someone lives a life. Under the influence of all kinds of imposed circumstances that unnaturally put pressure on a society, driven by powers and forces behind the scenes that are not recognizable to anyone, let alone definable, that person commits an act that causes someone harm. The pain inflicted, and the unacceptable feeling about that act, is locked up in a safety-deposit box without anything being done about it. The contents of this box, which really ought to be processed by the persons concerned are outsourced to Jesus. He bears the content.

If Jesus really does that, the conflict cannot be resolved. Because the pain wants to get out of the box. The pain wants to be liberated and felt. The guilt wants to be released. This requires a process of accepting and digesting, in whatever form. Only then can the perpetrator and the victim embrace each other again, thus resolving the karmic interdependency. In this assigned function, Jesus maintains the intransigence of the karmic charges. The result is that people cannot move on against their nature, which produces even more excessive events and actions. For all intents and purposes, karma accumulates and petrifies. It is quite possible that Jesus originally wanted to set a very different, loving example by encouraging people to process and reconcile. However, he still symbolizes the one who died for our sins. The deep-rooted dependency relationship that this creates, such as between a small child and its mother, was not foreseen on an individual level.

And certainly not in a context of reincarnation, because there is nothing meaningful (anymore) to read about that in the Bible.

ARE WE LED BY SUFFERING OR DO WE LEAD OUR OWN LIFE?

Religious domination, so stifling to so many, caused the advice from the heart to be exchanged for the precepts of the Catholic Church. You had to have the courage of your conviction to remain sovereign over your inner life. However, those who came to value the distorted meaning of Jesus' life, cunningly conceived by moldy men in miters, ended up in a millennia long trap. The blinkers that were put on in this way deprived those wearing them of the real facts behind the large-scale mechanism of subjugation. And the cycle of reincarnation continually provides new opportunities, new lives, to take off those blinders again thereby guaranteeing the migration of traveling souls. The interpretation that reincarnation is only intended to deal with old wounds throughout all kinds of lives and then transcend these earthly adventures, does not fit in with the experiences of clients. When interpreted in this way, the element of "life is suffering" seems to be constantly confirmed, while it was precisely that conviction that became one of the most important successes of the church in keeping people oppressed. I believe we are here to create a heaven on earth. I find it much more plausible that we are growing towards an era with series of human incarnations, where the starting point is living a life based on love and connection. In harmony with our environment and fellow creatures, in awareness of our spiritual nature before proceeding to any transcendence, it becomes "living a life." Now back to the filthy rich man and his beliefs.

Jesus, as the only son of God, is said to have the power and responsibility to take the sins of mankind upon His shoulders. For this He is willing to bleed submissively on our behalf out of unconditional love. After all, he is supposed to be the ultimate human sacrifice. It is also assumed that the blood sacrifice is necessary for the forgiveness of sins. The believer, once departed, now prefers to lie spooning in peace with Jesus forever and ever, amen. And that while the maggots are already enthusiastically and doggedly squatting his former home. Until 1963 there was even a papal decree from 1886 that forbade cremation. We evidently identify ourselves with our bodies even after death. We think that the location of where we are laid to rest plays a decisive role.

REWARDED WITH A PLACE OF HONOR

Jesus must secure your transition. He must prevent you from taking a wrong turn after your death and you will be offered a framed search area within a radius of a few tens of meters around the heart of a church. And not only that, whoever is closest to that core, the filthy stinking rich man, then has the best chance of being found. And whoever can find his last refuge directly under the chancel is practically guaranteed. His most devoted disciples, at the same time the straw men of the institute of the church, play a crucial role in maintaining this system. They are rewarded with a place of honor. In various places, such as Tuscany, they are even embalmed and mummified on the altar, like Snow White in a glass coffin. Or in a transparent closed box in a display case with bones on a velvet cushion. And have been for centuries. The family crypts of the Princes of Orange, as well as the Dutch royal family are also located under the *Nieuwe Kerk* in Delft. It's fascinating to wonder in what guise most of these persons have now reincarnated while their old bodies still adhere to a lapsed life of status, trapped in a zeitgeist of a great array of entrenched norms, values and interests.

The idea that the location of the deceased body matters encourages a belief system. Namely, that the soul must remain attached to it in order to secure its journey. It must be picked up, guided, preferably by Jesus himself. There is something passive and conditional about it. If that does not happen, the soul remains essentially connected to the earthly reality that surrounded its former death. As if you are waiting endlessly at the bus stop for the bus without realizing you no longer need the bus at all to continue your journey. The body, and later the bones, the family members, the customs, the tombs, the cemetery, the garden around the church, you name it, form the bus stop where many deceased people continue to stay. A place that is regularly kept alive by all kinds of services that must reinforce the place's function as a bus stop.

As these beliefs start to fade for the wandering deceased, a reality reveals itself that was previously there but remained obscured by its restrictive ideas. Now the wandering souls will perceive that a new, inviting world of light lies open to them. Let's say that the pasture with cows also comes into view, by which I mean that the bigger picture becomes visible, the real spiritual dimensions. This is how it is experienced during sessions. A world where you are incredibly welcome. Where you can find your way without conditions, you can have your encounters, you can receive insights. Once the façade of a conceivable hell dissolves, or just the mere surprise for the former atheist that he still exists after death, the mists rise, and one can see much further than before. What then becomes visible, tangible, and accessible is experienced as ultimate, as real, as free, and quite ordinary to the soul. Then one also observes loved ones who have gone before, or loving, luminous entities that sometimes even resemble a Jesus figure. I won't go into whether that is really the case. Because everything there is relative to earthly perception and understanding. If I were to remind the soul of its being in tune with the childlike fascination it had for Native Americans, then brilliant Native American entities could also manifest themselves. Such as the presence of an enormously loving and powerfully glowing Sitting Bull (during his earthly life a world-famous leader of the Hunkpapa Sioux Indians) for example, who on closer acquaintance appears to know Jesus well. All the same, they then represent the absolute beauty and purity of the new dimension that is being entered. It just depends on what focus there is at that moment, and which associations belong to it, and what meaning is attached to it. A world that reveals itself as soon as you let go of all your beliefs about who or what you are, and you just are.

I think it is so wonderful that we are surrounded by countless animals during all our earthly expeditions to help us gain some understanding of this. Animals cannot be anything other than what they are and don't have to make any effort to do so. They act and behave in accordance with their essence. That is their only reality. They are always the best version of themselves and are very often perceived by people in a guiding role during essential dreams, deep transformation, and transitional processes such as dying.

CHAPTER 34

Jesus, power places and Christ consciousness

"If you want to understand the universe, then think in terms of energy, frequency and vibrations."
– Nicola Tesla

Jesus, as the redeemer of our sins, is doing a mega job for countless earthlings. Although his selflessness is preached everywhere, in exchange for those absolutions one must believe in him according to conditions determined by the same institution that gave him the platform. And those conditions are quite harsh. Jesus is occupied with this illusion until the end of time, and he enslaves people into, no, far into the grave. It is so clever that masses of believers will also be unconditionally loyal to that system. Without conscious awareness, they therefore deliver their contribution in words, deeds and with a maximum investment of life energy, as a kind of repayment obligation. The canonized vehicle of the church thus continues to be supplied with fuel and horsepower and is enabled to steadily tour through time. The compelling messages of hell and damnation introduced by prayer and church service, which attach narrow conditions to human life at elementary levels, create a collective fear of life. An orchestrated leitmotif of melancholy and self-deprecation among the population, which provides fertile ground for a matching collective feeling of low self-esteem.

He who prays the *'Domine, non-sum dignus'* every week under church supervision, with his hand on his heart and head bent forward, a prayer in which the believer confesses his unworthiness: 'Lord, I am not worthy that thou shouldest enter under my roof but say in a word and my servant shall be healed ', undermines his self-worth to unprecedented depths. A prayer based on the premise that one is unhealthy and unworthy by definition and who through confession and sacrifice of enjoyment of life can still stay somewhat on the right track.

The substandard self-esteem that results from this gives rise to even more restrictive thoughts and beliefs which, like all thoughts, are creative. Even though people made the best of it, the sad reality of many generations was shaped in this way. 'I am no good', is the most effective initial undermining form of self-rejection. Without their noticing it, people slip into an attitude toward life shrouded in a gray haze. Drabness, poverty, joylessness, forms the (new) normal. Individuals become anxious, insecure, subdued, suspicious and underhanded. They do not speak their minds and only show the outside world an illusion of who they really are. Of course, not all of them, but just enough to determine the atmosphere in a community. Like a dish with too much salt is stripped of its original delicate taste, so that it can no longer be appreciated as a whole. On top of that, this subversive self-image also polarizes a society.

TRANSCENDING INSECURITIES

A minority sees an opportunity to enrich themselves in this power game and automatically elevates itself above the gray masses, pursuing the advantages that most people who are imprisoned in fear give them. Not because the self-image of these people is healthy, but because this unequal distribution of power allows them to rise above someone else, allowing them to transcend their own insecurities. And that gives rise to an unfair distribution of goods, resources, and opportunities. Power relations that produce aggrieved personalities and wounded bodies that, as the stories in this book show, then travel through time to new eras. And how many of these filthy stinking rich (and less rich) still end up dying in mortal fear? Even though their remains were close to the altar. 'One shouldn't speak ill of the dead ', where does the expression really come from? Who really dared to ask themselves, let alone dare to make it their work, to allow all unfinished exchanges to take place where possible by breathing life into the dead? Not many. Such matters fell under blasphemy and the devil's work with the associated punishments.

I have repeatedly asked clients about another image that compellingly manifests itself, just to be more certain. I have mentioned it before, but this discovery became so essential to me that I want to emphasize it again: wouldn't those masses of souls imprisoned in fear find themselves wandering in or around a church? Creating a kind of hole in the energetic field around it? As a spirit trapped in a timelessness constructed through the power of thought, still desperately searching for a way out, other than to hell. What do the weekly church services do for them? How innocent are the repetitive and hypnotic church hymns, the symbolically lauded rituals and monotonal affirmative statements and prayers that were sanctioned 'in the name of God' with a collective 'amen'? A word from Hebrew that means "so be it." Attended and endorsed no less by groups of faithful churchgoers, mostly descendants, who in schematic terms were practically ON top of these dead bodies in the crypts. What wasn't sealed and consecrated 'in the name of God' anyway? And to what extent does this ensure adherence and attachment to the system even before a deceased person is afforded the chance to weigh his own alternatives about his transition to other dimensions?

WANDERING SOULS

Are those Sunday worship services liberating? Or are they fixing the status quo of the wandering souls? And at the same time, using the same techniques, new generations of living church followers are already being groomed and made dependent on the idea of guilt and penance. With the confessional box as headquarters. Do you know someone who, during his current life, had his name struck from a church community register? There was a time when he innocently committed himself to it, like his relatives before him. The renouncement procedure is always accompanied by underlying feelings of guilt, all sorts of uncertainties and especially loyalty issues with family members who 'stayed behind', usually the parents themselves. Even when family members had already died, it still felt like a betrayal to them. As far as I have been able to ask the dead, the answer is unanimous: free yourself from any religion, because in the experience of the soul it has no meaning whatsoever. This often only becomes abundantly clear when the soul has managed to free itself from the earthly realm. Religions are designed to constrain people and are characterized by the presentation of an apparent authority that operates outside our field of vision, that exists outside of us and is conditional. Whether it concerns Catholicism or 'scientism '. Because every pyramidal, hierarchically functioning institution in which one is supposed to believe what is introduced from above, on which social decision-making and the organization of a society is then based, is a religion. One must remain vigilant whenever a power presents itself as "higher" and as authoritative, introducing a coercive agenda to which one must submit, however well-intentioned it may sound, and no matter how subtly it is drawn up.

What is also interesting in this context concerns the question of why so many churches are situated on mounds and ley lines. Locations that were by no means randomly chosen. The church has erected its edifices on ancient holy sites that already existed to suppress unwelcome pagan religions and wisdom, and to implement a new one.

Eelco de Boer, a Dutch writer and researcher, demonstrates in his three publications that the great majority of locations where churches were built on mounds, not just in the Netherlands, but also beyond its borders, are literally scaled up mirror images of constellations. In other words, places that are directly mirrored by stars, in exactly the same formations as the constellations known to us. The name of the capital city of Leeuwarden in the Dutch province of Friesland, for example, is comprised of the compound *leeuw* (lion) and '*wierd* (hill), so 'hill of the Lion', and is connected to the constellation Leo. Building took place around those locations and so settlements arose, followed later by villages and towns. These centers were already in use long before the church even made its influential appearance. These places were the fertile stage for rituals and ceremonies for the so-called pagans, naturopaths, witches, and mystics, who apparently knew about the importance of making these settlements in alignment with stars. Their energetic potential was used to reinforce and support important life processes, decision-making, and to preserve vital events for the community. From deep spiritual awareness. Was it perhaps the intention here to use these transformative, cosmic-dynamic force fields to help ancestors in their transition to the spheres of light where necessary? So that they didn't keep wandering around? So that they could become star children, as a metaphor for the ultimate homecoming of a sojourning soul after a series of incarnations? Could it be that the original capacity of such places was once hijacked and used under a 'false flag' for very different agendas? That the church sought its locations for its branches in existing places of power? The adapted message of Jesus, as 'redeemer of our sins', with which people had to be distracted from their original wisdom and divinity, could then be reinforced. The original uses of these sacred sites were suppressed. They had to make way for a well-thought-out religion. The pagans and witches, the conspiracy theorists of yesteryear, were bombarded as being the most sinful creatures ever.

JESUS CHRIST AND KARMA

The name Christ, "the anointed one," as it is connected to Jesus, could be called a title. Referring to Christ consciousness as a unitary source of pure love that a person carries within himself at his core. Instead of emphasizing that fact and affirming people in their divine nature, the church emphasizes precisely what one is not. And how unattainable this state of being is for an ordinary person. The road to it is then presented as a practically impossible route to take.

Assuming that Jesus had actually lived, He never had the platform that was accorded him. It only seems that way. And he did not proclaim himself the only begotten son of God. Even if he had wanted to, it was not an option. He was too wise for that, too holistically oriented, too permeated by his and our spiritual essence in an immense creation, and thus by the immaterial rules of earthly existence. You can help bring relief to someone, but not simply take over other people's burdens. Then you interfere in one of the most fundamental laws of creation, karma. Moreover, that would indicate a huge need for Jesus himself to be a pleaser, arising from a need to make amends because of a theme of rejection and self-condemnation from (one of) his own past lives. You never know, but I find it hard to imagine.

Since Jesus' life, as far as we know, testifies to the fact that he was deeply committed to humanity, unusually empathetic, lovingly compassionate, forgiving, and psychically gifted, it seems more logical to me that he acquired this through countless human incarnations. A whole series of them in which he experienced all aspects of being human. He had probably harmonized the possible karmic ballast he had picked up here and there before he was called Jesus. I can imagine that Jesus was an exceptionally gifted man far ahead of his time in terms of consciousness. That he reached a multidimensional state of consciousness and at the same time remained very human. Could that be the "Christ consciousness", which we all ultimately strive for while we are on earth as humans?

What made Jesus' incarnation difficult was that he was rooted as a man in a society that dwelled in a great deal of ignorance. That made him a prophet, an exalted one in the eyes of others. Although that must have been a conscious choice of incarnation at the time, as a human being he was also a perfectly ordinary person who (loved) his wife and (his) children and marveled at his materialization and the pleasures and mysteries of earthly existence. Some nuance regarding the significance of his exemplary role therefore seems justified to me. As well as a closer look at the concept of karma, by the way. That term is all too frequently given an ecclesiastic interpretation with a variety of religiously polarizing undertones in terms of good and evil, and guilt, punishment, and penance. How many people seeking to achieve piety forget and forgot to really live because of it? And who says that the frustration about that disappears after physical death?

CHAPTER 35

'I've Been Praying' for children

"Facts do not penetrate the world in which our beliefs live."
– Marcel Proust

The 'confession-or-your-life' formula acquired a boundless scope and proved to be an unprecedented success. There was *Ik bid al* (I've Been Praying), a prayer instruction booklet from 1924, written by the Dutch Brother Ambrosius, specially designed for children aged six and seven. My mother was that age then. For example, you read the following in the chapter *When I go to sleep*: "I wasn't good sometimes, but now I regret it. You (Dear Lord & Dear Lady) are so good, you give me so much. If I died now, I would be punished by You."

In several chapters, it is emphasized that "The Dear lord sees you, but not the other way around" and that "praying and trying with all your might to be good" is the only correct way of living. In the chapter, *For confession*, you read: "You are so beautiful. You are so good. I regret that I committed evil. I will never do it again. Never again, Dear Lord. I am filled with regret. WHAT DID I DO THAT WAS SO EVIL? Did I pray well? Was I good at church? Did I talk in church? Was I naughty with dad and mom? Did I fight with other children? Did I do my best in school? Did I ever say something that wasn't true? Did I ever do something nasty? Did I do that alone? Did I do that with others? Dear Lord, I say again. I am filled with regret. I will never do it again. I ask for your forgiveness."

And indeed, after confession: "Dear Lord, I am so happy. I have been going to confession. My soul is very clean now. Jesus, you love me very much now."

This is followed by the whole nine yards about what the child will never do again. The booklet is colorfully illustrated with pictures of deadly earnest-looking children's faces, depicted at a questionable level compared to pious figures chronically looking upward with apathetic facial expressions that instill fear and who engage in all sorts of rituals. It is not easy to find nothing wrong with this, but what is not at all difficult is to see that with an influential program like this, the autonomy of a child gets totally damaged. Not least because the parents of these children allowed this information to be believed and accepted, thereby also undermining healthy parental authority. After all, they themselves were programmed in this way. That brings the system of loyalty that children have towards their parents into even more treacherous waters. Children copy the lifestyles and views of their educators to a large extent. It is true that a lot of unnecessary ballast is eventually thrown out again at a later stage, which is the function of puberty. When the fear and threat of a sternly watching God has reached extraordinary proportions and has also become polluted by all kinds of abuse, then there is hardly any room for these natural cleansing processes to get through anymore. The programming then remains part of adult life without a critical revision.

Obviously, the degree of influence varies from child to child, depending on many factors concerning the nature and composition of a family. However, entire village communities are immersed in a sustained matrix of fear. The church council demanded that anyone who was forced to marry because of a pregnancy had to publicly announce that in church. How innocent is that? What does that mean for the people involved, the family and the baby itself? And in what way do these moments color these lives and those of their offspring? Can you taste indignation in these words? I may not be able to completely suppress it. How this kind of indoctrination affects the lines of cause-and-effect over generations, comes to my attention so often that I would like to shout it from the rooftops.

CASE HISTORY OF A DIALOGUE WITH GRANDMA

My client Ina has physical complaints. Things also occasionally do not run smoothly with her partner and children. We make contact with her deceased grandmother through Ina. Ina speaks with her grandmother's voice here.

Grandma and grandpa lost a four-year-old son in an accident on the farm. We discover that grandma had assigned her older son Tjeerd, who is about seven at the time, with the task of taking good care of his younger brother. She therefore holds him implicitly responsible for the death of her 4-year-old. I ask grandma questions.

M: "So, what you're really saying is, because your son died, you have come to regard it as God's punishment."

GM: "Yes."

M: “And then by making another, older son, responsible for that, were you actually hoping it wouldn’t be your fault. Which maybe resulted in having less of a chance of ending up in hell yourself.”

GM: “Yes.”

M: “But what happened from your point of view to the son you held responsible for this? What would happen to him then?”

GM: “He’s going to hell.”

M: “Have you ever said that to him?”

GM: “No.”

M: “No, but you felt it that way inside?”

GM: “Yes.”

M: “So, then there is something unspoken between you two that tells him that.”

GM: “Yes.”

M: “What kind of atmosphere is then created in your house from the day your son died?”

GM: “A lot of sadness and anger.”

M: “And grandpa, what is his role?”

GM: “He withdraws even more; he turns away from everything and is no longer accessible.”

M: “And when you’re in bed at night, where do your thoughts turn to?”

GM: “To God, the bastard.”

M: “But hey, if that’s how you think of him what does God think of you?”

GM: “That I’m a sourpuss, not a good person.”

M: “H’m, it’s really eating away at you, isn’t it?”

GM: “Yes, terribly.”

M: “If I remind you of your own childhood, grandma, when you were little yourself. What is the first memory or thought that comes to mind about that period?”

GM: “Hiding.”

M: “Hiding, from whom or what?”

GM: “From dad.”

M: “From dad, because if you don’t hide what then?”

GM: “He flails with his arms, he’s furious.”

M: “At whom and what?”

GM: “At everything and everyone.”

M: “Does it ever really get out of hand when dad does this?”

GM: “Yes.”

M: “And what happens then?”

GM: “Then he starts hitting people.”

M: “Who? You too?”

GM: Crying and shaking: “Yes, especially me.”

M: “Really? And where does he hit you?”

GM: “In my face, hard.”

The pain is palpably experienced.

M: “Does he say anything when he hits you so hard?”

GM: “I don’t hear any words, but only feel anger, anger. Like he wants to destroy me.”

An emotional discharge ensues.

M: “Grandma, can you sense what makes your father so furious that he just wants to destroy you? What’s in him that makes him vent his emotions on you?”

GM: Silence... “He is completely withdrawn in himself.”

M: “What role does the church play for you at that time?”

GM: “Sit well-behaved at the front and pretend everything is perfectly fine. While things at home are the worst they’ve ever been.”

M: “Are there other things important to mention when it comes to you and your father, except that he regularly beats you?”

GM: Silence... “Abuse.”

M: “What kind of abuse?”

GM: With a voice that trembles: “Sexual abuse”.

M: “Who does that?”

GM: “Daddy.”

M: “And how old are you?”

GM: “Five.”

M: “So, then you are still very young. And tell me, what happens then, what does he do?”

GM: “I feel he’s just really mad. Mad, mad, mad. It feels like he’s only mad at me. I feel so scared.”

M: “Yes, it’s ok to feel that. What does he do or say when it happens?”

GM: “That’s what comes to bad people. He thinks I’m very bad.”

M: “Oh, that’s what comes to bad people,” he says. “And what does he do with bad people?”

GM: “He puts his weenie in me.”

M: “Just try to make contact with that grandma, feel what’s happening.”

GM: “I just don’t feel anything.”

M: “How do you do that, not feel anything?”

GM: “Well, just not being with my body.”

M: “Because what else would you feel?”

GM: “Pain, tremendous pain.”

She cringes, expressing herself by making moaning sounds.

M: "Yes, grandma, of course that hurts. Just give it space, you have every right to feel it. "And you can't say anything about it to dad because otherwise?"

GM: "He'll hit me again."

A new wave of emotion breaks over her.

M: "And when all these things happen, Grandma, what's really the worst thing about it for you?"

GM: Crying: "That I'm not safe with dad."

M: "No, grandma, in fact, he is really giving you the message that's all part of being a bad person. As if you owe it all to yourself. "Grandma, how long does this go on, how often do these things happen?"

GM: Silence... "Until I was fifteen."

M: "So, from the age of five to fifteen, these things happened with dad."

GM: "Yes."

M: "So, your body, as young as it is, has to deal with these pains quite often."

GM: "Yes."

M: "Have you got used to it?"

GM: "Yes, if it hurts, I leave my body and I wait for it to be over."

She starts to clear her throat and cough loudly.

M: "And as far as your body is concerned, does papa put his weenie in your vagina?"

Gagging.

GM: "No, in my mouth too."

Loud coughing and spluttering then express an emotional discharge. Disgust and choking sounds come outside her body. Quite nasty, but then she calms down. She says,

"I feel much better now."

We skip a bit, then the question arises:

M: "Go to a moment in this whole exchange with dad, in which something happens that has the deepest effect on you."

In this way, we tap into an even deeper layer. It is quite literally palpable. As if the elevator, after we had already arrived at the basement, turns out to be capable of going to an even deeper level.

GM: "I'm pregnant. My God, I am pregnant."

M: "How do you find out?"

GM: "My mother tells me. She sees that I'm getting rounder, my breasts are bigger and my belly too."

M: "Did you notice anything yourself?"

GM: "Not really, I don't feel my body that way, I but did put on weight."

M: "Do you think mom knows who you're pregnant with?"

GM: "No, she has no idea. She was never there for me."

M: "What does your mother do now that she knows?"

GM: "She tells dad. She thinks I had sex with someone."

M: "Mom says that to dad? And where are you when she does?"

GM: "In the room."

M: "What happens now?"

GM: In panic: "He attacks me, he goes ballistic."

This heralds the start of a huge deepening in grandma's emotional experience. Grandma screams and cries at the same time. All this is still happening through her granddaughter.

GM: "He pulls me by my hair around the room and starts kicking me."

M: "Where do you feel him kicking?"

She points to her abdomen. Deep-seated pains and fears are openly expressed now. I put a pillow on her lower body and gently press to emphasize that part.

GM: "He keeps on kicking until it comes out.

M: "Okay grandma, feel that, even down there, that it is coming out. That the child comes out of your body."

From a therapeutic point of view, it is very important that the coming out of the (dead) child is consciously experienced. That attention continues to be paid, so that the consciousness of the uterus realizes that there is no longer a child in it. If this is not consciously experienced, the uterus can remain stuck in patterns of "I have to hold onto the baby", which can later, also in the offspring, result in physical manifestations in the uterus such as fibroids, cysts or worse. As such, the child is therefore still 'present' and needs to be fed.

Great energetic discharges keep coming from and going into grandma's body in waves, making it firmly shudder and shake. They seem to be spasms and convulsions.

M: *I encourage her.* "All right grandma, just express yourself, let yourself be heard, and let the body do what it feels it wants to do. Follow it, that's totally fine."

Things calm down after a while. Then a new confrontation follows when I say:

M: "Grandma, you told me that your child must have been about five months old. Then it already has a serious body. When it comes out, did you get to see the baby?"

GM: *With a new scream.* "Yes! I have to clean it up. It's lying in a pool of blood. I'm sticky all over."

Yet more outpourings of emotion.

GM: "I held it for a while."

M: "Yes, what do you feel?"

GM: "Tremendous sadness, but also tremendous love."

M: "All right, just make space to be able to feel that amid all that misery. Can you also tell if it's a boy or a girl?"

GM: "A little boy. He's still moving. I can still make contact with it. I calm down completely."

M: "All right, a little boy. Just be with him for a moment. Go ahead and feel each other."

GM: Lots of deep grief is released. "I have to clean up the baby, and all the blood. I believe I threw the baby away."

M: "Where?"

GM: "In the tub or in the water."

M: "Is it dead then?"

GM: "I don't know."

M: "Just feel deep down if your child has survived."

GM: "No."

M: "All right, let that sink in deeply. The baby has died."

This is of great therapeutic importance here. That the waking consciousness receives confirmation that the child has died. So long as this is not consciously realized, the child continues to live in grandma's deeper perception of the world. Which makes her continue to hold on to it, maintaining the soul entanglement. And the latter is going to bring about a reincarnation movement in the new generation of the same family, based on the old wound.

M: *I ask,* "What is going through you grandma at a moment like that, when you are throwing the baby away?"

GM: "Something inside me breaks."

M: "Where exactly do you feel that in your body?"

GM: "Everywhere, but especially here." She points to her womb.

M: "In your womb, because that's where the baby comes from, right?"

GM: "Yes, and I lose all my feeling."

M: "Just focus your attention on that grandma, on your womb. What doesn't your womb maybe still not get?"

GM: "That I'm not pregnant anymore, that it's over."

It relieves her to realize this. When all this is behind us and has taken place, we go a little further in time. I ask Grandma,

M: "How has all this history defined your life? For example, when you later become a mother yourself? How do you experience that grandma, becoming a mother?"

GM: "It's horrible, I can't connect with my kids. I name my eldest son after my father, Tjeerd, because father wants that. He has to carry on the family name."

M: "How is that for you, grandma, that your son bears the same name as your father?"

GM: "Disgusting, I keep my distance and can't be a mother to him."

M: "Do you see what you're actually projecting on Tjeerd?"

GM: "Yes, all the misery I suffered with my father."

M: "Let it really sink in grandma. What about your younger son?"

GM: “He is the apple of my eye, my everything. I protect him in everything. I favor him.”

M: “Can you imagine how he must have experienced that himself grandma?”

GM: Hesitantly: “Maybe like being smothered.”

M: “Yes, that could very well be the case. What could that have done to him, you being a mother who smothered him? Could it have something to do with his death?”

GM: “Maybe he didn’t want to be here anymore, I didn’t give him room for his own life.”

A deeper level of knowing now opens in grandma’s being. We consciously leave it at that. A substantial change occurs in her consciousness, in which the denial of her pain and guilt complex is lifted and a rearrangement of energies takes place. This will lead to the realization that there is a deeper context behind the ‘accident’ of her child and especially to the fact that Tjeerd of course bears no responsibility for this.

M: “If your father has been yelling at you from the age of five to fifteen that you are evil and worthless. That you were abused so often ‘in the name of God’ and had to swallow all his aggression literally and figuratively. And that you will be forgotten by God. How deep does it all go? What does all that do to you?”

GM: “I came to believe that I’m really bad. But it was lie, that lie of his that I came to believe.”

M: “And when later, to make matters worse, your child, the apple of your eye, also dies. What does that remind you of?”

GM: “Of my first child.”

That brings great sorrow.

M: “Yes, let it sink in. That you again lose something that comes from yourself. And what does that confirm deep inside of you again?”

GM: “That I’m really, really bad.”

M: “And then you’re going to hold Tjeerd responsible for that because you can’t bear all that yourself anymore.”

GM: “Yes, how terribly bad.”

M: “And grandpa, what is his role in all this?”

GM: “He distances himself from everything, he has not connected with anyone for a long time.”

M: “And when you get older yourself, and a grandchild is on the way while you yourself have become ill? How do you view your end?”

GM: *Tense:* “I’m going to hell.”

M: “Yes grandma, of course you have become convinced of that. What effect does such a belief have on your illness?”

GM: "It's going to be a very tough fight. I don't want to die because I'm going to go to purgatory."

M: "Can you feel where your body has started to get sick?"

GM: "Yes, in the womb."

M: "So, what made you sick?"

GM: "The abuse and all (self)reproach."

M: "What is your deepest conviction?"

GM: "I'm not allowed to be."

M: "Oh, listen carefully to what you're saying. Who deprives you of your right to be?"

GM: "My father... no, actually I do that myself."

M: "And if you're dying, and you don't feel like you're allowed to exist anymore, what happens then?"

GM: "Then I may not die, then punishment and misery await me." In panic she says: "I don't want to die; I don't want to die."

TEARS OF RELIEF

We guide grandma through her experience of dying. I place my fingers on her chest and throat, thereby touching the original point of suffocation and accompanying tightness of the chest. Grandma experiences her death again with a fit of coughing, after which the initial fear gives way to enormous enlightenment. Tears of relief are now rolling down her cheeks.

M: "What do you feel now grandma?"

GM: "I secretly went to another body then."

M: "Whose?"

GM: "My granddaughter's."

M: "Ina's? And how come?"

GM: "Because I'm still alive, and I don't have to go to hell."

M: "Yes, that's how it goes, right. And in which place in her body did you lock yourself?"

GM: "In her womb and in her heart."

M: "And what do you whisper to her about that?"

GM: "That she is mine, that she has to listen to me."

M: "And what do you tell her?"

GM: "Men are dangerous and that sex is dirty."

M: "All to jealously hold on to life, when yours is actually over."

GM: "Yes, I see it now."

M: "What would it be like for Ina if you didn't have to hold her anymore?"

GM: "That would change her life."

I help grandma get her bearings in the space, the dimension surrounding her, the world of the soul. She is intensely drawn to it and realizes that there is no hell at all. That it is a fabrication of human origin. Before we let grandma go, I ask her to contact her son Tjeerd at heart level. From a place of deep surrender, she speaks the words that spontaneously come to the surface from inside her: "Dear son, I love you so much. You didn't do it, I'm sorry. I didn't know any better."

For the first time, the condemnation between Tjeerd and his mother is lifted. Tjeerd has suppressed the guilt thrown at his entire life, which has seriously affected him and his fatherhood. As a result, Tjeerd could never really make genuine contact with his daughter Ina. When it comes to women, where his mother plays the leading role, he feels misunderstood, even 'dangerous', and therefore he always kept his distance.

After the session, granddaughter Ina is doing well. Her physical complaints disappear, and she experiences having come into a totally different flow with her partner and children. At the heart of the whole story, we again find the unmistakable influence of the Catholic Church. The belief systems that are inculcated literally manifest themselves below the belt. When our right to be is at stake, we become like a fish on dry land. Our natural basis of life becomes conditional and leads to excesses. People then come into conflict with themselves, and resort to such forms of expressions as abuse, with all the consequences that entails.

CHAPTER 36

The cloud, onze nieuwe god

"The fact that an opinion has been widely held is no evidence whatever that it is not utterly absurd."
– Bertrand Russell

Most indigenous peoples, but also countless inhabitants of the world in general, believe that we as humans have a soul, originating from a soul source. Father Sun symbolizes that source in physical form. For the soul the body is an applied shell, a vehicle, the raw materials of which have been supplied by Mother Earth, with your own biological mother as her unique emissary. When you can look at it that way, it's easier to understand that an innate need to experience the connection with that source and specially to celebrate it, is quite logical. Who doesn't know that? Every human being, every culture has its own original and sincere ways of expressing gratitude for the source of life that makes our existence possible. Not for nothing do we simply become happy, cheerful, and grateful inside when the sun starts to shine.

Expression is given to this depending on what characterizes a civilization in terms of customs, its environment, the climate, and history. With associated symbols and relics. Local animals, raw materials, meaningful colors, outfits, and other unique objects are used to express them with deep respect and dedication. Devotional dance and song, dedicated forms of prayer, temporary seclusion to receive messages from other dimensions, animated rituals and sealing ceremonies.

For centuries, the inner connection with our spiritual origins has been honored and empowered. Once on earth, after incarnation, the newly born, receptive child will initially adopt those frameworks from this need, which are given to him by his environment, within which, according to his (parents) ancestors this spirituality apparently resides. A child learns that the same life force lives in him as in an eagle or a butterfly. Or in fire and water, a birch tree, mountain, or ancestor. And not only that, but it teaches that that power interweaves the whole of creation, and that you can very consciously connect with it, for example during lucid dreams or certain rites. If the child learns this, it becomes the way he perceives things. He will build on this during his journey of development as a human being. His earthly journey is largely based on this legacy. He also learns to be free to build a very own, personal relationship with this creator. He may adjust, fill in and experience the interpretation of his experience as he pleases. In fact, that is precisely what he assumes the most important challenge of the life adventure to be.

A healthy image of God has a self-reflective effect. So that one ' grows towards him', without necessarily wanting to attach a masculine association to him. This god here mirrors his own spiritual essence, the memory of the creative power that we carry within us. And therein lies the pithiest discovery you can make – you are also divine in that essence. That the consciousness of Christ exists within you can be as meaningful to a Westerner, as it can be for an Indian to experience that the Great Spirit is his essence. The diversity of humans and peoples must leave room for different interpretations of the same principle. You feed upon it and grow through that awareness, no matter what it is called or how it is explained.

A CHILD LOOKS WITH UTMOST SIMPLICITY

When a child is presented with an image of a suffering and bleeding man nailed to a cross who died for our sins, with the accompanying explanation, that becomes the starting point. Its consequences are described in detail in this book. Although everything can be explained in different ways, that does not change the symbol that is central to the entire area of faith. And that's how a child looks, with utmost simplicity. It has no use for far-reaching, complicated ways of understanding and interpretation. It naturally seeks the most obvious, magical, and loving factor in every explanation. Even if it feels that certain developments need time, maturation, and perseverance, that should be the reassuring keynote. If the child cannot recognize this simplicity anywhere, if he always sees serious and gloomy persons gravely concerning themselves with matters of faith, then he experiences this as something that is not his own. The child distances himself from it. However, if his parents insist, even more that it really is like this, then the child will eventually split off from himself, from his original, pure perception. If it all goes on long enough and sinks in deeply, that split is then also experienced as normal, as 'one's own'. Then you are faced with the question of whether you are going to adhere to the image of God that has been introduced or whether you will continue to follow your own truth. And for children that is very difficult, because they usually accept their parents as a natural authority. And if they don't, then they catch hell and are reprimanded. In other words, it then becomes common for there to be incompatible contradictions within yourself.

Not believing in anything obviously does not mean that there can be no spiritual experience. People who live with a loving, respectful connection to the seasons, the elements, to each other and to the wonder of life do not have to believe in something that has a form, name, symbol, or doctrine. They just flow into the life they lead and experience that it is good that way, with all the ups and downs. For other families, where people believe in 'nothing', reason is in fact inconspicuously worshipped. Especially when there is an emphasis on not believing anything. Everything comes from rational thought, with using your brains at the forefront. Nothing else exists and there is no need to wonder about more than that. The brain must be well trained for this, usually in combination with several radical life experiences that result in everything being rationally explainable, so that it does not have to be felt. Ultimately, there must be a reason behind everything before it is given the right to exist for the person concerned. In this sense, science, with its technological progress, has become the new god for masses of people. After all, the brain is the place that is dissected to the core and people are in the habit of knowing what is happening in that gray sponge. The need to dissect, analyze and compartmentalize is fueled once people have learned enough to think in pigeonholes and boxes. A thought system, seen from a holistic point of view, makes it difficult to perceive things in a larger perspective. The focus is on specific points, rather than on the bigger picture. The end station is the brain specialist, the neuro-expert. He studied and took courses in it, so he should know. Unfortunately, he has nothing meaningful to say about spirituality.

IMPLEMENTING MICROCHIPS IN THE HUMAN BODY

Meanwhile, the smartphone has taken the place of the former cross above the entrance of the house. Or the rosary that every believer used to have in his pocket. At least that cross had something supernatural compared to the smartphone. It is only the result of advanced technology, although, perhaps developed with extraterrestrial knowledge. A trend has been set again. People feel the need to be somehow plugged into a source of knowing, a source of knowledge. It's a small step to switch from spiritual input to programmed, downloadable information. The less critically people accept this type of information, appealing to material and rational thought, the greater the benefits for the business behind it. Everyone stoically turns a blind eye to the downsides of these developments, such as radiation hazards and inability to make social contact. People adore the idea that all questions can be answered instantly and that there is an app for all important life matters. People blindly welcome the idea that we can be improved on all sides. For many, it is an attractive thought that the development of unwanted cells can be nipped in the bud by an inserted chip. Without wondering what the reason for such unbalanced growth could be. Or that we can suddenly speak Japanese or Russian through an inserted piece of technology without having to make any effort. We prefer to skip going through the experience and the effort that should normally lead to us learning to speak a foreign language. We prefer to plug directly into the end result, without having experienced the road to it. In this way you basically skip the most important reason to incarnate as a human being: experiencing, going through something in life. There is a fanatical movement within this fast-growing branch that considers it desirable to improve upon the object 'human' as such. The transhuman, robotized human, must become immortal and more perfect than the original by implementing extremely advanced and sophisticated technological microchips and the like in the human body, and then connecting them to 'the cloud', the controlling organ. An invisible being who, the word already betrays it, is once again somewhere in heaven. With technology that relies on algorithms, and that inputs predictable behavior without predicting what that will mean on a karmic level. It remains a belief, namely that people can be improved by external technology. It shows that a religion can manifest itself in countless ways. So long as ignorance about our divine nature is the starting point, and we do not see how we allow ourselves to be played, we remain dependent and especially receptive to the carrot being held out to us. And so, we surrender to an artificial god almost unnoticed. It may be part of this phase in our development as a human being, until we enter a new phase in which we no longer have a need for adoration for anything outside ourselves.

PEOPLE INVISIBLE BEHIND THE BUTTONS

'The cloud', in this context, is also a man-made 'intelligent god'. Behind the buttons people are almost invisible. Who has already figured that out? In that way each age produces gods that we ultimately appoint ourselves, depending on our needs. Those who are docile and do not see the revenue model behind this, easily let the often-questionable content of the information thrown at them take them for a ride. Similar in this type of religion is that the creators of the new faith seem to have the exclusive right to the sources of information from which the answers to life questions spring. How necessary and substantial those answers really are remains to be seen. A need can be created in a society with the help of all kinds of influences. Modern business operations have specialized more than ever in perception management. This cunningly convinces people to be dependent on all kinds of products and sources of information, preferably stipulated in a contract. Friendly or less friendly. Indians who adopted church ideology ultimately did so not out of a natural need, but because of the horrible repercussions if they didn't.

How reliable the source behind a doctrine of faith is, depends on the unconditionality and intentions that reside behind the symbol used. And that's where individuals are usually found. And it is not always clear at first glance how benevolent they are. It can take a while, sometimes lives. Wolves in sheep's clothing, gurus, they come and go. In fact, it does not matter which images are used to help market a story of faith. Whether it is a cross, tree, sun, medicine wheel, crescent moon, computer, or hypodermic needle. The representation of the things that really connect with our being out of love, will find real recognition and resonance. It is experienced as timeless and unconditional, supporting our growth. Just as you will continue to cherish a deep warm feeling throughout your life at thoughts of a grandfather or grandmother who loved you very intensely. Where noise comes on the line in the interpretation of a belief, in the long run the soul automatically clarifies the explanation of the image until it reconnects with the feeling of the heart. Even though you must completely detach yourself from something.

How many deaths, murders and misery have not taken place 'in the name of' something? And how stigmatizing is that in an experience of faith? That is why it takes several lives to be able to embrace yourself in love again. There was often no room to meander in your experience of God. The boiler was constantly under pressure. Prayer and idolization had to take place with relentless regularity. Even before you had an inkling of taking a break from it so that you could form your own conclusions, that menacing pointing finger was being waggled in your mind's eye. You watched your step. And the social control did the rest. The story behind the person whose place was empty on the pew, went through the community like wildfire. Do you see the parallel with Facebook and Google? They too know everything about your lifestyle.

CHAPTER 37

Corona, so long as fear rules

"A lie can travel halfway around the world while the truth is putting on its shoes."
– Charles Spurgeon

Preceded by innumerable considerations, it was of course a conscious choice to broach the subject of Corona in this book. Because during its completion, the world was invaded overnight by a pandemic that shook our whole society to its core. The many parallels with previous global disaster scenarios and situations, being described in this book that had consequences for us and our ancestors, were the deciding factor. In a short time, more than ever everyone was confronted with themes concerning the right to be, in which old, suppressed experiences from earlier times were rekindled.

We were met with doom scenarios, extreme measures, and social disruptions. Within weeks we were in lockdown, and everyone had to keep to a series of rules of conduct that were so different from normal human behavior that everyone could imagine this situation would have far-reaching consequences. Everything that normally connects people fell apart. In fact, connecting was punished.

Under rules laid down by the authorities and menacing drumbeats, people had to squeeze themselves into programs of behaviors and practices that fundamentally go against our natural, unifying nature. Togetherness, being free and touching one other are basic human needs. From a holistic point of view, this makes any proposed solution predicated on various forms of separation, automatically questionable. At the same time, it was made clear to us that all freedom-restricting measures and imposed bans on, for example, travelling or visiting places of entertainment, could as it were, be bought off by accepting vaccinations. Meanwhile, everything happened so fast that no one understood the ins and outs. It felt like a surprise attack.

The script for the whole scenario, however, seemed to have been written a long time ago and an extensive series of preparations had already been made in advance. An option that many do not think possible. Because then it would be a conspiracy. Anyone who had studied the website of the influential World Economic Forum had to scratch their heads in disbelief, because strangely enough a detailed description of the corona script had already been provided there, long before the virus erupted worldwide. And not only that, the expected consequences of a virus outbreak for the world were extensively studied and explained with a positive ending. A vision of the future that, with the aid of an incomprehensibly large plan of action, is called 'the great reset'. Besides all the measures that were introduced, what stood out was that anyone who expressed even the slightest difference of opinion, other than that held by the policy-making authorities, suffered greatly.

SUPPRESSION

When I sincerely emphasize that I do not want to offend anyone who has (had) to contend with Corona related illness or even death, with or without having been diagnosed as having it, that does not imply an apology for taking an extremely critical look at the genesis and actual extent of this wave of fear. In the context of this book, after all, the consequences for humanity are once again enormous. While we are not yet at the stage where the real effects and blunders of this global drama have been exposed, and we are able to look back and evaluate them, we can already see that the harmful impact on the development of our soul will be quite compelling.

We see an enormous number of similar characteristics with previously implemented nightmare scenarios and large-scale religions, all with extremely far-reaching consequences. These characteristics can be seen as symptoms. If noticed in time, they can result in a change of course or change of position, but often we only see afterwards what we could have done or didn't do. In any case, the following 'symptoms' are always central: 1. There is a great danger in which our right to be is fundamentally compromised, 2: Humans are considered responsible for this, and 3: Something must be actively 'suppressed', whereby one must comply with the plan that is supposed to provide the solution, including all its side effects. As long as there is the slightest need to suppress something, that justifies torrents of extreme measures and extremely untransparent political action. Every authoritarian institution knows that danger and fear are basic components for the implementation of a new political climate. And ancestors confirmed that to me time and time again. When I asked about what caused them to get so stuck in their past lives and be receptive to dubiously imposed ideas, I got all kinds of enlightening arguments acquired through trial and error. Without exception, these were all traceable to the effect of fear and the spiritual confusion that resulted in repressed processes of mourning.

The government authorities take for granted that the policy they have rigged around it, and the fighting stance they stake against this 'new enemy', is something that will receive unconditional support. In fact, this becomes the web in which people sometimes get ensnared for life and deprives them of their freedom. With a corresponding desired result: power and control. Every empire, of whatever size, is built on people, groups, and demonstrations that had to be 'crushed'. Whether it's the drama of Ruinerwold, an internationally notorious and sinister family drama that recently took place in the Netherlands or Mao Zedong's hunger for power that reportedly cost 70 million Chinese their lives.

THE INDIVIDUAL PROCESS OF DYING

When we take this big picture back to one of the core themes of this book: the individual process of dying, it raises several pressing questions. First, why is there so much need for aftercare for the deceased? Secondly, why does it rarely happen? And thirdly, what does this mean for the quality of life, the right of the families involved to be? On the one hand, crisis situations result in a great deal of suffering and death and at the same time they leave hardly any room for the necessary spiritual guidance. Meanwhile, this neglect of the process of souls making their transition undermines the energetic level of vibration for all those involved. In that way the human being and his immune system is chronically weakened. Whether it's about a demented grandfather who is permeated in every fiber of his being with the fear of the judgment of God as a result of a policy of church indoctrination, a doctor, who in his last moments painfully realizes that he has acted too much under pressure out of conflicts of interest, or someone for whom a series of vaccinations unexpectedly has fatal consequences while he was convinced that he would do well to follow the advice of medical authorities. How bystanders see it often deviates from the actual inner experience of the dying person in question. As soon as a disease that could prove fatal is cloaked and widely covered in the media with all kinds of frightening information, whether it is zooming in on all the external bells and whistles such as ventilators, the hands of dials popping up and down, stressed people in quarantine suits, and ambulances with screaming sirens, it automatically connects every process of dying to the name of the creature in question: Corona. And with it an inordinate amount of pressure, panic, and confusion for those who are having to deal with it now or in the future. Even when a coronavirus is not even the cause of someone's death. When all those impressions are also used to reinforce a medical battle plan and convince others of the importance of what needs to be suppressed, it even goes one step further. Unfortunately, many people only realize afterwards what the disruptive influence of certain circumstances was surrounding a process of dying and then also realize how it could have been approached differently. If a dying person believes that he is contagious, and therefore must be kept at a distance from his (grand)children 'for the greater good', these beliefs are also imprinted and can be transferred to new lives without revision. At all times, the most important conditions for a dying person and his family to make a transition as harmonious as possible are truth, understanding, love and space for contact.

JUSTIFICATION

If we were to deal with a life-threatening pandemic according to the picture outlined by governments, it would not only justify all the drastic measures taken, but also the traumatization of many millions of people. Precisely because the criteria for the definition of the term pandemic by the WHO were adjusted in 2010, so that Corona could not be called an epidemic thereby suggesting it posed a threat like Ebola. In the event of an outbreak, this is a gigantic responsibility that requires very careful action. Where death makes its appearance, especially under dramatic circumstances, there is still work to be done in terms of spiritual aftercare. In this way, it will also be increasingly possible to question souls who died from the consequences of Corona-related circumstances about their experience of dying and the run-up to it. Including all associated complications. We can ask them how, for example, they experienced their own funeral that had to take place digitally because otherwise too many people could be infected. Or what happens in our etheric bodies when medical procedures, such as the administration of vaccinations, take place, and what the effect is on the connection of the soul with the body. It is interesting to hear what consequences remain active for themselves and their descendants. You can bet those souls are going to tell us the naked truth. That might even be a new book.

According to the cycle of life, the many grandfathers and grandmothers who are discussed in this book and who carried the influences of their zeitgeist are succeeded by new generations of ancestors. That's us. And our posterity will speak of us as their ancestors who have experienced the corona crisis. But then in combination with all the background and outcomes that are yet unknown. So, let's learn a lot from them now, because we're just as likely to leave an imprint in our family systems to which our offspring will resonate. How are we going to fare this time? What are we going to pass on to our children and grandchildren? Does your life hold an opportunity for your soul, with all its incomprehensibly great spiritual potential, to free itself from a society that does not always seem as innocent as it is, and where large-scale behavioral experiments are imposed? Freedom and rules will never become friends, I read on a poster somewhere. It can be quite enlightening to look at what role each person plays when humanity finds itself in dire straits.

FOLLOWING AUTHORITIES AS A PHENOMENON

What makes it so easy for so many to give up their authority and uncritically accept what a government says. Our (grand)parents 'of the old school' usually blindly believed what the pastor, doctor, pope, minister, king, queen, or science claimed. How receptive they were to the speeches of dignitaries without realizing what kind of man was behind that outward display? Adolf Hitler, who became a father figure to many millions displaced by the First World War, is an example of this. And that's how artificial fathers and mothers constantly profile themselves among the population. They place themselves between the original connections of love people have with their parents, taking advantage of the damage that has arisen between them. They are ready with their solutions, fine words, promises and of course threats. Not all of them, of course, but enough to cause sufficient disruption.

Fortunately, there seems to be a serious growing trend among people who are starting to wonder whether everything we are told is correct. When the answers then trickle in, the next question is how truthful the social dilemmas we are presented with actually are. Just how correct is recorded history? Knowing that the perceptions on life of many are based on how the past was explained to us, should immediately remind us of our ancestors here. After all, we were generated from them, and our footprints followed theirs.

As my Native American teachers taught me, "We are the hands and feet of The Creator. We may make his creation manifest and create heaven on earth." Along the way, however, we can expect the necessary opposition, and we cannot always achieve this in one lifetime. The transition from Pisces to the Age of Aquarius contains a crucial step for humanity to take in order to grow.

FANATICAL RULERS

Could it be that what everyone ultimately must discover, even the most fanatical megalomaniac, is that life cannot be curbed or controlled by force and manipulation? That life regulates itself from a loving, indefinable principle. The vicarious control mechanism has now taken on global forms, and it has been in the making for a long time. The fears that are created are on a global scale. A flood of global crises: terrorism, climate disaster, shortages, debt and financial dependence everywhere you look, too many people on the planet consuming too much oxygen and therefore exhaling too much CO_2, and a global pandemic. Green sustainability for a better environment, pharmaceutically regulated global health, protection and safety through cameras and apps, and those who need a new organ can count on a computer-artificially generated 3D copy. A concept is gradually introduced and imposed in an apparent state of openness for a better variant of the creation that exists.

As soon as people discover which old circumstances have prompted them to adopt certain behaviors and certain choices, with the consequences that go with them, something fundamentally important happens. 'Armed' with the resulting consciousness, one avoids losing oneself in new situations of a similar order. In the end, you won't even be drawn to them anymore. Your alignment has changed, your worldview has been adjusted, and you can move on, an experience richer. This insight is reflected throughout this book.

CHAPTER 38

Everyone chooses a position

"A truth's initial commotion is directly proportional to how deeply the lie was believed. When a well-packaged fabric of lies has been sold gradually to the masses, the truth will seem utterly preposterous and its speaker a raving lunatic."
– Dresden James

As large-scale, impactful events and coercive belief systems seriously increase the pressure on the population, people's roles are shifting. As a result, they are forced to face choices. Everyone chooses a position. That was already the case when you decided to come to earth for an incarnation, and chose a specific family system, but once here, new moves have to be made on the chessboard of life. At the same time, it is pre-eminently such situations that challenge us to make progress in our process of personal growth.

The premature death of a parent, for example, causes a sudden shift in role patterns among family members. No one just happens to be in a certain place. This is just as much the case on a small scale as with a large-scale event, such as the outbreak of a coronavirus pandemic or a war. There is always group formation. In war, for example, you had the authorities, the opponents, the rescuers, the defenders, the outsiders, the hide-and-seekers, the followers. and the rank and file, to name a few. Each group is manned by birds of a different feather, different characters who occupy specific posts within them. Reincarnated souls, depending on the legacy of old lives, reclassify themselves on the map of their new existence. These remnants are unique per person but also bear collective themes because you always relate to others during events. Every human being forms a cell in the large, collective memory. Each position automatically connects you to a corresponding interest, to associated codes, habits, expectations, and a corresponding point of view and sometimes even associated clothing. It goes without saying in a more or less active role. Doctors attract the sick, authorities seek followers, soldiers seek enemies, whistleblowers seek sleeping listeners, traitors seek victims, shepherds seek sheep, the lost seek direction indicators, law enforcement officers seek the disobedient and those needing power attract those over whom they want power. The latter is particularly fascinating: power cannot be experienced without those who must be oppressed, 'kept down' by it. In short, everyone depends on others to go through a specific human experience.

CHOICES

The subconscious controls navigation to certain positions and every position taken challenges people. Choices must be made again, even though it may feel like you don't even have a choice. In fact, it concerns the choices you may once have wanted to make, but could not or did not, due to the circumstances at the time. If previous decisions were made based on interests that did not correspond to what your heart told you, now it must be different. It should be noted that in past lives you were also often the victim of manipulation and deception. This is how we ultimately learn to understand our own actions, and to control them. How many soldiers who ended up as cannon fodder were not convinced that they were fighting for a good cause, when the outcome of the battle could have been predicted in advance? Brainwashed by the idea that making a sacrifice for folk and fatherland is a supremely valued goal in life. The soul does not accept that. It does not want to live for folk and fatherland.

How many people still sincerely believe that pharmaceutical companies want to serve the well-being of people instead of the well-being of their own wallets? The soul wants the deceptions to be seen through because this sets it free. Just as a fish wants to be surrounded by water, the soul wants to be surrounded by love and truth. And where the soul has lost its natural habitat, it will go on an adventure to rediscover itself unperturbed.

CONFLICT SCENARIOS WITH SIMILIAR CHARACTERISTICS

Anyone who can imagine that with the emergence of a new conflict scenario old collective trauma fields are activated, with similar characteristics as before in which one lost oneself, can recognize it more quickly. And so, a circle can be broken. A new conflict with the possibility of experiencing a different outcome than the previous time.

Are you terrified of becoming infected? Perhaps that says something about previous experiences, for example with leprosy, the plague, syphilis, tuberculosis, or Spanish flu. Does a vaccination passport unconsciously remind you of an *ausweis* from World War II? Does Ikea's proposal to put a yellow sticker on your chest if you can't or don't want to wear a mask rub you up in such a wrong way you totally lose it? Are you afraid of being 'spotted and apprehended' if you don't wear a mask in a supermarket because you were once singled out and taken away? So then realize how scenes from World War II or other eras awaken in you.

There is an enormous stratification of things that can touch you in your personal archives. Some are unknowingly thrown back into their fear of shortages when they see the shelves empty in the supermarket. They expect the curfew again, with the proof of identity that goes with it, or scenarios of great insecurity loom on the horizon, with the prospect of looting and raids when uniformed civil enforcement officers, armed with night sticks, walk the streets. Many experience the resemblance between the Star of David and the mandatory face mask, so that the patch itself calls up enormously deep repressed emotional worlds. Or they foresee that only someone who has been vaccinated will have access to social life, so that old experiences of being excluded will immediately manifest themselves. Others are germaphobes. Anyone who feels an uncontrollable urge to wash their hands countless times a day is probably still stuck in an old personal guilt complex about unsanitary conditions that once arose that resulted in death. Think of the death of a child from spoiled food. For him, the current pressure to prevent infection by keeping a distance, and the confirmation that hand washing really helps, is a very stressful extra layer that will be superimposed on the themes that already exist. Not to mention all those who are afraid of becoming infected with Corona because they succumbed to an infectious disease in a previous life. Remnants and traces of fear of a (new) form of infection, of having physical contact, or of losing yourself in isolation, still churn under the surface. Strong emotions can still resonate in someone when something comparable arises. Intense grief over the loss of loved ones who were unreachable in quarantine, or fear of certain medical procedures. And a slavishness to the one who claims to provide security and solutions. This immediately recalls striking similarities with the current coronavirus. No matter your position, regardless of the circumstances and confrontations, you are always in the right place.

That is a gauge: the greater the resistance or fear that is evoked, the more likely your connection is to something old. And the latter offers perspective in the sense that it can be investigated, it has already taken place, and is processable. It is better to be open to an old painful truth than to drift along in the fog of ignorance. Have a look at what follows below, the division of the different positions in which people could end up in the corona outbreak sketched in black and white. It is not my intention to pigeonhole someone with this. It's about understanding that people don't choose positions randomly but are driven by the soul. This offers opportunities and therefore challenges.

A position that does not fit you (anymore), that keeps you trapped in something, requires a breakthrough to get rid of it, and at the same time a temptation to linger in it. Can you feel recognition somewhere? Or on the contrary a strong aversion?

ROLES AND POSITIONS TAKEN DURING THE CORONA CRISIS

'Perpetrators and those in power' and related people concerned play a role in many ranks in organizing, directing, and maintaining a major defining event. There are interests that motivate their actions and drive how they act depending on their (power) position. Often through deep-rooted and private trauma, they are disconnected from their feelings and thus from any awareness or conscience. They wish to rise above their pain and insecurities forever by exercising power over people (and animals) who in fact represent their own shortcomings. In their world of experience dominated by reason and obsessions, there is no awareness that they will one day be confronted with the consequences of their actions.

'Followers' who meekly accept what those authorities claim see no connection with catastrophes that have arisen and the possibility that they might be deliberately orchestrated. They follow the reports and measures uncritically, deeply believe in the interests of a government in control, and thereby actually feed the degree of success of the narrative on display.

'The down-to-earth citizen' who doesn't just let himself swallow everything, looks at affairs from a distance and objectively weighs the pros and cons of the various sources of information, mainstream, and alternative. They still follow their intuition sufficiently so that they will not be easily overwhelmed by hypes and doom scenarios that have been introduced. Because they cannot so easily be knocked off balance, they can continue to weigh the alternatives and find out afterwards that they are right without that having been their intention. They must often painfully deal with loved ones who are less or uncritical.

'Alternative types' create concepts in which all painful and difficult impressions are converted in an almost compulsive way into positivity, semi-logical explanations or that even acquire a spiritual meaning. The 'everything will be fine in the end' forms the basis of this. No mention should be made of pain and uncertainty. The advantage of a curfew is that it is nice and quiet on the street, right? Or that the air becomes cleaner because there are less airplanes flying. And because nature regulates itself and there are too many people, a pandemic is a logical consequence. That's how it has always been.

'Those forced to be involved' such as scientists, dignitaries and title holders who are supposed to have a certain expertise regarding a situation that has arisen, are put on the spot. As credible authorities for the people, they are pushed forward publicly. They are expected to propagate well-researched theories that underscore the necessity of certain actions and underpin the narrative of fear that has been introduced.

'Public service officials', such as doctors and nurses, are unexpectedly confronted with a reality that they have not experienced before. Having to follow imposed measures, they are expected to perform their services, while at the same time finding themselves in a workplace which is bristling with authoritative instructions, and fraught with serious conditions, while also concealing a truth about which it would be better not to talk.

'Law enforcement officers' see their opportunity to prevent disobedient people from not complying with the rules. In this way, they experience playing a valuable role in preventing chaotic situations. They must combat the chaos with which they themselves were once confronted, with disastrous consequences. Being an extension of official bodies may well give them the security they did not once have in a past life, which caused them to lose out. Or where others once came out worst, for which they felt responsible. As soon as they go overboard with the powers they have acquired, thus enabling them to live out old recognition complexes, they line their pockets without being aware of it. Every act that caused suffering will one day have a resounding impact.

'Whistleblowers' want to alarm people about impending calamity because they themselves were once too late, or too naïve. Or complicit of course, thereby in fact warning people about themselves. On the other hand, the insiders who know the ins and outs of the system, are the best devil's advocates and therefore provide precisely the kind of information that goes over many people's heads.

Then there are the 'outsiders' whom you could almost forget to mention. They are somewhere on earth where they don't hear a word about a certain event that is going on all over the world.

Winston Churchill's statement 'never waste a good crisis' indicates that emergencies can also bring benefits. The British statesman thus indicated that the United Nations owed its existence to the less pleasant period that preceded the establishment of that organization. Without the Second World War, the institute would never have existed, according to the British prime minister. It indicates that every crisis provides a necessary foundation for projects, initiatives, and developments that under normal circumstances could not grow because there is no reason to do so. Under the guise of an international need for reconstruction and a collective sense of 'together we are strong', it was believed that they would be able to cope with future disaster scenarios. Apart from the logical question as to whether disasters are premeditated for these reasons, it is in any case abundantly clear that 'the profiteers' enrich themselves in all kinds of ways with the business that produces those conditions of abject misery.

And then, of course, there are 'the victims' on many levels. You can be a victim in many ways. This concerns the numerous people who die along with their families and those involved with them. Amid a jumble of clinical, medical interventions, with or without loved ones who may only be present under certain conditions, the inflicted person undergoes a miserable process of dying in solitude, full of unspoken words, in an atmosphere of emotional neglect. As a result, both the deceased and the descendants cannot break free in harmony, and no one can work through what has happened in a good way. Anyone weighed down by the pressure and under the yoke of the situation is ultimately a victim. They carry with them the legacy of an enormously stressful program that was spread among humanity in a certain era.

These are some of the kinds of posts that everyone can take up, as it were, making it extremely interesting to find out what your ancestors did under the circumstances that were topical and threatening in their day and displayed similarities to now. Did they follow their heart, or did they camouflage their motives for fear of reprisals? When you learn to listen well, do they then whisper their advice to you? A comforting truth is always available to you and your situation that stems from them. But to reach that they first had to detach themselves from the ballast they had once incurred.

CHAPTER 39

Pitfalls and deceptions

"The darkness is light enough for me."
– Juan de la Cruz (1542-1591)

As soon as breakthroughs occur during sessions, a suppressed understanding of the circumstances of certain conflicts manifests itself almost immediately. I have described it in detail. I am continually baffled by the proximity of the crucial insights that can bring about deep changes in one's patterns. Although I officially practice reincarnation therapy, my working method is fundamentally different from that of colleagues in many areas. I have readjusted quite a few visions and have mainly explored and worked out the areas that relate to our ancestors. I interpret the phenomenon of past lives in relation to our current existence very differently than before and see more and more that the unfinished emotional triggers from past lives are embedded in the connection with our (ancestors) parents. Here, too, wisdom is constantly on its way. Within the world of reincarnation or regression therapy there are also many disagreements, dogmas, old-fashioned and newfangled views. That's what it means to be human. The logic behind 'the perpetrator and the victim', for example, can be explained in so many ways. So long as one has not really lived through what that means, the term remains too black and white for many.

PARALLEL LIVES

Some speak of parallel lives. Which means that you can live different lives at the same time in the same era. The soul splits up and takes on an incarnation with very different circumstances, themes, and events on two (or more) tracks. For us humans 'thinking in three dimensions' it is a possibility that is difficult to grasp. I am by no means ruling it out. At the same time, I never needed to adjust the outcome of a session one way or another. In the end the outcome is self-explanatory. Some experience being a Jewish girl who has been seriously harmed during the Second World War, while research that probes somewhat deeper shows that the identification with this innocent creature is meant to conceal the true SS man. To explain such a time discrepancy, since the Jewish girl and the SS lived at the same calendar time as it were, these clients then say that it is about parallel lives. I do not believe that myself, but in fact it does not matter so long as the impact of the session(s) yields the desired changes. Moreover, it is quite enriching to discover that this SS character was a role that also stems from a previous severe experience of being a victim. One which can be found on the known timeline before the life, and therefore the birth, of the SS man. In other words, first one dies, after which the other is born. If it does not turn out to be the case, it has no result, which is a reassuring thought. The human mind turns out to be infinitely creative, also at these layers. It is even able to sabotage itself on levels that one attributes to an inner knowing. Meanwhile, people let themselves be fooled. That 'inner knowing' appears to be constructed based on cleverness. It is reduced to a subtle survival strategy in a spiritual jacket, often surrounded by the necessary fuss, theories and acquired gradations within a certain spiritual discipline.

INVOKING LIGHT BEINGS

To reinforce their sessions, some therapists and care providers invoke the assistance of light worlds and (arch)angels. This is done in terms that to an unprecedented extent call upon the most enlightened forces of love from the entire cosmos. Not infrequently with the help of all kinds of symbolic and magical frills. Here I often see an adoration of the therapist for authorities from his own family system. The awesome light beings actually represent those they themselves missed very much in their younger years, when there was a great deal of insecurity. So much grandiosity and counterforce had been needed, in the experience of the inner child of the therapist, to undo the miserable situation that had been his share at the time. It is also possible that the light being is the counterpart of a dominant, aggressive parent who forcefully set the boundaries at home. It is questionable whether these invoked light beings really manifest themselves as concretely as the therapist requires of them. A call to unseen and unknown forces enclosed in a ceremonial setting resounds further than one often realizes. And therefore, also to various shadowy regions. It depends on the real intentions and hidden agendas of the one summoning them, of which he himself is not always aware. And confused, malevolent spirits are also smart. They're practically human. As soon as they feel that their true nature goes unnoticed, they can manifest themselves differently, for example as an angel or guide. This can then work out in various ways. Either it gives these spirits an even firmer position in the auric field of the client (or therapist), where conditions are even set for their help, or they see an opportunity here to continue to interfere with the earthly world so that they do not have to dwell on the fact that they are actually dead. When a high-ranking official shouts 'God bless us all', and sometimes means the population of an entire country, he also appeals to a large group of people for a power that he cannot oversee from the limited comprehension that his conditioning has hammered into him.

SENDING LIGHT AND LOVE

Sending too much light, love and positivity to certain areas and people under veiled coercion can be very counterproductive. In an extreme form, this happens in films about exorcism. The invaded mind is automatically considered evil, usually by someone who represents the church, and thus 'the good'. With all kinds of ceremonial violence, the 'evil spirit', which is soon called a demon, is exorcised, and sometimes even directed to the deepest regions of hell. Everything is done in the name of the 'All-mighty God'. But the word "might" can be misinterpreted quite quickly. That way, a mind only becomes more desperate and angrier. You must not shine a spotlight on someone who has been locked in pain, fear, isolation, and self-blame for a long time. This should be done subtly, with understanding and with a measured amount of light. What makes spirits angry, menacing, and unrelenting stems from the totally misunderstood and extraordinarily painful events they went through during their earthly existence. Once dead, they still jealously cling to the earthly realm – as we have been able to read – through a living person who is receptive enough to their presence and often has similar issues. A respectful, curious approach, in which genuine inquiries are made about the circumstances that damaged his life, helps let the spirit process, after which letting go comes naturally. As soon as an extreme display is made about protection with light and love, the need of the care provider to undo a certain pain with someone in his circle comes to the fore unnoticed. The actual healing therefore does not occur. Rather, there is a demand for even more treatments of this caliber. It should not result in spiritual treatment of symptoms.

I'm not suggesting that spiritual forces from loving places do not have anything to do with humanity because that happens at all levels. It is just that the subtlety and extent to which that happens often exceeds our comprehension. They don't have to be called or to be called in, like the AAA when your car breaks down. They are already involved if the right climate was created during a session or healing process.

If therapists or healers rely on the psychically obtained information from alleged spirit guides or other invisible sources, it is useful to exercise a degree of vigilance. It is also human in this field of work to show bias in interpreting statements, theories, and wisdom that people have learned in all kinds of literature about reincarnation. After doing some experimental work, they then sometimes develop a whole working model around it with very questionable standards, conditions and working methods. Such as for example, 'sending to the light', or energetically combating unwanted emotions or other charges. You can play with this model all you want so long as the client is impressed by it and at the same time in need of help, and you can use it at will. It is not so complicated to 'get someone into a past life', nor to draw conclusions about the inner workings of ancestors. What matters is entering these fields of work with a great deal of humility, determination, and prudence – in the right balance, in which the therapist has a guiding, instead of a directing role. Then the appropriate answers will automatically manifest themselves with the corresponding processes of change and logic. The client needs to experience that he or she themselves have been the most important agent of healing and change.

CHAPTER 40

The third, fourth and fifth dimensions

"Impatience requires the impossible, the attainment of the end without the means."
– G.W.F. Hegel

I once read a story about a Western researcher. During an expedition he comes into contact with shamans who live very secluded in the Altai Mountains. He writes down the special spiritual experiences he gains daily in a blog on his laptop. When an otherworldly shaman asks him what that glowing object on his lap is, with all those moving symbols, he says that this is a technological invention from the modern world. "This allows you to use a large electronically installed network to be connected to people and places around the world by air," he explains a little euphorically. The shaman responds dryly: "Oh, do you need such a device for that?"

That such an artificially manufactured network is actually a technological interpretation of an already existing principle is an interesting thought. After a step-by-step introduction, in which the advantages were blown up to such an extent that the disadvantages remained hidden in their shadow for a long time, an already existing divine principle was replaced among mankind by a counterfeit intelligent system. In its original form, we know it as telepathy. In this artificial version, however, one does not see that there are questionable human intentions behind it. The Lego Forest with plastic trees replaces the real forest for the child. As a result, the child becomes alienated from the original creation with all its wonders, lessons, smells, and colors. The similarity with these 'internets', the original and the replica, concerns the possibility to be online at any time and to able to contact information sources and persons, anywhere in the world. For a soul this is normal and also for an embodied person who is still awake enough in terms of consciousness and therefore sufficiently embedded in the fourth dimension too, because he still sufficiently remembers the origin of his soul. The difference, however, is that the "natural internet" only functions based on the source of God from which the soul originates. Here one can connect with sources and relationships without any technological interference, knowing that exchange at these levels is essential for an earthly existence. The soul itself selects which connections are essential, and which are not, and at what times and in which stages of life. The artificial system, on the other hand, provides people with a continuous overload of selected and processed smart information. After a period of several decades in which it has crept up on them, people have been made completely dependent on it and tied to all kinds of binding contracts. The initially innocent and welcome provision of information presented to humans as a tool, turned out to be the cover of a computer octopus that literally restricts people. We are now going to experience it for ourselves: a total submission to a digital network, totally dependent on electricity, which regulates the international infrastructure of life at every conceivable level.

THE GREAT RESET

While generations of young people learned that the answer to every question that arises must be directly retrievable, they were imperceptibly sucked into a dubious but seductive stream of possibilities, where it remains to be seen how it affects our well-being. As attractive as it all appears, the purpose of this system is to distract people from their process of inner growth, and from the lessons that Mother Nature offers to understand yourself. It also means that our absorption capacity and processing system is constantly under high tension, with the associated harmful burden on our health. We are simply inundated with mental stimuli and information that are not relevant, and that we are not able to corroborate with the center of our feelings in the heart. Our telepathic abilities are still in their infancy in terms of development, so there is not really much confidence in them yet. After all, an appeal has never been made to them in our lifetime.

An artificial substitute for a divine basic principle that already exists, but is yet unknown to many, is therefore still a tempting option. A welcome intruder. We already embrace it, without thinking about where it will lead us. With tons of technological fiddling, it seems as if we can face our personal and social problems in the future without seeing that it in fact causes us more difficulties. Cyborg man, a man 'improved' by technology, who in a previous era was called an *übermensch*, is therefore the ultimate prospect. The inevitable new standard of living that goes with it is thus heralded with much unequivocal fanfare. According to spokespersons of AI (Artificial Intelligence), we are on the eve of a great, 'inevitable', reset of humanity. Klaus Schwab's already immortal words, with his characteristic accent (pronounce it out loud): 'Secret reset', speak for themselves. He is not referring to the transition to a fourth dimension of consciousness, but to a 'fourth industrial revolution'. A message now resounding with increasing emphasis thanks to the assistance of the artificially constructed web. The web with all its threads, spun by a spider remarkably and skillfully capable of hiding itself, is the main means for the introduction of the new normal. However, the suggested transition to an artificially intelligent episode of humanity is a falsified variant of the actual transition we make as humans: from the third to the fourth dimension.

A GIGANTIC PERIOD OF TRANSITION

But what are we in fact talking about when we use the term dimensions? I've touched on it before. According to indigenous people like the Mayans, we are in a time when we are moving from the Age of Pisces to the Age of Aquarius. Synonyms for time spans of thousands of years linked to the characteristics of the constellations. We are traveling from the third to the fourth dimension with 2012 as the equinox and are currently in the middle of this gigantic period of transition. A period filled with a multitude of exceptional planetary constellations, all of which have a major influence on our actions. Taken as a whole, a dimension is a state of consciousness that is available and accessible to all, once the main part of the preceding dimension has been lived through and understood to a certain degree, as a logical consequence of development and growth. A dimension is not so much a destination in the sense of a place where you can go. Dimensions vibrate in fluctuating resonances, like the colors of the rainbow merge according to the color spectrum red-orange-yellow-green-blue-indigo. In addition, each color represents a level of consciousness, just like with our chakras, or energy centers. If a certain chakra becomes blocked so that there is no good flow to the next chakra – say dimension – an experience also remains incomplete and cannot integrate. At the same time, life force, consciousness, always tends to want to move further, to expand. Perhaps all a bit abstractly explained for our comprehension, but in simple language: when the penny has dropped, you no longer long to go back to the phase in which that was not yet the case. We are attracted to a new phase with new opportunities for development. Here, the prerequisite for this growth and development is also characteristic for a different human perception and focus, belonging to the fourth dimension: a literally groundbreaking field of vision that shines through greater than before. A new dimension reveals itself in how things are perceived, so that we can no longer only take our own perceptions as a starting point for our visions. All four wind directions of the medicine wheel now play a role in perception, literally completing the circle. One now appears truly capable of seeing someone else's viewpoint without getting entangled in one's own opinions and views. It makes it immediately clear that this is not without conflict, since old notions with their corresponding interests and issues of identity are no longer sustainable.

TRANSCEND OR CONNECT?

I have already touched on whether in the writing of the final chapters I had not strayed too far afield from the main thrust of this book. It was also a question I constantly asked myself. It was my intention from the start to cause a stir in people's old patterns of belief, so I thought it would make sense to let this excursion, with the following concrete example, again merge with all the previous chapters. Hopefully, the usefulness of an explanation about Corona and shifts of consciousness, expressed in dimensions, becomes clearer regarding our 'right to be'. The example is a general one. It could adequately describe all the deeply hidden and repressed experiences that keep us from growing spiritually, and which many people still prefer to deny. Consciously or unconsciously.

When grandpa sexually abused his granddaughter, damaging this girl's lower chakras, something which extended into her adulthood, that still gives grandpa access to those chakras after his death. Grandpa forced his way into this biologically basal, sexual area, crossing her line in the process.

Grandpa's "advantage" is that he can remain earthbound through the life energy leaking from one of his offspring and continue to exert a dominant influence on his granddaughter. That way his shame and guilt, or his pangs of conscience, do not have to be experienced. He planted such deep-seated fear in his granddaughter with the threatening language he used to tell her what would happen if she talked about their little secret, that it persisted well into her adulthood. That is why she clammed up about her emotional experience for such a long time, refusing to talk about it. Thus, an old trauma is perpetuated long after it actually took place. The boundaries he violated remain so chronically violated, it clearly reflects the effect of a threat over time. Only when grandpa's own pain comes to light that his transgressive behavior engendered, most likely through influences from the church and war, does his granddaughter's blocked life force start flowing again. This means the granddaughter must confront her past. For both (the soul of) her grandfather, as well as herself, processing such trauma from the abuse enables them to break free of old wounds. Now grandpa can finally let go, merge into the realms of souls, and the released chakras of his granddaughter may now begin to heal. Incidentally, all family members involved will reap the benefits of dissolving these types of trauma clusters, since they all had a lateral connection to them because of their blood relationship. Only now is there really room for 4D consciousness to flow into the energetic system of this granddaughter. This goes hand in hand with a profound, lasting sense of liberation, a flood of pennies dropping into place, and an awareness of all kinds of entanglements in which she had ended up during her life because of this abuse. All shamans know that our diseases and disorders are without exception related to (ancestors) parents who died under traumatic circumstances. So, transcending old traumas is not desirable. Instead, it is a kind of seductive diversionary maneuver that disconnects us from what is also ours. What is desirable, however, involves reconnecting with situations in which we once lost ourselves, to become whole again.

CONSPIRACY

The present transition from the third to the fourth dimension is based on the same principle, on a large scale. That means that all the old wounds, arising from eras as described in detail in this book, including the corona time, have built up in the filter of 3D consciousness among people. They simply wish to be lived through and thus liberated. Living through them only means that life goes through them, so that liberation occurs. So long as most people think that organized crime of this magnitude, on a global level, is a conspiracy theory, this plays into the hands of those who are pushing for an artificial replacement of our society, making it increasingly impossible for us to clean up our old mess. So long as grandpa, who no one could have imagined was capable of such acts, and anyone pointing that out is a conspiracy theorist, can invisibly take up his position in his granddaughter, the influence his power has is guaranteed. The field of trauma is thus maintained in such a way that the 4D frequencies can scarcely flow in. That is why it is good to always remain widely informed and to continue to investigate carefully. Because conspiracy or not, it is quite clear that Corona already gives a great deal of nourishment to the birth of new areas of trauma, and that we had better minimize them where possible for ourselves and our offspring.

3-D HOLOGRAM, HEIGHT, LENGTH AND WIDTH

So, our consciousness seeks connection to these new frequencies, and vice versa, creating a different awareness about everything that we previously did not think possible. For example, that it becomes natural to connect yourself with a deceased ancestor to clarify certain matters. That telepathy is very normal, and you can pick up on other people's frame of mind, and you are now learning to distinguish between what is yours and what is not. Or that it becomes logical that you learn to understand your own past lives and, where necessary, process them for the benefit of your current well-being. Before you gain access to these realities invisible to the naked eye, you must of course first realize that you are more than just a body in a material reality. A great deal of writing devoted to this subject amply testifies to that. Still, human experiences are required that reveal these spiritual worlds. A monk, in his desire to be close to God, can spend a lifetime in abstinence, meditation, and contemplation without having a real spiritual experience, while a villain can have a near death experience that completely changes his life. How the three-dimension works in the perception of the person connected to it may be better understood by imagining a 3D hologram. A schematic representation of a person's world of perception: the height (thinking), the width (body) and the depth (emotions). But now, with the revelation of a fourth, spiritual dimension, the mind also becomes an integral and conscious part of one's existence. A whole new world literally opens, and a lot of old conclusions suddenly turn out to be extremely relative and unfounded.

We are going to experience living, to move based on our free will from our spirit, and no longer by randomness and chance from a survival mode. Just as the granddaughter, after her detachment from grandfather's influence, ends up in very different waters, and regains her self-determination, so too will the fourth dimension have a similar effect on people.

BAREFOOT TIME

What we notice about the shifts is that we can no longer cling to old values and beliefs. We have to surrender to something new, something that we cannot yet fully interpret. At the same time, we already have a gut longing for a world in which we deal with each other and our environment very differently. The omens in and surrounding us have already been noticeable for a long time. But it feels like we must throw away our old shoes before we have new ones. To bridge the gap, we find ours in a time of going barefoot, diligently searching for the new footwear with which we can continue on our life paths. Leaving an era means that we are going to adjust, reevaluate the logic about the world, each other, and ourselves and about social structures and manners. At the same time, we have become familiar with the old, and many of our educators to whom we remain loyal for a very long time were riddled with three-dimensional ways of acting and thinking. One of the specific characteristics of 3D belief is that a certain rigidity structures our lives. And that our thinking, acting, and feeling play out in linear time. Linear time as a system of belief that allows us to 'live', with an experience of past and present... and then we die. Because this belief is a standard assumption of mass 3D consciousness, and events seem to confirm this; most people think and react as if this is true. In fact, they project this limited view onto their still shaky spiritual awareness. Nowadays you can become quite the spiritual bigwig by following expensive training courses, making step-by-step plans, and using meditation techniques. A 3D movement interpreted in 4D or even 5D clothing. Because many people even long for the fifth dimension. With the help of working models and exercises, one can already work towards this according to methods that have long been discovered by some progressive chosen ones. As if the fourth can be passed over. But underlying this view is a three-dimensional, linear focus. It is as if you want to experience adulthood by skipping the puberty that is necessary to reach maturity. And so, I see shy teenagers in my practice who have a hard time expressing themselves in words but have a palpable spiritual awareness compared to the self-proclaimed 5D healers surrounded by an impressive array of diplomas and theories implying all sorts of high degrees of enlightenment. Chasing these 'higher attunements' often helps them to remain disconnected from, for example, an aggressive father or sickly mother, because the pain in their childhood was too overwhelming. Like in the example of the grandfather and his granddaughter. With the message of 'the right to be' in the background, you can only really move into a new phase, when you have also reached a degree of acceptance with those parts of yourself that 'remained behind' in old eras, of even past lives sometimes from the second dimension. This ballast concretely consists of the burdens and restrictive beliefs incurred from previous lives, and the energies transferred from the parental home. In addition, your father and mother, as emissaries of your ancestors, are what matter most, while for many they are undervalued or even forgotten. The greater the craving for the fifth dimension, the more often we are drawn to the past.

ONE WITH ALL THAT LIVES

Many visionaries and seers have foresight about coming eras and can already talk about it. *The Prophecy of Red Floyd* appeals to me personally, from an Indian point of view. But there are many, of course. The new consciousness mainly contains the realization that we live in a world where we mirror each other, in which we cannot exclude anything. That we reap what we sow and that we have consciously chosen to incarnate in the footsteps of our parents. That everyone's right to be belongs to themselves and should not be determined by persons who appropriate that right to decide that for others. It is no coincidence that the current technological dominance goes hand in hand with the transition to a fourth dimension. Once sufficiently touched by the vibrations of the fourth-dimension consciousness, one quickly begins to see through the facades of the old power structures. And with it, its own sabotage mechanisms that are based on power. Many people are currently in the process of preparing to reach their own breakthroughs. The power elite, meanwhile, will stop at nothing to prevent humanity from moving with the flow of the fourth dimension. A massive implementation of all kinds of control mechanisms in the form of laws and rules (of conduct) must keep people as they are, and that is precisely what we must discover. As the four-dimensional vibrations of consciousness become sufficiently incorporated, the old will automatically lose its grip. We will then pick up the shards and surrender to new challenges and hopeful prospects. That souls recognize each other by vibrations, and not by appearance. And that every 'no' is okay, so long as it's a 'yes' to yourself.

THE ROAD TO ROME

To remain faithful to one of the main themes of the book, reincarnation therapy is but one of the many roads that lead to Rome. As far as I'm concerned, a promising one. It is true that this road does not lead to Rome, but another destination instead: the right to be. The therapeutic methods and insights that I have described are of course seen through my eyes and are therefore not the complete picture. I do however feel a genuine satisfaction because I believe I have given a real representation of all those stories with their underlying messages and translations of a bigger picture. I also know that I will be corrected wherever that isn't the case. I do not lay personal claim to any cure, success, or result. That which I ultimately only make use of in my work is not mine in 'to possess'. Frequently working and looking beyond the boundaries of modern man's orientation to the exterior in his materialistic habitat, is something that is still extraordinary for most people in this day and age. It gives insight into a reality that is always there but must be entered.

Quantum mechanics shows more and more concretely that matter arises from energy, from emptiness in our perception. The next step is that we discover that we ourselves control that energy with our thoughts. The resulting formation of our physical reality is therefore actually in our hands. Disruptive and limiting thoughts form from traumatic life experiences and indoctrination. Loving, creative thoughts are the basic principle of our existence. They reappear when old pain can be released. They are the shining remnants of trauma healing and for me also the most important reason to love my work in both all its simplicity and complexity. Our society may not yet be truly imbued with the infinite power of love, the potential our soul possesses, but when I see the soul constantly working through all those people to rid them of old limitations, a beautiful image arises in my mind's eye of a near future. The world is now mainly organized based on our ignorance of this in favor of a singular group of power-hungry people, who think they can take advantage of it from some inbred form of cleverness. But change is only a matter of time. The present time. We move from an old to a new destination like the monarch butterfly travels from North America to Mexico. For that journey of thousands of miles, it needs several generations. Once it has reached its destination it gratefully realizes every intermediate step that its ancestors made. And many of us are here on earth to help them reach the final stages and passing into a new world. Let's thank our ancestors for that and embrace them with our wings.

Epilogue

Where's Wally?

"To rise above your old self is to descend to the depths to transform into a form that suits you NOW."
– Ingspire

Are you familiar with Englishman, Martin Handford's book *Where's Wally?* Colorful books of detailed double-page spread picture puzzles with a guy in a red-and-white striped T-shirt and jeans, as its main character. Wally is practically unfindable amid countless other figures in all kinds of living situations. You really have to do your darndest to find him because that's the whole point.

Imagine a new edition of *Where's Wally?* The theme of that book is: the misunderstood pages of our history. Where were you? The book contains several picture puzzles with images of circumstances from eras that were the result of major disruptions in human society. Perhaps a region or community immersed in fear, as a victim of the dark sides of the church. Or an illustrious secret society where nefarious plans were forged. Various war scenarios. Perhaps a battlefield or a large group of high-ranking soldiers who came up with strategies they fortunately did not have to take part in themselves. Bank buildings with the suits and ties working in them, lining their pockets. A society plagued by leprosy or some other malady or a print from a period when it was normal to have slaves, or to be a slave. An orphanage with lost children, or an Indian tribe that was expelled from their land. A people plagued by hunger. Where were you? You were also involved in one way or another and you also bear a bit of responsibility for this history. This new edition of Where's Wally? is a living workbook. Only people who have the courage and wisdom to make the world a better place by starting with themselves, dare to purchase this or receive it symbolically as a gift by a dear friend who understands the art of touching you.

GRIM HISTORY BOOK

The challenge is to occasionally have a look for yourself into a grim history book that you know you appear in. The book can of course be found within yourself and through self-examination, acquired self-knowledge, by opening yourself to inner processes and reconnecting with old, unfinished, and sometimes even split off, painful experiences. Wally, here you yourself, doesn't have a red and white T-shirt right now. No, sometimes a ball of lead is chained to one of his ankles. Or is he sitting in a dungeon, dangling from a rope, hiding himself in the fog, numbing himself or disguising himself almost unrecognizably in a costume full of medals and ribbons. Sometimes it really is quite a task to find him, and at the same time you are the only one who can do that. And every time you succeed, and you realize that it wasn't all that bad, the picture puzzle once lost comes to life in a surprising way, and with it the entire book. It transforms into a luminous, colorful, joyful environment. By going through your own transformation processes, each in your own way, by finding yourself again and becoming more complete, the static old image you had of yourself starts to discolor and fade.

As I said, this book is alive and kicking. Your rediscovered Wally's can go to a new time, to the now. The recovered Wally's no longer have to knock on your door. They make the old puzzle of which they were once a part pale into insignificance. In this way, there can be an exponentially rapid breakdown of the old humiliating occult systems dragging people down that are still active in the catacombs on which our society is partly built. We can welcome back our lost life streams. Licking our wounds and plugging our leaks. With our loved ones, friends, children, and the animals, in a beautiful world in which the seasons colorfully alternate, we rally around the fire. With tasteful food, surrounded by the music of our hearts, we show each other and our ancestors the life trophies we have acquired. We raise our own voice in song, which shows everyone who you really are, and how that came about. Love is our deepest state of being. And out of all the Roman Catholic clerical attire, the military costumes and other outfits that once represented something dark, we make a huge patchwork quilt under which we let a long episode of humanity rest, without ever forgetting it. Celebrating our 'right to be'.

AHO MITAKUYE OYASIN

(In Lakota 'All our relations', prayer of unity and harmony with all forms of life: all people, animals, birds, insects, trees and plants, the stones, mountains, valleys, and rivers.)

AFTERWORD BY EWALD STÖTELER

I felt honored when Maarten asked me to write an afterword to his book.

In 2003, the mapping of the human genome, our genetic blueprint, was completed. There was euphoria in scientific circles. It was assumed that with this human genome in hand, the cause of all diseases could eventually be found. The idea was that genetic defects that would then be detected could now be remedied and so in the long term almost all diseases could be cured. This turned out not to be the case. Genetic structures are apparently so subject to change that healing with the help of genetic engineering has turned out to be a vain hope. A little later, a new term, 'epigenetics', made its appearance – a field that studies the effect of environmental influences on the formation of, and changes in, DNA. The interplay from a person's environment arranges the genes and is therefore a contributing factor to their character, their structure. Virtually unnoticed, this introduction resulted in a total paradigm shift within the scientific worldview. After all, science always tries to find a material explanation for all observable phenomena. But now, with the advent of the concept of epigenetics, suddenly a non-material reality was taken seriously. Something that up to that point was unthinkable.

Epigenetics now makes it possible to turn a gene on or off, with the result that a disease may or may not develop. Here, of course, the question immediately arises, who turns what on or off and how or why? A question that raises many moral questions in trying to gain a greater understanding of this new reality. After all, it confirms that the body is an expression of something that is immaterial at its core. Is it the intention that a disease due to gene manipulation may no longer have a physical expression?

THE BODY IS THE VEHICLE FOR THE HUMAN SOUL

Incorporeal force fields, referred to in such terms as the human mind, the spiritual, '*vis medicatrix naturae*' or Qi, are thus a driving force behind the formation of the unique physical body. In other words, the body is in the deepest sense the vehicle for the human soul. In the law of nature this is a fact. For example, it is also a law of nature that man has a body. After all, every human being has one. And that we have a father and a mother, or a masculine and feminine principle, that lays the foundation for the formation of our body. And, because we live as human beings, we all have a biography, a unique course in life. After all, every human being has one. The detailed descriptions of personal biographies of people, as extensively documented in this book, are therefore automatically essential to better understand ourselves.

LIFE EXPERIENCES CONTINUE TO IMPACT SUCCESSIVE GENERATIONS

Human life, meanwhile, can be affected in countless different ways. Being influenced in a healthy and healing way, but also in a pathogenic, damaging, or destructive way. Recent studies from epigenetics have shown that our genetic structure changes partly due to the different impressions and living conditions to which we are exposed during our lives. And since new DNA is formed from the DNA of our (ancestors) parents, their life experiences continue to impact subsequent generations. Our (grand)children can therefore physically experience the consequences of events from previous generations in their current lives. Nearly all diseases are caused at this immaterial, energetic level. And so, the importance of understanding our immaterial, spiritual life gradually becomes more important and clearer in relation to our health.

In homeopathy, it is mainly the 'nosodes' that address themes dealing with ancestral issues. They are prescribed for all kinds of specific diseases in relation to previous generations.

PROFOUND SELF-EXAMINATION MARKS A TURNING POINT IN LIFE

For most of us, this invisible world of the human soul is not easy to reach. We usually have to be shown the way by someone who went before us. Until we have developed the necessary abilities to become somewhat familiar with it. The distressed current social situation in which many people find themselves and the stress this causes the soul, even though one might not call it that, shows the necessity of this. Deep self-examination, often over multiple incarnations, represents a turning point in many people's lives. A turning point towards more self-awareness, more self-knowledge and healing. This process is described in many vivid variations in this book. A personal mirror of the soul for the reader. A true-to-life description of how the soul is expressed through the human body and its biography, in and over different generations and incarnations. This information deserves to be made accessible to a large audience. That's what this book does!

DEEP CALMING AND LIBERATION OF CLIENTS

Maarten's experienced, lucid, and truthful approach to his clients creates an impressive picture in which we see how the past, in the form of previous generations and past incarnations, confronts the individual soul again with current life situations. This with the aim of becoming aware of it. In this way we can heal 'from' our soul. The soul, in its yearning for wholeness, always creates circumstances in the maze of life to find deeper awareness and meaning. The reactions documented by Maarten of the deep calming and liberation of his clients, the sincere stories, the profound awareness and the healing, therapeutic consequences of the sessions described, are so telling, true, and recognizable they come across to the reader as quite natural and deeply palpable. By taking seriously the misguided paths people took during their lives out of self-protection and overcompensation and approaching them with respect, Maarten imbues them with significant meaning, thereby rendering them superfluous.

THE SPECIAL CHARACTER OF THIS BOOK

Themes such as upbringing, war, religion, education, regression, and reincarnation are subjects that recur. Since these are important elements in our collective heritage, collective memory, and our personal biography, it is almost inevitable the necessary attention will be paid to this. No doubt because healing can take place in their transformation.

Maarten takes you by the hand into the deeper layers. A deepening that is so based on everyday reality and therefore so obviously logical that the reader could even lose sight of the special character of this book.

We are confronted with our own reality, our own past, our upbringing, our unresolved and repressed elements, and our family issues that we are usually not even aware of. With the ultimate goal of reaching ourselves, our own identity, our own life goals, our own self-respect, our own meaning, in short, our own right to be.

Ewald Stöteler

Internationally known Classical Homeopath, practicing since 1981. Ewald teaches at training institutes in Japan, Germany, and the Netherlands.
He is the author of several books on homeopathy, including Hahnemann's Homeopathy – The Classification and Treatment of Diseases According to Dr. Samuel Hahneman, published in 2019.

APPENDIX

Client's Case Histories

"I allow myself to succeed now"

Since undergoing therapy with you, I have also become a regression therapist myself. That says it all. My problem was unresolved anger and self-sabotage that caused me to have a propensity for depression and only moderately succeed in what I undertook. I had no idea in this life why that was. But during therapy I came into a life as an SS man who had done horrible things in Poland, and then started to drink and wanted to escape. That was not possible. In the end he told what he had done to his own people and was shot to death. By experiencing and processing this again, I can now allow myself to succeed, and I do not have to control myself so much since I no longer have to be afraid that I might otherwise make wrong choices. Now fifteen years later, having realized all these things, this part of me has completely disappeared. After all this time I cannot thank you enough.
– Anonymous

"I could let go of my fear"

I was very nervous my first time with Maarten, I didn't really dare. But I was so stuck after having had my baby and being sent from pillar to post that I was open to trying something else. Maarten asked me: "If you close your eyes and you feel where you can go, what comes to mind about what happened while giving birth?" I saw my grandmother's mother – my mother's grandmother. She died when my grandmother was very small. I saw her walking into the water in a white robe. The birth had triggered that death. Maarten was able to guide me effectively to that life and to relive that death. This allowed me to let go of my own near-death experience and the fear of dying after having just become a mother myself.

In a second session I encountered a different life. A man who had killed a lot of people including children in the war. Heavy. I incorporated that session into a painting and a poem. I don't remember the words myself; they came through me, and I donated them to Maarten for his practice. A journey into "deceased time," as I've come to call it, has helped me to fully accept and embrace my inner man, allowing me to write a book. I am very happy and proud of this!
– Indira van Tongerlo-Fokkens, author of the book *De Vrouw Zonder Hoofd* (The Woman with No Head)

We looked at you then
With our empty eyes
When you killed betrayed
And deceived us

We can forgive you
Because we too are alive again
We're the wiser for it
The burden on your shoulders
Has long been processed

We're looking at you now
With loving eyes
Full of passion and compassion
Let's go now
We don't blame you anymore
Love remains
And will always flow
Go on feel it
You're not dreaming

It's all of value
To be able to live
To be able to give love
Here on mother earth
Love yourself again
Stand up for who you are
Like mother earth
Has known you for ages

– Petra 2012

“No longer go through life blindfolded”

I was regularly overcome by feelings of insecurity, fear, and uncontrolled anger. During a session with Maarten, my grandfather turned out to be the way inwards, totally unexpectedly. My grandfather fought during the battle of Stalingrad. I was able to get to know my grandfather and grandma from up close. This will stay with me forever. The edginess is gone, and the strong hatred vanished instantly. As if a layer has fallen off me. I look after myself more and the situation I find myself in, because I realize that everything is interrelated. I no longer go through life blindfolded.

– Laurian Eras

‘Never had problems ever again’

I had been suffering from ‘restless legs’ for at least twenty years when I visited Maarten. Especially just before falling asleep, my legs started twitching and I got the feeling like bugs were crawling around inside them. Medication did work but had side effects and without it I used to walk half the night outside on the street because I simply couldn’t stand lying in bed. Maarten put me in a trance. I saw myself in a previous life in a dungeon of a castle, with my left leg chained to the wall. Hardly any room to move and just enough food to stay alive. But it was quite clear to me that I would not make it out alive. Maarten let me relive my death in that dungeon, which was pretty hardcore. The next day I stopped taking the medication. It’s been three years now, and I have never had problems with my legs ever again.

– Piet Steijn

“Second chance to heal”

During Maarten’s sessions, through looking at, embracing, enduring, and experiencing my dark side – via travelling back to my distant past in the regression sessions – I found the relaxation in the here and now from my learned manifestations. In the here and now I felt freed from the burden that wasn’t mine and I was given a second chance to heal. This also had a healing effect on my offspring.

– André Heuvelman, performs worldwide as (solo) trumpet player and played with the Rotterdam Philharmonic Orchestra and the Nederlands Blazers Ensemble (Netherlands Wind Ensemble). www.andreheuvelman.nl

"More peace, self-insight and direction"

In 2018 I had to deal with a breast tumor, which both my mother and grandmother also had to deal with before me. Parallel to the standard advice from the hospital, I felt a strong desire to look at a deeper layer in myself to see which issues were underlying this. In addition to some other physical complaints, I also suffered from a huge feeling of anxiety and a fear of making myself visible. During the sessions we worked on the ancestral burden that I carried with me. This was mainly focused on issues of sexuality, premature infant mortality, and bottled-up emotions about them in the women in my family line. This was related to my breast tumor, I discovered. I also have been able to process trauma from a past life, in which I was involved in healing as a woman and for which I was severely condemned by the religious convictions of the time and eventually died. The sessions have helped me to gain more peace, self-insight, and direction in my life. I am incredibly grateful that this has come my way.

– Rianne Bakker, Transformative coach

"Stopped taking medication"

My request for help had to do with intense neuralgic pain in both my lower legs and feet. When removing growths caused by running, I had suffered surgical damage. Bad luck. I had a nice job but could no longer work due to the pain. Regular healthcare could not help me further and I was given narcotic medication that controlled my life. What story clung to my pain? I went to Maarten, and it was serious. This Rotterdam Indian with wings (meant with respect) was so decisive that I had run out of options. I was allowed to focus on my hellish pain and go back to the moment it started. To my surprise, I was suddenly lying on a field in the hills. As a soldier in a war. Both my lower legs were gone, and I experienced a burning, searing pain. Just like I have in this life. Under supervision I could experience my death again, this time free of panic. After a healing ritual, in which the lower legs I had lost were reconnected to the body and anointed, I was able to leave myself resting in a beautiful place in a completed past. All this touched me deeply.

At first the pain increased, but after a few weeks there was suddenly inexplicable room in my lower legs. That's how I got the idea to stop taking my medication. Just surviving for the kids gave way to a more livable life. The pain became more bearable. I live medicine-free, can breathe again and I keep going. And all this after two sessions, a good six months ago. My condition continues to improve, and I have become even more curious about myself.

– Ineke, 'Lady on sneakers', hypnotherapist in training

"My life has undergone a complete transformation"

During an interactive day with Maarten, I suddenly started violently shuddering and shaking. Maarten took me aside. I was allowed to close my eyes and connect with my deceased mother in my mind. The shaking became even more intense. Maarten asked me to lend my voice to my mother, so that I could directly engage in a dialogue with her. My mother was still in the icy, dirty water of the canal. Those were the vibrations. I saw her and all the details. She tried to resist dying, a violent scene full of struggle. "I don't want this, what did I do?" she uttered through my voice. Maarten stimulated me to feel with my body what happened to mom while she drowned. This caused severe coughing and spluttering. Choking mucus in my chest area and throat. Eventually, a blissful calm came over me. Through a window, a huge shaft of sunlight penetrated the room that shone on the neck and back of my head. I can still feel the smile through my tears.

Mom continued with huge expressions of regret for having left us behind alone. She didn't want to but had been doped up on medication and was so wounded, orphaned and had missed so much love. I have always kept loving her, despite the heavy tasks and consequences that have scarred my life. She desperately wanted to keep everyone with her. She remained attached to her relatives. It felt so good that I was allowed to help with her final process of deliverance.

I also saw my two sisters and brother standing in front of me. They were younger again than when we had been brutally separated in real life. They reached the ages of 20, 31 and 51. A loving farewell followed, with an expression of admiration on their part for what I have borne. Maarten was able to tell me that dad was sitting in my chair, smiling, and radiating love. I was totally consumed with love. My sisters and brother cried out to me: 'Go enjoy, go live!' Rest assured, I do. I bring out my inner creativity through writing, painting, and making fairy houses. My life has undergone a complete transformation. I get up and live!

– Sjaan

"Willpower turns into real power"

"For years I constantly felt as if there was a plexiglass wall between me and life. I experienced a lot of turmoil, fatigue and unexplained feelings of inner grief and sadness. During several sessions with Maarten, I regressed to a life in the Second World War. A life as a resistance fighter that was characterized by intense stress, deep fear, and loss of loved ones. A life that suddenly came to an end – a death that was not accepted then. By going back to these moments and consciously reliving that dying, peace has come inside me. Life back then has been given a place. The willpower which kept me going through life before has

made way for real power, enabling me to live more from just 'being'. My *joie de vivre* has increased enormously. That makes me intensely grateful."
– Nathasja Schadron

"His armor had vanished"
My son Harmen, born in 2004, was extremely feisty as a child. One of extremes, very black and white in dealing with people, authoritarian and extremely sensitive. At times it felt like he was being taken over by another kind of energy. As a child and even up to the age of 16, he played a lot with weapons and was utterly fascinated by the war. When this subject was dealt with at school, he was sad and unreasonable for days. In elementary school, he changed from a happy child to a child who was always afraid and hardly spoke at all. He was overstimulated, had no filter, couldn't handle pressure, authority, and many people in one space. He also wet his bed until he was 12 and often had terrible nightmares. To him it felt as if someone was sitting on his chest, and he had nowhere to go. Because 'the system' has no knowledge of sensitive/paranormal children, let alone of unprocessed abuse from the parents/ancestors, they labelled him 'autistic'. This made him feel even more misunderstood. And as a mother, I felt distraught and powerless.

That's why I went to Maarten. During my session I made contact with my grandfather. He died three years after I was born. It felt like he was already waiting for me. An intense anger flared inside me, which really shocked me. "You stupid asshole!" I shouted. The moment I delved into his story, it turned out that as an 18-year-old in World War II, he was forced into military service. It was as if I was grabbed by my throat, it was sickening. The powerless feeling of having to do something you don't support, literally hurt my heart. My grandfather saw horrible things, including many dead people he had to walk through. I felt the fear and pain intensely and seeing the images was hugely confronting. My grandfather repressed everything and couldn't process it emotionally. I felt a heart-breaking sadness with him, but especially also guilt and shame.

After the war he married and had nine children. His youngest daughter drowned when she was 7; I am the reincarnation of this. Then he lost another son to leukemia. Grandpa could not handle the responsibility of the large family and the grief and ran out on them. My father then had to become the family breadwinner as the eldest son of 17 years. At the age of 54, grandpa died of bone cancer. On his deathbed he asked about my father, but my father refused to come. So, there was never any closure. Grandpa now said during the session, "I'm so sorry," and asked for forgiveness, which I was able to give him from my heart.

After this session Harmen ran up to me with joy and flew into my arms. How intense was that! It felt so good, I'll never forget this. He had never done anything like this before of his own accord. On top of that he kept seeking me out to give me a big hug. Really special. The edginess was gone and there was a different look in his eyes. His armor had vanished and there was literally more (breathing) space. He became more open, and he dared to show his soft side better. At school at the time, they also felt that he had changed – was more open and cheerful. That he is the reincarnation of grandpa was not mentioned in so many words during the session, but I do have the feeling that this is the case.

He told me recently that he would like to join the army. "If only there was a war on", he said. I asked if he felt he had anything to finish. He confirmed that he did. He said he wanted to fight again and preferably against the Russians. In the long run he will eventually find his way.

– Diana

"Breastfeeding without being pregnant"

I was in the final stages of healing from a hormonal abnormality I had from birth. The homestretch seemed to be the hardest and take the longest. Everything made me feel that more was needed. More research, more depth and insight. I knew: there's more to it, but what? My first session with Maarten was right on target. Among other things, it came to light that in my previous life I died heavily pregnant in a gas chamber. This explained more than I can describe now, and I experienced this as coming home. Maarten told me that this session would have a longer-term effect, even become physically visible. My body had to become unpregnant, the old programs were still running through my current body because everything had ended so abruptly at the time. I would gain weight and even breastfeed (without being pregnant). After this, my body would regain its natural balance. And that's how it went, picking up momentum. Hard to believe. The result was full recovery! I now go through life hormonally balanced. I am eternally grateful. I realize it is a given that you have to allow yourself to (re-) experience it, before you can acknowledge it and have an opinion about it!

– Maaike Middelweerd

"Things have been solved that have been stuck for years"

The request for help that finally brought me to Maarten was the fact that I had not had a serious relationship for so long, with someone who I would like to grow old with. My first session with Maarten was about my father, who died just before my divorce. My father had not let me go. It seemed as if he was unaware that he had now passed on to another world. During the session this became clear to him and with a lot of emotion from both sides he let me go. Immediately after the session I felt relieved, light, and cheerful. It was an emotional but very liberating experience. In the months that followed, I started eating healthier and exercising more and I lost twelve kilos effortlessly and without dieting. My self-image improved because of this, a fantastic feeling. My weight has stayed the same ever since.

At the next session I got in touch with my grandmother and my fear of commitment and abandonment were dealt with. The third and final session was with my late mother. There the expectations and disappointments in her life and love came to the fore. These two sessions were also concluded with a healing movement for all involved: towards the reality of death and feeling and experiencing the relationships to each other in a different perspective.

In the last session Maarten also led me to a past life in which I ended up as a young boy in the trenches of France in the First World War, all alone with comrades who were all shot or bombed to death in a dizzying rapid succession. I also died after a few months from a piece of shrapnel in my stomach. That trauma is now also part of my consciousness.

After the third session I immediately felt it was enough. Things had been solved that had been stuck for years and now I can continue on my life path. A few things have been set in motion by the sessions with Maarten, on a non-rational level that I could not have reached on my own. I am very grateful to him. I can't explain how this all works, but the changes are genuinely significant. Very shortly after the last session, I met a fantastic man through Tinder, the first person I had contact with through this medium. We have been together for ten months now and have a loving and mature relationship. A man I want to grow old with.

– Annette

"Finally, I feel that I have a right to be"

From an early age I had the feeling that I had no right to be. And whenever I exerted myself, I had problems with my heart. Cardiologists never found a cause. As a child, I was the odd one out in our family of eight children. I withdrew and lived in my own, invisible world where I felt perfectly at home, until my father died unexpectedly of cardiac arrest. He was in the hospital for his lungs and was supposed to come home in a few days. In the night before his earthly death, he came to say goodbye in my dream. He told me he was dying but would stay with me. His sudden death caused our family to fall apart, because my mother became ill with grief and could not cope with the situation.

After his death, I started sleeping badly and dreaming a lot about my father. At home, no one believed in predictive dreams. I felt like it was my fault that he had died, because I already knew it at night and hadn't warned anyone. Otherwise, he might still have survived. They were right about what I was constantly told at Catholic primary school: I'm no good.

During my session with Maarten, it turned out that I am the reincarnation of my father's mother who died young. My father also made his appearance. He had resisted his death and had decided to continue living on Earth through my open aura. His energy settled in my heart. After that I had more and more palpitations and I felt as if a block of concrete was pressing down on my heart region. During this session Maarten asked my father if he was willing to accept the situation and if he could help my father to let go of Earthly life, because I suffered from his clinging. My father was willing to do that. I then experienced what it's like to fight against your impending death. I always thought that a heart attack was the easiest death, but I am no longer convinced that is so. If your soul resists the earthly end, then the body fights a huge battle, so that the transition of the soul back to the 'source' is experienced as heavy and painful in the body. It was not a pleasant experience, but certainly worth it. It has relieved me of my father's heart problems. My guilt has completely disappeared and the concrete block on my heart, which I always felt, has also been lifted. It feels like there is more room in my heart. Since that session, I am no longer the reincarnation of my father's mother, but the one I should be in this life: me. Finally, I feel that I too have a right to be myself and I am very happy and grateful for that.
– Henriëtte du Bois

"Quite profound healing has taken place"
The sessions I had with Maarten have brought me more than I could have imagined. I had signed up because of regularly recurring back problems and dark periods. In the chair it quickly became clear that I was still tense and frozen in my body. I immediately knew what the cause was and thought that I had already completely healed it. During the session I experienced complete integrity, security and trust which allowed me to fully open to the process. I have been able to feel the experiences of sexual abuse in my body energetically. While feeling that, I gained insights I had not had until that day. The number of times the abuse happened and what happened. It was more than the frozen image I had in my memory. I also gained insights into why my father did what he did. These insights provide a great deal of clarity and above all peace of mind.

The result, a few weeks after this session, is that my hips and pelvic area are looser. I was also very relaxed at the dentist while my wisdom tooth was filled. I used to sit gagging, fraught with tension and clenched jaws. After a course of treatment with the 'anxiety dentist' this had already become less but now I was so relaxed in the chair that the dentist could easily do her work. She was also very surprised.

The event that caused my back pain in a past life has also healed. I consciously felt this person's process of dying. My back now feels more supple and stronger. In the sessions I found out what the cause of the dark periods is. This turned out to be my grandmother. In World War II, as a little girl, she had to be hidden in the basement, where she had to be quiet, because her father was afraid that she would betray what he did. She stopped having fun and playing. After her death she came into my energy, so I sometimes stood along the railroad tracks because I no longer wanted to live. After this session I woke up the next day with a sense of purpose in life, a desire to have fun and enjoy myself. And I still feel that way now. I am grateful that I took the step to go to Maarten. From complete integrity, safety and trust, quite profound healing has taken place.
– Karin

"I focus on myself now"

I am 22 now and have had quite a few complaints since I was born. Ranging from chronic colds and chronic ear infections to not being able to defecate and nightly anxiety attacks. Things were not easy at school either; I attended two playgroups, four primary schools and three secondary schools. I could barely, if at all, tolerate the authority of female teachers. I've been given a lot of labels, from autistic to ADHD with socially emotionally disturbed behavior and whatnot. What I clearly know now is I am a highly sensitive person who thinks in images. And that I have lived before.

As a child I had problems with my right knee all the time. If I started running it would buckle and I would lose my balance, and fall. There was also a lot of eczema surrounding my knee. It itched and I was ashamed, it looked like hell. The stuff the doctor gave me did not help. Through sessions with Maarten, I now know that in my previous life as a soldier I suffered a serious knee injury.

Things got worse when I was a teenager. I experienced things differently than my peers and had a hard time holding my own with them. I wanted to avoid arguments between others, I was afraid of violence and afraid of everything, but I could specify why. I often dissociated and hardly noticed what was really going on around me. Things got out of hand, something had to be done, my parents came up with the idea to go to Maarten.

I was nervous as hell at my first session, but everything fell into place. The fears, the sadness, and the search for my 'brothers in arms'. I had been an SS man and was a ruthless soldier. This was caused in my youth as a German boy by my cruel father, who had become mentally disturbed by the influences of the First World War. The preparation at the *Hitlerjugend* was completely in line with his policy and so I was selected to become an SS man. Then you were someone. But the horrors that I had to deal with, and that I also performed myself, were barbaric. A real nightmare. I was just part of a workforce which carried out the bizarre orders.

The worst part is that in the beginning I also believed that this was the right thing to do. But when you see your comrades die for nothing, you begin to realize that you, as a human being, do not count at all. This was the moment for me that I no longer believed in the war. Shortly thereafter, I met my end in a terrible way. That's where my fears came from. In my current life I was totally afraid of the dark. Now I understand why.

The two sessions with Maarten have helped me enormously, I have pieces back from my soul. After the first session I was left with a lot of sadness, shame, and anger. During a second session we saw that it had to do with women, to whom I was misogynistic to say the least. Here, too, I gained an insight: that my compulsive need for women had to do with the loss of my mother in childhood. Confronting to live through but very enlightening. Maarten helped me a lot with this, by looking without judgment and staying with it, so that I could feel what had happened. That's how we ended up discovering another life before my German life, in the same situation but on the opposite side: an English soldier in the trenches of the First World War. That also ended miserably, but this showed the overall picture, why I had made certain choices in matters pertaining to the soul.

I experienced great relief after the session. It was as if these two men/boys had received recognition for their existence, their commitment, their deaths. It may sound crazy, but they have been given a kind of rest and don't have to fight anymore. I have become calmer, and I focus on myself now. My eczema is getting better. It has practically cleared up around my knee and been substantially reduced around my anus and genitals, in combination with using homeopathic ointment. I am now making contact with my heart and am busy with heart energy, which makes me feel good. Processing takes time but I know inside myself that everything is alright. I'm proud of who I am with all the trimmings. With the light and the dark.

– J.V.

"Everything is clear now"

While reading Maarten's article *The Tears of Our Ancestors*, all sorts of things were touched upon. Did I have them, ancestors? Yes, there was something about a grandmother who had died in an asylum. And something about one of my father's brothers who died young... After my first consultation with Maarten, I stood outside swearing like a trooper. There was clearly work to be done. My sadness was frozen, I see in hindsight, and my anger

swallowed, because I had not been told anything about my history. Everyone thought at the time there was no need for anyone to hear about a manslaughter. So long as things turned out well, during the war. But it is important to be honest about it because the family system does not tolerate this, even two generations later. All kinds of things appeared to be hidden, but everything is clear now. Maarten took my feeling seriously. People are given a name at birth, and those names should not be forgotten. They form my foundation and roots of life. I have no secrets because silence and denial hurt like hell.
– Hendrikje ten Klooster

"I got my voice back"
Maarten came into my life at the right time. The sessions in which we went back to my ancestors have brought about a very big change in me: I got my voice back. I had a feeling of being stuck and not being heard for years. I had a huge fear of expressing myself. This became increasingly clear. During workshops that I followed, where the issue arose about letting yourself be heard, not a sound came out of me. I couldn't function in the group. All this frustrated me enormously. Previously I had gone to several people with my issue, but for the time being the lock remained firmly in place. Maarten let the secret that hung around my family come out in a regression. All I can say is that I am eternally grateful for this. My life is slowly taking a new turn, I can now finally live my truth and stand in my own strength.
– Leen Tack from Belgium

"Corné 's development has progressed by leaps and bounds"
When he was around a year and a half old, if he got angry or something wouldn't work, Corné, started banging his head on the ground or wall. Nothing helped to make him stop, you couldn't get through to him. The head banging stopped when he was around 3 years old, and he started running away and hiding. This was often accompanied by him saying things like "I'm doing everything wrong" and "I can't do anything at all." After a while he started to roll up in a ball, like a hedgehog, preferably crawling away in a corner. Even after a simple remark like "Will you please use your fork when you eat." If you asked why he did this, he never knew an answer. He was tense, sucked his thumb a lot and his development began to stagnate. He forgot words, started talking less well and became more reliant on getting help just to do things. His cheerfulness and open-mindedness diminished and the twinkle in his eyes vanished.

As a parent, you are faced with a conundrum: what am I doing wrong? His younger brother doesn't react like that. Is Corné just seeking attention? But with a stricter approach, the behavior only got worse. It gave us such a powerless feeling, when we saw the helplessness in his eyes when he was rolled up and there was nothing you could do for him. Besides that, you want to keep the balance in the family from derailing by letting him get away with things that his younger brother is rebuked for. We had to seek help. Because of our own experience with Maarten, we thought, that's where we'll start. Corné, 6 years old at the time, was immediately enthusiastic.

When we arrived at Maarten's house early, Corné, who had his favorite stuffed animal Stekel the hedgehog with him, walked around the garden with his father. They all found sweet chestnuts, still in their prickly pods. Quite symbolic, it turned out later. Based on a drawing Corné made, he and Maarten came to the heart of the story. During the session, Corné told loudly and clearly what had happened to him during the birth. He had not rotated in the womb properly and got stuck for a moment. He blamed himself for not doing it right and took it very seriously. Because of this, he found it difficult to grow up and wanted to stay small. By rolling himself up, he felt safe and small again, like in the womb. Safe like a hedgehog, which rolls up and sticks out its spines.

On the outside, the birth went by the book. He was born at home within a few hours without complications. So, we didn't expect this. After the session Corné was very relieved. He is now happier and less tense. His eyes gleam with pleasure again and he deals better with setbacks or a comment about his behavior. His development has progressed by leaps and bounds. His reading has improved, his vocabulary increased rapidly, and he has started doing things independently again. And: he never rolls up like a hedgehog when something doesn't go right.

– Jurriaan, Kim and Corné Schot

"From the invisible to visible right to be"

Hidden information was released through me. The moment I felt that the time had come to do something about the fact that I was not comfortable in my own skin and often had feelings of depression, Maarten came my way three times. The title of his lecture Tears of Our Ancestors immediately touched me, even though I thought: what tears?

I wanted to look at my father's family system first. Were there feelings of depression there? Sitting in a lovely chair, Maarten took me on an inner journey. *Beppe* (Granma) Albertje immediately came into the picture. She apparently wanted, through me as a conduit, to release information that had been hidden for a long time. Soon there were a lot of emotions and sadness, it was very intense.

Beppe Albertje was the mother of eight children and lived with her husband on the farm where she was born. She died during the war at the age of 36, which was a trauma for all the children. The youngest was 1 and the oldest 12 years old. My father, sixth in line, was 4 years old when she died. My father later took over the farm and I was born there too. Grandma was eager to pass on that she had experienced deep love for a soldier, but that she could not express her sensitivity. I got an image of a bale of straw in the hayloft. In that batch of straw, I was hidden away as a 'fruit', because Beppe had gotten pregnant out of wedlock, aborted herself, and this was immediately hidden away. In the context of reincarnation, I was given an image in which I, Hedwig, as a soul, was hidden away and was not allowed to be there. In short, I was once the child of my Beppe, who was not allowed to be there. This hiding away was totally the theme in my life now!

Grandma indicated that the family story that she had died of kidney problems, was not correct. The session continued and I felt so miserable and nauseous that I wanted to get out of the situation. Beppe said: "I decided to end my life with all the strength I possessed." Beppe did this in a place in the hayloft where I preferred not to come as a child, although I did not know why at the time. With her death, she wanted to identify with her lost child by killing herself in that attic. That's why she was still glued to me in that old pain. Gradually, everything fell into place. Beppe had not closed this period properly and there were still loose ends. My feelings of depression were not allowed to be there. That feeling of love, when you love someone so much, was something I immediately recognized in my life. Because of the tears of the ancestors, who had been flowing through me for years, I could not name where this feeling came from. Profound healing flowed into me. A while after the session I began feeling happier and happier. I had let go of a few things. The message Beppe gave me was: "Follow your heart, I had not been able to do that. What I could not live for, you now can. You have now realized your practice *De Stroming*, (The Flow) in which you can express your passion." The many tears that have flowed have made me a happier person. By becoming aware of this, you break lines which enables you to live your own authentic self. "Like grandma says – follow your heart – I had never been able to do that."
– Hedwig Ydema

"Chocolate no longer gives me the same satisfaction"
I visited Maarten because I was overweight and had an eating disorder. My challenge was that I ate much too much chocolate. During the session I discovered that in this way I was looking for security and comfort, which I had been deprived of as a baby and later as

a child. It had to do with my mother. I experienced a deep conflict in the bond with her, already in the period of the pregnancy. The traumatization my mother suffered during World War II, in which her self-image was greatly affected, became transferred to me for deeper reasons that had to do with a past life of my own, in the same period of 1940-45. We went back to the first moment I tasted breast milk. It tasted bitter and was disgusting. Maarten asked me: "If food had a color, what would that color be? And what color is the food you eat?" Surprisingly, both types of food did not have the same color. The color of the food I ate was the color of my mother's food, which in essence represented her self-condemnation. I learned how a deep disapproval was passed on by her mother, my grandmother. Because I realized the connection between her and my issues, I was able to give all the 'non-own' color back to my mother in energetic form. For the first time ever, my mother was equal to her own mother, and so I could also feel love for her. Since then, eating chocolate hasn't given me the same satisfaction as before. And believe me, I've tried. I have tasted every kind of chocolate I could find, including cake with chocolate. After 48 years of my life, my craving for chocolate has disappeared, even now, a year and a half after the session.
– Nicole Hentschel

'The disease-energy of my housemate was still there"

One of Maarten's workshops I attended had to do with the death of my housemate, in June 2019. She had used medication such as morphine for the pain. The last weeks of her time in our apartment I gave her my study because there is a bathroom adjacent to it. After her passing, I felt very clearly that I no longer wanted to enter those spaces. I kept the office door constantly closed, and I only opened it when I had to pick up something. A disgusting smell came from the bathroom, even after I cleaned it several times.

During the workshop we talked about the impact that certain medications such as morphine can have on death. Had everything really gone as well as we thought during the spiritual care of my housemate? During the session, in which I opened myself to her soul, it initially seemed as if everything had gone well. However, a fly kept on landing on my face, just like a fly had always kept landing on the face of my dying housemate to my great annoyance at the time. Because of her illness, there was a foul odor in and around her body, especially when she exhaled. This session took place in a learning setting with several students present, and everyone suddenly smelled a filthy, penetrating odor. In my role as housemate, I was unable to smell it. Together we concluded that fractions of her disease energy must have remained in the office and bathroom because she was not able to fully surrender to death, because of the disturbance of consciousness due to the

administration of morphine and painkillers. The stench clearly made these fractions palpable. My deceased housemate had to call back this energy, which was originally hers, to complete her soul again. In her realignment, this 'disease energy' could be transformed. That energy would negatively affect my life if she stayed behind in the house, which had been clearly felt for some time, but now also became understandable. When I came home later, I immediately felt that something had changed. I had no trouble opening the doors of the study and bathroom. I was able to redecorate the study and to this day I work there regularly. The stench has completely disappeared.
– A.

FAKE HUMAN HISTORY – *IT'S ALL COMING OUT!* – GRAHAM HANCOCK

TEACHING OF CONNECTION – GRANDMOTHER SARA

HOME CALLING – ILSE OVERSIER

BESTAANSRECHT – LISANNE SPAANDER

RUNNING WITH WOLVES – EL PERIQUIN

INDIGENOUS NATIVE AMERICAN PROPHECY

©Mira van der Sanden

MAARTEN OVERSIER

Maarten A. Oversier (1962) lives in the rural town of Roden, in the northern Dutch province of Drenthe, but originally hails from Rotterdam, where he was head chef at a renowned hotel. His true vocation however was of a more spiritual nature. As a regression and reincarnation therapist he has given over 15,000 sessions. He publishes articles, gives lectures and teaches at various locations in Europe and in Canadian Indian reserves. Maarten maintains warm personal relations with members of native peoples whom he regularly invites to come to the Netherlands to share their wisdom.

www.maartenoversier.com